UNIVERSITY OF DERBY

ONE WEEK LOAN

MUST BE RETURNED TO SITE BORROWED FROM

FINES for late return of items:

> 50p per DAY or part day (Full-time)
> 50p per WEEK or part week (Part-time)
> MAXIMUM FINE APPLIES

Non-payment of fines, or repeatedly keeping items overdue may result in suspension of borrowing rights.

| 1 5 DEC 2003 | | |
| 1 4 DEC 2004 | | |

A:\A9DATE1.DOC
02.01

New-Product Development and Testing

New-Product Development and Testing

Edited by

Walter Henry
University of California, Riverside

Michael Menasco
University of California, Riverside

Hirokazu Takada
University of California, Riverside

LEXINGTON BOOKS
An Imprint of Macmillan, Inc.
NEW YORK

Maxwell Macmillan Canada
TORONTO

Maxwell Macmillan International
NEW YORK   OXFORD   SINGAPORE   SYDNEY

Copyright © 1989 by Lexington Books
An Imprint of Macmillan, Inc.

Lexington Books
An Imprint of Macmillan, Inc.
866 Third Avenue, New York, N.Y. 10022

Maxwell Macmillan Canada, Inc.
1200 Eglinton Avenue East
Suite 200
Don Mills, Ontario M3C 3N1

Macmillan, Inc. is part of the Maxwell Communication
Group of Companies.

Printed in the United States of America

printing number

2 3 4 5 6 7 8 9 10

Library of Congress Cataloging-in-Publication Data

New-product development and testing / edited by Walter Henry, Michael Menasco, Hirokazu
Takada.
    p. cm.
1. New products—Management. I. Henry, Walter (Walter A.) II. Menasco, Michael.
III. Takada, Hirokazu.
HF5415.153.N47 1989
658.5'75—dc19   85–46004
                                                                          CIP

Contents

Preface

Business managers and marketing academics alike agree that an essential element of long-term survival of any organization is success in new-product development. What are the key success factors? A 1986 workshop brought together new-product managers, market research practitioners, and marketing academics to explore this issue and to access the state of the art in new-product development. Papers and ideas presented at that workshop and key selected articles already in print are presented in this book to provide the reader with a broad perspective of the current state of the art and a review of the leading edge of new-product–development technology in each of six keys to success.

Six keys were identified:

1. *Management of the development process:* This was selected at the workshop as a critical area of success while at the same time the area most in need of further advances.

2. *Design:* There is growing realization that design has become a critical success factor.

3. *Conjoint and related analysis techniques:* Attribute analysis and optimum-benefit-bundle estimation is an important phase in concept evaluation.

4. *Pretest-market models:* Advanced pretest-market models for share-of-market predictions are necessary in market-introduction planning.

5. *New-product–diffusion models:* Recent advances in diffusion-rate models for new-product-substitute situations and cross-culture introductions make rate-of-growth estimates more realistic.

6. *Consumer-behavior models:* New consumer-behavior–modeling approaches provide further insight into new-product acceptance.

The reader will find that the chapters in the book, just as the key success factors themselves, vary from management issues, to issues of practical application, to issues that explore the more theoretical boundaries of concept testing, diffusion prediction, and consumer–new-product–evaluation modeling. Readers who have less need for the detailed theoretical presentations found in chapters 6, 10, 12, and 13 may wish to skip over these chapters and read the overviews found in the introductory comments for parts III, V, and VI of the book. Readers interested in the quantitative aspects of testing, prediction, and modeling will find the four chapters provide a look at the leading edge of technology.

The workshop of new-product managers, market-research practitioners, and academics, which was the genesis of this work, was held in February 1986 at the University of California, Riverside. It was jointly sponsored by the Education Division of the American Marketing Association, the Product Development and Management Association, and the Graduate School of Management at the university.

Many people make a book such as this possible. The editors wish to thank the participants of the workshop for their efforts and patience. Their contributions of time and expertise were invaluable. We are also grateful to the authors who allowed us to add their works already in print to the book. Many members of the faculty and staff at the Graduate School of Management provided assistance when needed. We salute them as well. There is especially heart-felt thanks to Dr. Michael Mokwa of the Education Division of the American Marketing Association and to Dr. Thomas Hustad of the Product Development and Management Association for their support and advice in bringing the workshop and this book to fruition.

Part I
Management of New-Product Development

I t is significant that "Management of New-Product Development" is the title of the first part of this book. Among the business decision makers, research practitioners, and the academics present at the workshop from which this book evolved, there was a unanimous opinion that the key success factor that was least well developed and in most need of advancement was the management process itself. Strangely enough, the workshop was void of papers dealing with this fundamental issue. It is unclear whether the problem lies in many people's assumption that we are dealing with the "art" of management and therefore it is not a topic appropriate to scholarly papers or that it is so idiosyncratic that it cannot be generalized into a normative model.

The following chapters do begin to develop a prescription for effective product-development management. Chapter 1 by Feldman and Page (first published in a 1984 issue of *Journal of Product Innovation Management* reviews the accepted textbook model of the product-planning process of (1) exploration, (2) screening, (3) concept testing, (4) business analysis, (5) development, (6) testing, and (7) commercialization. It then examines the deviations found in practice in a selected industry. The authors suggest that the variance observed stems from the inherent complexity of the process and from our inability to effectively manage it.

Cooper and Kleinschmidt (1986), published in a latter issue of the *Journal of Product Innovation Management*, presented data on both the extent and proficiency of the process activities as reported by 123 firms in a Canadian study of the new-product–management process. New-product success, in their investigation, was found to be closely linked to what activities were carried out, to the completeness of the process, and to how effectively the process was managed. A well–thought-out structured-development process, carefully followed by avoiding what appears to be expedient time or money shortcuts, can significantly reduce the risks inherent in new-product introductions. Marketing studies early in the process, done to estimate market potential and the keys to consumer acceptance, are particularly critical to success. This information allows an initial go/no-go assessment based on market considerations. If further work is warranted, it also provides a consumer orientation to later product development activities.

Chapter 2 by Johne builds on the importance of management control in new-product development. In a 1984 issue of the *Journal of Product Innovation Management,* Johne stressed the necessity of separating the initiation phase of development from the implementation phase. Johne stresses the appropriateness of the loose-tight management style first popularized by Peters and Waterman (1982). In chapter 2, based on Johne's study of active and inactive product-innovator firms, we shall see that experienced product innovators usually incorporated loose structures during the initiation phase and shifted to a much tighter structure and control during the implementation of business analysis, development, testing, and commercialization.

However, the serial nature of the well–thought-out process rigorously adhered to brings its own unique set of management problems. The diverse goals of finance, engineering, manufacturing, and marketing sequentially applied can lead to suboptimum performance and create a less than unified effort. Heany and Vinson (1984) proposed a fresh approach to the management problem of bringing together an effective new-product–development team. They accurately point out the problems of parochialism and serial decision making.

Management must first identify new-product goals in terms of customer wants. Second, these customer-oriented goals must be linked to design logic and to the manufacturing processes. Third, the new-product manager must play an active facilitator role, continually stressing the new-product goals over individual objectives. Heany and Vinson's approach reflects important insights into the management of people in the innovation process discussed separately by Stefflre (1985) and More (1985).

Stefflre (1985) dealt specifically with the decision process within large organizations and its tendency to produce suboptimal innovations:

> The larger the organization, the higher the probability that its collective decision processes will focus upon short-run, internal problems, and select minimally dissatisfying solutions to these rather than focusing upon external, long-run opportunities, or those aspects of the alternatives that relate to their consequences.

As Stefflre correctly pointed out, firms exhibiting this focus tend to produce products that exhibit characteristics that fit the internal line of least resistance, rather than focus on the characteristics that can provide a true competitive advantage from the consumer's point of view.

More (1985) took Stefflre's premise a step further and suggested that major barriers to successful innovation were endemic to intraorganizational behavior. He suggested that the following six "dislocations" may be causal in inhibiting and constraining the innovation process:

1. Dislocation of risk and accountability. (Decisionmakers may not be ultimately responsible.)
2. Dislocation of temporal continuity. (Key decisions may be made by different people over a long period of time.)
3. Dislocation of power and expertise. (Decisionmakers may not be the people with greatest expertise.)
4. Dislocation of risk and information. (Information may not be available when decisions are made.)
5. Dislocation of functional role interface. (Phasing of specializations may not be appropriate.)
6. Dislocation of risk and payoff. (Time phasing of negative and positive cash flow.)

Although More dwelled on each dislocation in some detail, the final prescription was: "The organizational structure and reward system must repair the dislocations by explicitly and behaviorally tying together the critical decisions, resources, and inputs to the successful outputs for a new product."

That there is much art in the management of innovation is apparent. Central to the issue is not the lack of a well-prescribed process. The central issue is how to bring about the appropriate management of the complex tasks leading to successful product development. Managers must be cognizant of the quality of process integration. To this end, procedures must be in place to provide the maximum openness to and search for new-product ideas not only from the traditional inernal sources but from the external environment representing the final consumers and their intermediaries. Screening procedures should be formalized to insure objective review of each idea's role and position in the overall strategic-marketing plan. And, finally, there must be a well–thought-out structure for implementation without missing key development tasks or rigorous examination at each phase.

The art of management is more than the management of the process. It is also—and perhaps most critically—the leadership of the people involved. Incentives and motivation that focus on the quality of teamwork required to bring about a new product with a competitive advantage in the eyes of the consumer may be management's greatest test. Chapters 1 and 2 offer a beginning to meeting that challenge.

References

Cooper, Robert G., and Elko J. Kleinschmidt (1986). "An Investigation into the New Product Process," *Journal of Innovation Management* 3 (June): 71–85.

Heany, Donald F., and William D. Vinson (1984). "A Fresh Look at New Product Development," *Journal of Business Strategy* 5 (fall): 22–31.

More, Roger A. (1985). "Barriers to Innovation: Intraorganizational Dislocations," *Journal of Product Innovation Management* 3 (September): 205–07.

Peters, Thomas J., and Robert H. Waterman (1982). *In Search of Excellence*. New York: Harper & Row.

Stefflre, Volney (1985). "Organizational Obstacles to Innovation: A Formulation of the Problem," *Journal of Product Innovation Management* 2 (March): 3–11.

1
Principles versus Practice in New-Product Planning

Laurence P. Feldman
Albert L. Page

New-product planning involves the determination of the company's basic new-product objectives along with the type and specifications of the products that the company will make. While the basic methods and concepts of new-product planning have been known to the business community for nearly a quarter of a century, many corporations still have not made effective use of them, encountering problems that appear to be directly attributable to their new-product planning. Consider the following examples:

In the late 1960s, Polaroid Corporation began development of a product that, a decade and $250 million later, was to become Polavision. In many ways, the product was an outstanding technical achievement. But when first introduced, it had numerous fundamental flaws. The images produced by the film were excessively grainy and could be seen on the special projection equipment only if the viewer stood directly in front of it. A single reel of film lasted for only two-and-a-half minutes, and there was no sound. Furthermore, the hand-held camera contained a bright light that tended to annoy small children—the most likely subjects of Polavision home movies. These shortcomings were highlighted by direct competition from videocassette-recorder technology that, while somewhat more expensive, offered home movies with sound, up to six hours in length, on convenient, reusable cassettes. Shortly after the introduction of Polavision, Polaroid brought out improved film and a more versatile viewer, but sales fell far short of expectations and it was withdrawn from the market. Even before its withdrawal, one writer described Polavision as " . . . a striking failure in both technology and marketing."

As late as 1978, A.O. Smith Corporation, a manufacturer of automobile frames, dominated the market with a 40 percent share that accounted for 40 percent of its sales and about half its profits. Its principal customer

Reprinted with minor alterations by permission of the publisher from *The Journal of Product Innovation Management* 2, no. 1: 43–55. Copyright 1984 by Elsevier Science Publishing Co., Inc.

was General Motors. As a consequence of the move toward smaller, more fuel-efficient automobiles that used unitized (integral–body-frame) construction, Smith began to lose its market. In 1979, Smith tried desperately to convince Detroit that its frames could be adapted to smaller cars without a weight penalty. It spent $300,000 to rebuilt a just-introduced GM unitized body Chevrolet Citation with a separate frame. The demonstration car actually rode more smoothly and weighed seven pounds less than the standard Citation. Despite these efforts, in 1980 GM informed Smith that, after 1983, it would no longer purchase the auto frames on which a major portion of the vendor's profits had been based.

Each of these cases is indicative of the need to improve the product-planning process, reflecting sins of commission and omission, respectively. In the case of Polavision, Polaroid persisted in devoting time and money to a product while ignoring events occurring in the highly dynamic environment posed by the consumer-electronics market. For A.O. Smith, the problem appears to have been overcommitment to a major existing product line in the face of significant market changes. So strong was this commitment that they ignored the needs of their OEM customers, who were switching to unitized construction not only to save weight, but also to gain a more solid small car that could be built with greater use of industrial robots.

New products are at the cutting edge of corporate strategy, because they are one of its primary means of producing new growth and because they define the future direction of the firm. Its new-product planning also reflects the way the firm has chosen to cope with change in its business environment.

Today's business environment is more dynamic and more potentially threatening than it has ever been, making it more difficult to predict accurately the needs of buyers and respond to them with successful new products. At the same time, in many sectors of the U.S. economy, vigorous foreign competition is making its presence felt, and successful new products are necessary for U.S. companies to remain competitive in their markets. In this more difficult business environment, the direct cost and other consequences of new-product failures grows and heightens the need for more effective new-product planning to produce the required successes.

As early as 1968, Booz, Allen & Hamilton (BAH), in the introduction to their widely circulated publication *Management of New Products* stated:

> The principles of New Product Management are now almost universally accepted. The pioneering concepts stated in the first edition of 1957 have been adopted, tested, and proven in continuing experience of many major companies in the U.S.—and worldwide.

In the discussion that follows, we shall compare the new-product–planning practices of nine major companies with a normative approach to the new-product–planning process based on three principles. First, we shall review these three principles as they derive from modern management practice. Then, we shall examine actual management practice at these companies in the light of these principles. Finally, we shall review possible reasons why actual management practice at these firms deviates from the normative approach, and we shall suggest ways that the practice of product planning can be improved.

Three Principles of New-Product Planning

Three principles can be derived from the contemporary literature on new-product planning. New-product planners should:

1. Use a new-product–planning process that is orderly, logical, and sequential.
2. Formulate new-product plans that are strategically based.
3. Utilize sophisticated management techniques.

Let us now examine the derivation of each of these principles.

The New-Product–Planning Process

There are a number of normative models of the new-product–planning process.[1] The most widely accepted of these is the one originated by Booz, Allen & Hamilton (1968). It described a six-stage process consisting of:

1. *Exploration*—the search for new-product ideas,
2. *Screening*—the elimination of obviously unsuitable ideas,
3. *Business analysis*—evaluation of each surviving idea as a business proposition,
4. *Development*—conversion of the idea into a working product,
5. *Testing*—experimentation to determine the marketability of the product, and, finally,
6. *Commercialization.*

Since the original specification of this model, another stage, *concept testing*—exposure of specific versions or descriptions of the product idea to potential buyers to gauge buyer reaction—has been added by some practitioners between the screening and business analysis stages (Kotler [1980]).

As conceived by BAH, this multistage approach to new-product planning is orderly, logical, and sequential. It suggests that all new-product ideas go through the process in the specified order. The logic of the process rests in the fact that costs tend to increase at an increasing rate as ideas move through the new-product–planning process. Therefore, it is desirable to eliminate clearly unsuccessful ideas as early in the process as possible. It is sequential because it suggests that each stage serves as a hurdle that must be successfully surmounted before passing on to the next stage. By establishing objective criteria for each stage, management insures that only projects that meet these criteria survive to continue through the process.

The Strategic Basis for New-Product Plans

As was recognized in the 1982 Booz, Allen & Hamilton update of new-product–planning practices, strategic planning establishes the basic direction of the firm. It is the means by which the firm adapts to long-range environmental challenges, such as those posed by the energy crisis, or foreign competition. A cornerstone of the strategic planning process is the derivation of new-product plans to meet these challenges. It is these plans that assure that products will emerge to take the firm in the desired direction. Ideally, appropriate criteria based upon the strategic objectives expressed in the new-product plan are developed for each stage of the process and are used to evaluate each project.

Use of Sophisticated Management Techniques

Given the high stakes involved in the new-product–planning game, one would expect that today's manager would bring to bear sophisticated weapons from the arsenal of analytic techniques. For example, it is reasonable to assume that every effort would be made to minimize subjective influences on the new-product–planning process through the use of systematic evaluation methods such as rating scales. Also, one would expect advanced marketing research tools, such as multidimensional scaling and conjoint analysis, to be used for uncovering new-product opportunities, and computer models such as DEMON, TRACKER, and ASSESSOR to be used for predicting new-product performance. In addition, an era of high interest rates should place a premium on the use of sophisticated financial-planning techniques such as Internal Rate of Return and Opportunity Cost of Capital to evaluate the potential payoffs from new-product projects.

The Reality of New-Product Planning

Our observations about the reality of new-product planning are based upon recently completed in-depth interviews with product-planning executives from nine major corporations. These companies were selected because of their use of a dynamic, electronics-based technology and their relatively large size. All have names that would be widely recognized by the general public, and all but one, a subsidiary of an overseas company, are listed on the New York Stock Exchange. At least three were market leaders in the line of business for which the research was conducted. Their number includes six industrial- and three consumer-goods manufacturers.

Key personnel, some at the division and some at the corporate level, with knowledge of the new-product–planning process were interviewed at each of these companies. The lengthy interviews were structured around an outline of the product-planning process, and detailed information was obtained on the nature of the process at each company or division. The size and resources of these companies, and the dynamic nature of the environment in which they operated, were such as to suggest they would apply advanced management practices in their new-product–planning activities. To preserve anonymity, disguised names that describe the essential business with which each of the respondents was associated will be used in the following discussion.

Disparities in the Process

Exploration. For most companies, the search for new-product items may be the most difficult part of the product-planning process. Yet, like other stages of the process, the generation of successful new-product ideas can be improved through the application of management techniques. As table–1 illustrates, new-product ideas may spring either from a source internal to the company or from some outside source. They may also results from the company's efforts consciously to structure (i.e., manage) the idea flow. Or, they may just occur fortuitously or on an ad hoc basis.

Table 1–1
Origins of New-Product Ideas: Sources Internal or External to the Company

Structure	Source	
	Internal	External

Formal	R&D
	Creativity techniques
	  from strategic plan
		Marketing research
		New-product
		  consultants

Informal	Ad hoc suggestions
	  from anywhere in the
	  organization
		Customer suggestion
		Volunteered suggestion
		Accidental intelligence
		Competitive reaction

Despite the promise of improved performance offered by a planned, proactive approach to idea generation, in general the idea-generation process occurred on an ad hoc basis, with no real attempt at formal management of the idea flow from either internal or external sources. Particularly noteworthy was the lack of reliance on R&D as a new-product–idea source. Instead, the emphasis of this function was primarily on development either of new ideas obtained from other sources or of existing products on an evolutionary basis. In fact, Information Retrieval Corp. had been so disappointed with the performance of this function that it had been abolished at the corporate level, with R&D at the divisional level focusing almost entirely on development.

By way of contrast, Electronic Games Corp. had two separate R&D groups. Their primary function was also developmental. Despite the considerable resources devoted to these groups by the company, two of its most successful products were licensed from other sources.

With one or two exceptions, there were few attempts at formal management of the idea-generation process. One of the exceptions was Communications Terminal Corp. This company, which had the most formal approach to the product-planning process overall, derived its new-product ideas from opportunities identified in a strategic plan. This involves strategic thinking about customers' markets, with the ideal being "to develop capabilities in advance of customer needs."

Information Retrieval Corp. and Switching Devices Corp. also made some use of their strategic plans as a basis for the generation of new-product ideas, but to a lesser extent. The latter company was unique in that it had a formal bonus-incentive program to encourage submission of ideas from anywhere within the organization. However, at least half of its ideas came, informally, from customers. Surprisingly, this heavy reliance on feedback from customers was found in only one other company. Metalworking Controls Corp., where it was the sole source of new-product ideas. On the other hand, Home Entertainment Corp. obtained the majority of its new-product ideas by following the product lead of competitors.

There were two other interesting points. First, we had expected that using marketing research to identify new-product opportunities would be the norm rather than the exception. No use was made of marketing research for this purpose by either industrial- or consumer-goods companies.

The second was that despite the occasional use of brainstorming on a rather informed basis by two companies, none of the respondents indicated that they use the more formal techniques of creativity stimulation such as attribute listing, Synectics, and other techniques that have been popularized in the literature on product planning. Two did make occasional use of brainstorming. For example, at Communications Terminal Corp., an across-lines task force was set up once a year to pursue a "blue-sky" approach to idea generation. In these meetings, the spirit was "you know products, know markets, read trade journals—what have you got?"

Screening. Reduced to its essence, screening involves the preliminary evaluation of new-product ideas, with the rejection of those ideas that, for one reason or another, appear to be inappropriate. There are many different bases for conducting this type of evaluation, ranging from informal to formal. An extreme example of informality is the product planner who evaluates an idea on a "gut-feeling" basis. At the other end of the spectrum is the use of a systematic, uniform procedure in which all of those involved in the evaluation process apply the same criteria in the same way. This practice reduces the element of subjective judgment and also helps determine the relative viability of each idea.

In large, complex organizations, where many people may be involved in product-planning activity, it is desirable to formalize the screening procedure as much as possible, but we found little evidence of this formality in the screening procedures used by the nine companies. In ascending levels of formality, they fell into four groups. The least formal was Systems Communications Corp., which had no explicit screening procedure. Decisions as to the probable viability of a new-product idea were likely to be made on an interpersonal basis—for example, over lunch. Slightly more formal were the two companies that screened ideas intuitively, making a subjective evaluation in holistic terms. Thus, at Electronic Games Corp., three executives subjectively considered the overall merits of the proposal for a new product based on their knowledge, both intuitive and from marketing research, of the general requisites for such products. At Home Entertainment Corp., on the other hand, a single individual screened ideas against a criterion based on a highly subjective three-point scale: whether the idea was "ludicrous, viable, or dynamite."

A third group of companies used groups of executives who applied general, but discrete criteria to evaluate an idea. However, these criteria were neither standardized nor written down. For example, Office Products Corp., one of the four companies in this group, might consider such things as market size and channels of distribution in appraising an idea. These criteria were not explicitly defined and standardized across products, however, and no objective means of evaluating the relative merit of different ideas was used.

The companies that come closest to the formal approach to screening indicative of good management practice constitute the fourth group. In one instance, Information Retrieval Corp. applied screening criteria that were derived from priorities set out in its strategic plan. These included such things as technological developments, likely competitive strategies, contribution to corporate objectives, and cash-flow considerations. However, no attempt was made to assign objective weights to these criteria. The other company in this group, Switching Devices Corp., used a two-stage screening process. Initially, ideas were screened on a "gut-feel" basis. Ideas that survived this highly subjective phase were then assigned to the appropriate product manager, who applied a highly formalized screening procedure developed by a consultant. This procedure, which used explicit criteria in a uniform way, might be applied repeatedly over the lengthy development period as additional information affecting the product's viability was obtained.

Concept Testing. The concept-testing stage represents the first attempt to define a specific product, based on an idea that survives the screening stage, and to expose that product definition, in the form of either model, mockup, or description to potential customers to determine their reaction. This step is performed prior to the commitment of major financial resources to either product development or business analysis and provides a relatively inexpensive way of determining buyer reaction to the product concept.

Despite the advantages of concept testing, in terms of the information it provides and the relatively low cost, only two consumer- and two industrial-goods companies used it at all. Home Entertainment Corp. concept tested all the ideas that survive screening, using shopping-mall interviews. Home Appliance Corp. also did some concept testing. Switching Devices Corp. sometimes concept-tested either informally or formally. Occasionally, these tests were conducted both by in-house personnel and contract-research suppliers and the results were compared.

Perhaps the most interesting approach to concept testing was initiated by Systems Communications Corp. Seventeen attributes of a proposed product were identified using both managerial experience and the input from focus groups. Five field-research teams, equipped with Apple Computers, applied a specially developed conjoint-analysis program to identify the product features and benefits potential users were willing to trade off.

It is remarkable (given the relatively low cost of this stage of the product-planning process and its potential for high profits in terms of information on market reaction) that only four firms appear to use it. There are two possible explanations. One is that companies may be reluctant to expose their interest in a particular new-product area because competitors may learn about their concept-testing activity. That is especially true when the product-development process is very protracted, with considerable time elapsing between concept testing and commercialization. However, Switching Devices Corp., which used concept testing, also had the longest product-development time.

A second explanation is that although formal concept testing is not conducted, at industrial companies testing may be done on an informal basis, with salespeople approaching customers informally to determine their reaction to a product concept.

Business Analysis. Business analysis is the stage in which surviving product concepts are evaluated for their viability as business propositions. This involves such activities as market-segmentation studies, sales forecasting, pricing, and financial analysis, and it marks the point at which substantial costs begin to be incurred in the planning for a new product.

Apart from one company that did no business analysis, the remaining eight fell into two basic groups: those that combined business analysis with screening and those that considered it as a separate stage after screening. Of all the companies conducting business analysis, at whatever stage, only one, Metalworking Controls Corp., had any formal financial hurdles. It required that new-product proposals promise a minimum 30 percent ROI to receive further consideration.

Among the four companies that combined the two stages, Information Retrieval Corp. started with sales and ROI projections expressed in its strategic business plan. A detailed financial analysis for the proposed product was incorporated as part of the screening process. ROI projections being one of the screening criteria considered. One problem this company encountered was that the internal competition for new-product resources fostered a situation resulting in inflated estimates of ROI. According to the corporate director, business development, the performance of new products in achieving targeted ROI was "deplorable" because of this "institutionalized optimism." Metalworking Controls is another company that combined consideration of ROI with other nonfinancial criteria in the screening stage.

Home Appliance Corp. and Switching Devices Corp. also combined screening and business analysis, but in different ways. In the case of the former, financial projections were successively refined as part of the committee process that reviewed new-product proposals. At Switching Devices Corp., the individual product manager who conducted the screening process was required to perform specified financial analysis including return on assets employed, contribution analysis, payback and discounted cash flow, which were considered as part of that process. However, the levels of performance on these financial criteria were not specified in advance, and products forecast to perform poorly on one or more of these criteria might still be acceptable on the grounds of competitive necessity.

Among those conducting business analysis as a separate stage, there were several different approaches. The most sophisticated was taken by Office Products Corp. It was the only company among those interviewed that used computer simulations to test revenue and cost projections and derive a "mini business plan." As an interesting sidelight on this process, this company was one that explicitly excluded ROI from its analysis. Two other companies developed cost and revenue projections as part of specific sales forecasts. Another company, Home Entertainment Corp., based its business analysis on a "design to cost" approach, in which costs and proposed product features were successively traded off in an iterative process until the desired profit potential had been reached.

Development and Testing. The management practices we found implemented by the nine companies at the development and testing stages of the process were essentially what we expected to find. The companies kept good managerial control over the authorization and spending of the funds required to develop the idea into a working product, and they used market testing more or less appropriately in conjunction with their development activities.

Features that we found characteristic of financial control at the development stage included a general rule that expenditures to commence the development of a new idea into a product would not be made before formal approval by a committee and/or senior executive resulting in an explicit decision to fund the development project.

Nevertheless, at three of the industrial companies, small amounts of discretionary, ex-budget funding was available prior to the authorization decision for ideas that were felt to need some R&D work on them to aid the screening and business analysis. At one of these companies, Information Retrieval Corp., as much as $100,000 could be spent on an idea before it was formally authorized as a project. An executive expressed the opinion that more of this informal funding of development work probably went on than the formally oriented corporate staff would like to acknowledge.

Furthermore, once a financial commitment to a project was made, this did not mean the commitment was cast in concrete. At most of the companies, projects would be terminated if they were not found to be feasible for market, technical, or financial reasons at any point during their development. This was possible because evaluation of the project continued after it passed through screening and business analysis while the development process was going on. At two companies, this continued-evaluation process was formalized into a sequential development system that projects entered after they successfully passed through the initial business analysis. At each step in the development process, the project as reassessed and cost estimates refined. These systems also insured that the firms kept very close watch on the continued development of the project once it had been authorized. At Electronic Games Corp., after an idea was developed into hardware, it was evaluated by a management team on eight to ten performance dimensions. On the basis of this evaluation, a product that was as much as 70 percent developed might be shelved despite the investment to that point.

Another management and control device that we found being used for larger development projects was the appointment of a special-projects manager or new-product manager to supervise the development activities and do the continuing evaluation work.

Development and market-testing activities go hand in hand. A major role of market testing is to determine the market's response to the product and particular aspects of the product such as its features, appearance, and price. Such testing can occur first after the development phase. In either case, the results from market testing may indicate an area where something about the product is seen as unsatisfactory and cause further development work to be undertaken to correct the situation.

Among the nine firms we interviewed, seven made use of some form of market-testing activity in their new-product–planning process, including the three consumer-products companies whose uses of testing were more extensive and varied. The four industrial companies all used field tests or field trials of their new products with customers, but nothing else. Still, the vice president for corporate planning at Communications Terminal Corp. recognized that more research and testing of their industrial products was possible when he told us he would like to be able to work out a detailed introductory marketing strategy for new products based on marketing research.

The three consumer-products companies all did a variety of market testing of their products including employee use testing, testing of style, features, and appearance in shopping malls, location tests, and exposure of new products to distributors to gauge their reaction and interest. No test marketing was done by these three firms because it is more difficult to test durable goods than package goods. An example of a company doing development and testing hand-in-hand was Electronic Games Corp., which tested its products in the market after 60–75 percent of the development work on them had been completed and it had an operating product. The remaining development work to strengthen the overall product was then done based upon the input provided by this market test.

Shortcomings in Strategic Direction

We expected to find that the new-product activities at the nine companies in our sample would be guided by strategic inputs so that the output of the process would represent an accurate expression of the firm's chosen strategic direction. What we found was substantially different from that expectation. At six of the nine companies, there was either no linking of the corporation's new-product activities with its strategic plans or no strategic plans at all. While at two of the others, the firm's, strategic planning had some impact upon new product planning, it was less than it should have been.

Only at the Communications Terminal Corp. was the product-planning activity driven by the corporation's strategic plans. There, the vice president of strategic planning was responsible for both corporate and product planning, and marketing planning was done as a part of the strategic planning. The result was a five-year product plan driven by strategic thinking that identified new business opportunities. These identified opportunities comprised the scope of the target areas where R&D could then begin its search for new-product solutions. In contrast, Home Entertainment Corp., one of the six companies, also developed a five-year product plan to guide its new-product activities, but this plan was not guided by any overall sense of the corporation's intended strategic direction.

On the other hand, another company in the same group, Metalworking Controls Corp., gave no strategic direction to its new-product planning and did not have a new-product plan. Instead, its new-product activities were customer-driven. Customers would ask the company to develop new products for them. While this was being responsive to market needs, the company went in whatever direction its customers chose to take it since it had no strategic basis of its own for deciding what types of products it should or should not be developing.

At the two firms between these extremes, strategic planning's input into the new-product–planning process was similar. There was no explicit link between a strategic business plan and a new-product plan. Nonetheless, they recognized that the directions spelled out in the broader strategic plans constituted the basis for criteria for evaluating new-product ideas at the screening stage of the new-product–planning process.

The vice president business development at Office Products Corp. recognized the value of strategic inputs at the screening stage when he told us his group was trying to get the company to develop a strategic plan so they would be able to evaluate new-product programs against it. In this way, only new-product ideas that fit within a mission and strategy would get through the screening process. The obvious weakness was that strategic direction would be provided one stage later in the new-product–planning process than it should have been. That is because strategic guidance would narrow the scope of the area within which the search for new ideas, whether technology- or market-driven, should be conducted.

Our research suggests that many large corporations still have a long way to go before their new-product planning is effectively tied to, and directed by, their strategic business plans.

Neglect of Sophisticated Techniques

It is our observation that little use is made of sophisticated managerial or analytical techniques in new-product planning. As we have already indicated, the fundamental value of strategic planning in guiding the new-product search-

and-development process was either ignored or underutilized. Furthermore, structured methods of idea generation and screening were almost totally neglected.

Only one of the respondents used multivariate statistical techniques, such as multidimensional scaling or conjoint analysis, to explore the structure of the market for net products or as a guide to market preference for product features. That was Systems Communications Corp.'s use of conjoint analysis for concept testing described earlier. Of course, a prerequisite for the use of such techniques is the use of marketing research to obtain the necessary data, and only a small minority of companies engaged in this research.

Only one company made use of computer simulation to test its assumptions about the prospective performance of a proposed product. Other than this, a broad array of simulation and forecasting models were ignored. Similarly, only one company utilized a variety of sophisticated methods of financial analysis to evaluate product proposals as business propositions.

Conclusions on the Observed Product-Planning Process

The preceding description of the new-product–planning process, as it applies in eight of the nine companies, is summarized in table 1–2. To the extent that the new-product–planning operations of the companies we observed were typical, there are several conclusions that can be drawn.

We found that the process was characterized by a relatively high degree of informality that bore little correspondence to any normative model. Little use was made of strategic planning at several stages where its application would be beneficial. Marketing research was underutilized, especially in the areas of idea generation and demand estimation, and there was little use of technical research as a source of new products. There were few explicit criteria against which product proposals were appraised, and those that were used were, most often, not strategically based. Furthermore, no provision was made to insure that these criteria were commonly understood or applied in the same way.

Formal concept testing, with its ability to supply an abundance of market information, appears to be the exception rather than the rule. Business analysis is often combined with screening, frequently using financial techniques that are rudimentary and without the benefit of detailed demand forecasts.

An extreme example of failure to manage new-product activities effectively is provided by Systems Communications Corp., the company omitted from table 1–2 because of its complete departure from the product-planning model used there.

Traditionally, this company had a technical orientation toward new-product development. Engineers designed a prototype that they would turn over to

Table 1–2
Comparison of the New-Product–Planning Processes at Eight Companies

	Industrial-Products Companies			
	Office Products Corp.	*Information Retrieval Corp.*	*Switching Devices Corp.*	*Metalworking Controls Corp.*
Exploration	No formal method. Ideas may come from anywhere in the organization.	No formal method. Ideas may come from anywhere in the organization. Interdivisional brainstorming. Some direction from strategic plan.	Ideas from many internal and external sources. Formal bonus incentive system. Strategic planning searches for areas of market opportunity and anticipates market needs. 50–60% of ideas are customer-generated.	Ideas for evolutionary developments come from customers.
Screening	Two stages: (1) Prescreen by small group using general (unwritten) criteria subjectively applied. (2) A committee evaluates in general terms including "ball-park" financial estimates.	Criteria are derived from priorities in strategic plan in qualitative terms. Rough sales and ROI projections also used as criteria. Combined with business analysis. (See below.)	Two stages: (1) "Gut feel," kills 30–40%. (2) Uses consultant-developed systematic appraisal. Includes a variety of financial analyses, but with no preestablished financial-performance levels. Combined with business analysis.	Four unwritten criteria applied informally by committee. Combined with business analysis. (See below.)
Concept testing	None.	None.	Informal and formal. Both in-house and by contract-research suppliers.	None.
Business analysis	Do detailed "mini business plan." Use computer simulation. No standard financial criteria. ROI never used.	Combined with screening. Standard venture-analysis form is prepared with detailed financial-performance projections. They are compared to criteria in business strategy.	Combined with screening.	Combined with screening. Use 30%-minimum-ROI hurdle.

	Consumer-Products Companies		
Communications Terminal Corp.	*Electronic Games Corp.*	*Consumer Appliance Corp.*	*Home Entertainment Corp.*
Ideas for new business opportunities identified in strategic plan. Projection of customer needs. Also "blue-sky" approach.	From creative group "skull sessions" within two R&D groups. Also from engineering, other executives, and licensing.	From anywhere inside or outside the company. Standardized form for idea submission. Also trade fairs and shows.	No formal method. Ideas may come from research engineering. Imitates competitive products.
Unwritten, general criteria applied informally by individuals. Also includes "coarse forecasting cuts."	Implicit criteria applied by small group based o intuition and knowledge from marketing research. Preceded by some hardware development.	First for technical feasibility by engineering. Then, subjectively by individuals without specific criteria. Finally, committee evaluates in general terms, including preliminary financial estimates. Combined with business analysis. (See below.)	Subjective, holistic by an individual.
None.	None.	May be done where more information is deemed necessary.	Used generally.
Costs and sales forecast developed for each product passing screen.	No business analysis until after market test. Resulting sales forecast is basis for detailed financial analysis. Prior to market test, financial performance evaluated intuitively.	Concurrent with development. Financial projections are refined successively as additional cost information is obtained from development.	Employee use testing done regularly.

Table 1–2 *continued*

	Industrial-Products Companies			
	Office Products Corp.	*Information Retrieval Corp.*	*Switching Devices Corp.*	*Metalworking Controls Corp.*
Development	As a general rule, financial commitment made only after business analysis.	Financial commitment to development generally not made until after business analysis. For really new products, will do preliminary development work before committing to manufacturing development.	As a general rule, financial commitment made only after business analysis. Marketing-research studies continued during development.	Make ten prototypes to be used for testing.
Market testing	Field trials with customers.	Field trials with customers.	Field trials with customers.	Field trials with customers.

Note: Radio Communications Corporation was omitted because its new-product–planning process did not conform to the sequential procedure outlined in the table. A description of the process at that company appears in the text.

manufacturing with little consultation with marketing or sales. The result was a product that was overengineered and too expensive for its markets. Today, the company is moving toward a marketing orientation. It has a manual outlining a formal product planning system, but it is not used because "management doesn't apply the discipline to require the rules to be followed." In fact, there is no formal product-planning process. Instead, an idea for a new product originates and survives solely as a result of a "product champion," whose major efforts are directed toward "selling" the idea to others involved in the process. There is no formal screening of these ideas. The basis for selecting ideas for engineering development is political rather than rational. It can take a year, or more, of advocacy before the selection decision is made.

This all adds up to a considerable gap between actual practice and the principles of sound new-product planning. It also suggests something about both the nature of the problem and the actions necessary to improve the process.

	Consumer-Products Companies		
Communications Terminal Corp.	*Electronic Games Corp.*	*Consumer Appliance Corp.*	*Home Entertainment Corp.*
Three stages: (1) Agree on hard specifications. (2) R&D proves technology. (3) Design acceptance.	Substantially completed prior to business analysis. Hardware evaluated on 8–10 dimensions using a standard form.	Development not begun until after approval of business analysis.	Employee use testing done regularly.
Field trials with customers.	Consumer use tests.	Additional market research on desirable features.	May do style, feature, and appearance tests in malls. Products displayed to distributor panel for feedback.

Sources of New-Product–Planning Problems

There are numerous reasons why the new-product–planning practices we described might deviate from those suggested by the three principles we have enumerated. From our observations, however, we believe that these deviations stem from two basic sources: the complex nature of the process itself and the premium that it places on the need to manage it more effectively.

Complexity of the Process

While the problems we observed are, to some degree, a reflection of the unique circumstances faced by each to the companies themselves, a major source of difficulty with the new-product–planning process is that it is inherently entropic. It tends toward disorder because it involves people with different skills and varying perspectives as to how new-product problems should be solved. A further complication is that much of the process involves dealing with an intangible concept rather than a tangible product. The process also requires the management of creativity, and it is particularly easy to succumb to a technological infatuation with new-product ideas and projects.

The problem that this poses is likely to be particularly pronounced at companies with a strong technological base, such as the ones we have described. In this environment, there is a temptation for engineers to believe they can design and execute anything, while R&D people can become enamored with the latest technological breakthrough. As a result, they lose sense of market needs, often producing technological solutions to phantom problems.

In some cases, the dominance of a technological orientation in the new-product–planning process, or its misdirection, is caused by a failure to communicate strategic-planning considerations to the engineering staff. The result is a general lack of direction in research and development that wastes technical resources and dissipates new-product efforts.

A final element that adds to the complexity of the process is the fact that creativity, which is difficult both to foster and direct, is an essential aspect of new-product planning. Yet, as many have observed, the bureaucratic organization not only does not know how to foster it but often finds it anathema. This is at least partially confirmed in our examination of the nine companies, which indicates that they do much better in the later stages of the process where the need for creativity diminishes.

Managerial Shortcomings

Given its complexity, the product-planning function offers a particularly difficult challenge to management. Many of the problems with product planning stem from the failure of management either to recognize and/or live up to that challenge.

In the companies we observed, there did not seem to be much order in the process. Few had documents spelling out the procedure, and if they had them, they were more often honored in the breach. In several instances, those involved in the process had difficulty in describing the organization, and, in one instance in particular, it appeared not to exist in any reasonable form. One got the impression that the various product-planning organizations, rather than being a rational response to a planning problem, had just evolved over time into a form that might hinder rather than help.

In some companies, managers may see problems in their new-product process, but may not see the means to improve it because they are not aware of the appropriate advanced managerial practices. There are two possible explanations for this. One is ignorance of their existence. This is particularly likely at companies where managers with new-product responsibilities have technical backgrounds. Alternatively, management may be aware of them but have little faith in their application to the solution of practical product-planning problems. A factor contributing to the unwillingness to rely on these techniques may be an uneasiness that stems from the arcane nature of some computer-based analysis.

Another source of problems was the corporate emphasis on consensus rather than conflict. We believe that one effect of this emphasis was an unwillingness to entertain ideas for really new products, because the introduction of such ideas without preclearance might invite resistance. That was true even though absence of prior constraint is the very essence of the creativity that is likely to result in really new products.

Improving the Product-Planning Process

It is not enough, however, to recognize the causes of the problem. It is also necessary to put forward a broad framework for their solution as it relates to strategic orientation, the need for ordering the process, and increasing information input.

Strategic Orientation

The place to begin improving the new-product–planning process is to recognize the essentially strategic nature of new-product decisions and to establish a framework that suggests both the nature of the decisions to be made and the criteria against which they will be evaluated. Without the planning discipline to establish basic direction, although there may be an overall sense of the business that broadly constrains the direction of new-product effects, the constraint is implicit and easy to overlook. This oversight may lead to unwise ventures into entirely new product areas, either through internal development or unwise acquisitions. Or, rather than risk finding themselves out of their depth in a new product field, the tendency is to play it safe by staying in the shallows of new-product planning. The consequence may be new-product efforts that are staid and conservative in a market that demands daring. The companies we observed had yet to reach the stage where there was adequate linkage between strategic plans, if any, and new-product activities.

Ordering the Process

Making the product-planning process more uniform and systematic is another area of potentially high payoff. Uniformity in the process, in terms of both procedure and content, permits all product proposals to be evaluated in the same way so that their merits as business propositions are strictly comparable.

More than many other activities in a company, product planning is a "people process." Its multilayered, cross-functional interdisciplinary character places great demands on the human skills of creativity, negotiation, and perseverance. In large organizations, however, this leads to what might be called "the product-planning paradox." Despite the need for individual advocacy and interpersonal exchange, the product-planning process should deemphasize the subjectivity of individual advocacy and incorporate measures designed to maximize objectivity. While no one should be so completely detached from the process that they feel that they have no stake in the outcome, the main problem in the companies we observed was the reverse. The investment of personal capital was potentially so great that people either would avoid the introduction of possibly embarrassing ideas or, conceivably, would be loath to kill an idea as additional commitments were made to it.

For the procedure as a whole, only four of the nine companies had a document formally spelling out the process. When there is no formal process description, the people involved will reach an intuitive understanding about what the process is. As a result, their product planning may exhibit the kinds of problems we have described. Spelling out the process is not enough, however, if management does not apply the discipline to require the rules to be followed.

It is also necessary to reach agreement as to the criteria that will be applied in the evaluation of each idea and to achieve a relatively high degree of unanimity as to the meaning and relative importance of each criterion. At least at the screening stage, the criteria are such as not to require any additional information on the part of evaluators before making their decisions. In addition, business analysis has some characteristics that distinguish this stage from screening, i.e., it is not merely a process that screens new-product ideas against a specialized subset of (financial) criteria, although that is what it does.

In contrast, the proper conduct of business analysis requires the assemblage of a large amount of financial and marketing-research information to determine whether the proposed product has the potential for viability as a business venture. When the screening and business-analysis phases are telescoped, as occurred at several of the companies we observed, the probability of arriving at two equally undesirable outcomes is enhanced. One effect of combining the two stages is that the high level of information required for a sound business analysis will go unrecognized. That is, the relatively superficial appraisal of the screening stage will be carried over, failing to examine the full ramifications in terms of market potentials, forecasts, segmentation, and other matters vital to evaluating the prospective success of the proposal. The other undesirable outcome is that the level of information desired for a sound business analysis will be brought to bear too soon, resulting in major expenditures too early in the process, with all the pressure for premature commitment that they can bring.

Increasing the Marketing-Research Input

Another method by the product-planning process can be improved is to increase the level of information provided by marketing research. Sound strategic planning for new products requires the availability and appropriate use of marketing information. In most of the companies we observed, marketing research played a negligible or minor role rather than being part of a systematic and continuing information-gathering effort.

The marketing-research function should be integrated with product planning on a continuing basis. It should be used to identify market opportunities and to gather information on market demand for use in business analysis. It should also be used to its full potential for both concept testing and product testing at various stages of development. Without information of this type, a company, at best, relies on its salesforce or customer complaints as indicators of market need, and it has no systematic way of dealing even with these sources of information.

Conclusion

Although we found product planning that ranged from sophisticated to naive in the nine companies we surveyed in depth, the preponderance of practice tended toward the latter. Yet as recently as 1979, a Booz, Allen & Hamilton report, referring to the new-product process, said that "in the past 10 years both consumer and industrial product manufacturers have become far more sophisticated and results have improved."[5] How can one account for these differences?

One possible explanation is that over a wide range of sophistication, the companies we surveyed were technology-based. As a consequence, they tended to ignore the imperatives of the market in their product planning, thus short-circuiting various aspects of the product-planning process that depend on market input. Another explanation is that mail surveys of product-planning practices, such as the one reported by BAH (1982), tend to report what people say they do rather than actual practice. Significantly, although the 1982 BAH report concludes there is now greater efficiency in product planning, this improvement was not reflected in the new-product success rate of those that are commercialized, which has stayed constant over the past two decades.

If we accept the former explanation of lack of market input, our findings suggest an urgent need for improvement. The consensus among the companies we interviewed was that new products would account for a substantial proportion of their sales within the next ten years—a conclusion totally consistent with that reached by BAH. If the new products of these, and U.S. companies generally, are to succeed given the current environment of strong international competition and shortened product life cycles, then product planning generally (especially those aspects of it relating to market input) will have to be improved.

It is encouraging to note that there is a growing awareness of the urgent need to change. The Video Products Division of General Electric has begun to expose its design engineers directly to feedback from the consumer. As John R. Rockwell of Booz, Allen & Hamilton put it: " 'Growth will be market driven,' only those companies that 'figure out how to drive that change instead of just reacting to it' with thrive" (*Business Week* [1983]). Application of the three principles of modern management practice as they relate to new-product planning will help to insure this outcome.

References

Booz: Booz, Allen & Hamilton. (1968). *Management of New Products,* 4th ed. New York: Boozx, Allen & Hamilton.
———— (1982). *New Product Management for the 1980's.* New York: Booz, Allen & Hamilton.
Kotler, Philip. (1980). *Marketing Management,* 4th ed. Englewood Cliffs, N.J.: Prentice-Hall.
"Listening to the Voice of the Market Place" (February 21): 90–95.
Sommers, William P. (1982). "Product Development: New Approaches in the 1980's," in *Readings in the Management of Innovation.* Michael L. Tushman and William L. Moore, eds. Boston: Pitman.
Wind, Yoram J. (1982). *Product Policy: Concepts, Methods, and Strategy.* Reading, Mass.: Addison-Wesley.

Notes

1. Several of these models are discussed in Wind (1982, chapter 8).

2
How Experienced Product Innovators Organize

Frederick A. Johne

Product innovation is becoming an increasingly important competitive activity in many industries, while more and more firms with little or no experience with the tasks involved are having to organize themselves for this purpose. Managers are faced with finding answers to key questions such as:

- To what extent should idea generation be encouraged as a freewheeling activity as opposed to being constrained by market-planning guidelines?
- How much importance should be placed on testing an idea in concept prior to making a major financial commitment in favor of a particular product development?
- How closely and how regularly should product-development activities be monitored and controlled by top management?

This chapter reports the results of an investigation into how product innovation is organized in one high tech manufacturing industry in which competition is particularly fierce. Examples are provided of organizational practices used in active and experienced instrument-manufacturing firms that are admired and often copied later by other firms. Two main types of structure are discussed: (1) formal structures, such as new-product committees, departments, and groups, and (2) infrastructures, which make up the substance of work organization in terms of how it is defined and controlled. The results show: (1) how the organizational formats of active product-innovator firms are quite different from those of firms with less experience with the tasks involved and (2) why the structures of active and experienced firms in the instrument-manufacturing industry are particularly suited for efficient product innovation.

The main message of the findings for managers who want to streamline their product-innovation procedures is that the substance of organizational

Reprinted with minor alterations by permission of the publisher from The Journal of Product Innovation Management 2, no. 4: 210–23. Copyright 1984 by Elsevier Science Publishing Co., Inc.

arrangements (and not solely the formal organization structure) should be examined. Specifically, the findings suggest that firms with little or no experience with product innovation stand to gain considerably by tightly organizing certain subactivities, such as product development proper, test marketing, and launching. On the other hand, quite different organizational arrangements are likely to encourage staff to suggest appropriate new ideas and to explore these in concept prior to top management making a major financial commitment to support a particular product innovation.

Before describing findings and discussing the managerial implications in full, I shall provide information on: (1) the relationship between organization structure and efficient product innovation, (2) ways in which structures can be measured, and (3) the design and execution of the investigation.

Efficient Product Innovation

While both product and process innovation are important in manufacturing firms, Utterback and Abernathy (1975) have demonstrated analytically that process innovation—which is concerned with lowering the manufacturing costs of existing products—normally follows product innovation. Product innovation involves the development of radically or incrementally new products. While every firm needs to strike a balance between product and process innovation, it is product innovation that provides the key to long-run survival for firms operating in fast-changing technological environments. If a firm operating in such an environment fails to undertake sufficient product innovation, it will find—as its products mature—that the scope for even process innovation is reduced, because many customers are likely to switch to buying from more progressive sources.

Because product innovation is so important, it is essential that the activity is undertaken efficiently to meet specific corporate objectives. Cooper (1983) has suggested that two main objectives underlie product innovation in firms. First, there is the objective of developing successful individual new products (both in technical and market terms). Second, there is the objective of making a success of the overall new-product program in terms of its impact on total company sales and also in terms of its ultimate profit contribution.

Identifying and measuring the factors associated with success in the development of individual new products is a well-established research area. Consequently, there is now available a rich body of literature that examines the relative importance of the various factors involved (Chakrabarti and Rubenstein [1976], Cooper [1979A, 1979B, 1982, Hopkins [1981], Rothwell [1977], Rothwell et al. [1974]). The following factors have been identified as being particularly important:

1. Good contact with the firm's market environment to accurately determine users' requirements.

2. Good internal cooperation and coordination between engineering (R&D), production, and marketing.

3. Careful planning and control.

4. Efficient development work.

5. The will on the part of top management to innovate.

6. Provision of good after-sales service and user education.

7. Existence of key individuals such as a product champion, a business innovator, and a technical innovator.

While all firms commonly aim for tactical success in developing individual new products, there is no general agreement on the level of resources that might optimally be spent on this activity. This is not really surprising because firms pursue different strategies, particularly as far as product innovation is concerned. Some firms, for example, want to be technological leaders—which implies greater emphasis on product innovation—whereas others want to excel in terms of marketing older products. Hence, the literature on factors determining success in a firm's overall new-product program can only be applied for practical management purposes if careful account is taken of the strategy a firm wants to pursue.

Work in the area of corporate strategy suggests that manufacturing firms can pursue one of two main types of technological-product–innovation strategies. For example, Freeman (1974) conceives firms pursuing offensive or defensive product strategies; Miles and Snow (1978) speak of prospector and reactor firms; Miller and Friesen (1982) of entrepreneurial and conservative firms. The difference between these two types of strategies has been well expressed by Ansoff et al. (1976) and by Nyström (1979), who suggest that such strategies fall into two main modes: (1) innovative or entrepreneurial and (2) competitive or positional. Each major mode or strategy represents a distinct competitive stance: a firm competing in the innovative mode addresses technological growth opportunities in the form of product innovation, while a firm competing in the positional mode addresses the problem of achieving greater efficiency in current operations.

The investigation reported in this chapter examines the way product innovation is organized in high tech manufacturing firms that have been pursuing an entrepreneurial product-innovation strategy for a number of years. Such firms are called active product innovators and they are more likely to be efficient product innovators than less active firms because of their accumulated experience: efficient product innovators being conceived as getting new technically advanced products to market quickly and successfully. Specifically, the managerial practices of active product-innovator firms are compared with those of firms in the same industry that have been less active product innovators. The purpose of this chapter is to highlight best current organizational practice as far as efficient product innovation is concerned.

It is now evident that many firms are getting better at developing new products. Studies of industrial new-product development by Crawford (1979), Hopkins (1981), and Cooper (1982, 1983) have shown failure rates to be much lower than previously thought. Interestingly, all these studies stress the wide deviation from the current average failure rate of some 35 percent, which suggests that some firms are much better at managing product innovation than others.

My investigation concerned itself solely with one factor contributing to success in industrial product innovation. While organizational matters are known to be important in this respect, no attempt was made to assess their importance relative to other factors. This was a deliberate decision, because the aim of the investigation was to reveal differences in organizational practice between firms that are active product innovators and firms with less experience with the tasks involved. The assumptions underlying the research approach were that: (1) active and experienced product-innovator firms can be expected to have learned a considerable amount about organizing themselves for the tasks involved and (2) what has been learned in this way is of interest to firms that are less active and less experienced product innovators.

Loose–Tight Structures

The way firms organize product-innovation tasks can be studied in concrete terms and also in conceptual terms. The most straightforward way of looking at a firm's organization is to consider only the formal titles given to groups of persons involved in product innovation. Concrete examples of such mechanisms are "new product committees" and "new-product–project teams." However, such names solely describe the trappings of organizational structuring. What formal descriptions cannot indicate, on their own, is how organizational participants actually function; that is to say, they do not provide information on the substance of structuring.

In an endeavour to discover more about the intricacies of organizational structuring, researchers have made use of various analytical schemas (discussed shortly) to reveal details of informal or "hidden" structures. Such hidden structures are also referred to as "infra"-structures to differentiate them from concrete "super"-structures (Khandwalla [1977], Mintzberg [1979]). Analysis of organizational infrastructures suggests several interesting propositions concerning the efficient organization of product innovation.

For example, Zaltman et al. (1973), Baldridge and Burnham (1975), Dewar and Duncan (1977), and Cummings and O'Connell (1978) have all argued that the *initiation* of innovation in an organization is facilitated through a loose structuring of activities. Some of these writers have gone on to assert that for effective *implementation*, a singleness of purpose is required that can be achieved by a tight structuring of activities. These are interesting assertions because they suggest that certain structures might be better suited for particular organizational tasks. If this is indeed so, it implies that innovative organizations need to insure a shift occurs in the infrastructures used.

In fact, the notion of a shift in an organization's task structures was explained well by Shepard as long ago as 1967 in an example of a military raiding unit operating in the Pacific during World War II, which made use of alternating organizational forms. He described how planning (initiation) was a joint activity involving the entire unit with the private having as much opportunity to contribute as the colonel. However, during the execution (implementation) of a raid, the same group operated under a strict and tightly controlled military command structure. More recently, the notion has been popularized by Peters and Waterman (1982), who have suggested that corporate performance can be aided by simultaneous loose–tight organizational structures.

Hence, an important purpose of the investigation was to examine (1) whether firms that are active and experienced product innovators do, in fact, use dual organization structures and (2) if so, in what ways their infrastructures are different from those found in firms with less experience.

Initiation and Implementation

Whereas the focus of study was the firm (defined shortly), the focus of analysis chosen was the group of persons involved in product-innovation tasks. Exploratory interviews indicated that product innovation can be conceived as the outcome of two main phases. First, there is the *initiation* phase, which embraces (1) idea generation, (2) screening, and (3) concept testing and development. Second, there is the *implementation* phase, which embraces (4) product development proper, (5) test marketing, and (6) launching.

For the purpose of examining how firms undertake particular product-innovation tasks, the research used the following infrastructural variables developed by organizational researchers in Britain and in the United States (Pugh et al. [1963], Hage and Aiken [1970]):

- *Specialization:* the degree of division of labor achieved internally in terms of functions and roles.

- *Formalization:* the extent to which rules, procedures, and structures are written down for defining roles and for passing information.
- *Standardization:* the degree to which roles are defined for carrying out tasks in a certain way, i.e., the consistency in reviewing related tasks and the frequency in doing so.
- *Centralization:* the degree of dispersion of power by the chief executive officer (CEO).
- *Stratification:* the degree that status differentials are adhered to in the execution of tasks.

Each infrastructural attribute was operationalized by constructing multiple three-point scales to capture the essential elements in undertaking initiation and implementation tasks. The actual scales used are reproduced in the appendix. Using these particular infrastructural attributes allowed more specific operational data to be collected than is possible within the more general analytical schemas developed by organizational researchers such as Weber (1921/1947) (bureaucracy), Burns and Stalker (1961) (organic and mechanistic structures), and Lawrence and Lorsch (1967) (differentiation and integration).

Choosing the Firms to Study

The sample of firms for study was drawn from the population of firms manufacturing and marketing electrical and electronic test, measurement, and control instruments in the United Kingdom under Standard Industrial Classification (SIC) category 3442. Instrument manufacturers were selected because this industry contains some of the world's most active industrial product-innovator firms, which can be expected, because of their accumulated experience, to provide examples of the best current practice. It was decided to focus on a single manufacturing industry to control for some of the contingencies affecting operations: market complexity and turbulence, as well as operating technology, for example. It was also decided to control for size, so that only firms with one hundred or more employees were included to enable investigation of interdepartmental interaction, which is difficult to study in small firms.

A firm was defined as a manufacturing unit trading in its own right—either as an independent company or as a division or a business unit of a holding company. However, even when firms are drawn from a SIC four-figure industry classification, there can still be considerable diversity in their operations. For example, some instrument firms have much wider product ranges than others. To overcome this problem, the population was narrowed to include only firms manufacturing stand-alone instruments such as oscil-loscopes, logic analyzers, multimeters, and digital voltmeters.

Instrument-industry experts (who included manufacturers, persons sell-ing components to these manufacturers, trade-association personnel, and users of stand-alone instruments in government, industry, and the universi-ties) were asked for assistance in categorizing firms into one of two groups. The first group comprised only firms that are active and experienced product innovators; the second group only firms that are not known for taking the initiative on product innovation.

The specific question asked of the industry experts was:

Some firms are known to be more innovative than others in terms of offer-ing customers new and improved products. In these firms, recently launched products account for a high proportion of total sales revenue. From your knowledge of the stand-alone test and measurement industry, which larger firms do you consider to be the most active and experienced in terms of launching new technologically based products?

The question was readily understood by industry experts because it re-ferred to firms' activities in a particular product market. In consequence, the experts mentioned not merely the names of large multidivisionalized com-panies such as Hewlett Packard, Gould, G.E.C., and Tektronix, but identi-fied actual divisions or business units in them responsible for competing in the stand-alone test-instrument market. In fact, eight firms were most fre-quently mentioned as having been active product innovators in the industry in recent years. Of these, four were U.S.-owned, one was Dutch-owned, and three were British-owned. These eight firms were then balanced out with a convenience sample comprising an equal number of British firms from the same industry that had not been mentioned as being active product innovators.

A semistructured interview schedule (part of which is reproduced in the appendix) was administered in face-to-face interviews with persons involved in product-innovation tasks in the sample firms. Interviews were conducted between January and December 1982 and each firm was visited on several occasions to insure that we met with all relevant personnel.

It is worth reporting that all firms agreed to cooperate in the study, probably because considerable care and preparation went into the initial contact with each firm. First contact was always made with the chief exec-utive officer by a letter explaining the purpose of the study. On the occasion of the first visit, the CEO or its representative was asked to provide impor-tant background information, which is summarized for all firms in table 2–1. Thereafter directors, managers, and project leaders/engineers were in-terviewed on a "snowball" basis.

In the case of each firm, representatives of the development (R&D) and marketing functions were interviewed as a bare minimum. On average, four respondents were interviewed in each firm. Each respondent was interviewed individually, whenever possible within one hour, so as to keep the door open for return visits. Any differences in replies to the precoded semistructured questions (see appendix) were reconciled in return visits or in telephone calls until a common score was obtained for each firm for each infrastructural variable. Because each interview was tape recorded and included a discussion of a specific case history as an example of current practice, it was not too difficult to reconcile apparent differences by carefully analyzing the contents of individual interviews.

Active Product Innovators Are Different

Important and statistically significant differences in achievement were found between the eight firms categorized by industry experts as being active product innovators and the eight firms in the control group. This is an interesting result because it lends support to the research approach used in the investigation. Specifically, it was found that active product innovators rely far more on recently introduced products for their sales revenue. Not surprisingly, therefore, they claim technological leadership for a higher percentage of their product sales. They export a higher proportion of sales and compete in markets having considerably higher growth rates than those addressed by less active product-innovator firms. The actual differences between the two groups of firms are shown in table 2–1.

It is appropriate at this point to reiterate that it is not the intention of this chapter to argue that the clear differences between the eight active product-innovator firms on the one hand and the eight less active innovator firms on the other are caused directly by differences in their organization structures. The purpose of the investigation was limited to showing why certain organization structures are better suited for efficient product innovation. However, it is not surprising, in my opinion, that the structures identified as being best suited for efficient product innovation are found predominantly in firms that are active product innovators. After all, such firms can be expected to have learned more about structuring themselves to achieve desired product-innovation objectives.

Formal Structures

Although infrastructures were the main focus of the research, I also examined formal organization structures in the two groups of firms. In this connection, Randall (1980) has identified three main types of formal organizational mechanisms used for product innovation: (1) new-product com-

Table 2–1
Major Differences between the Two Groups of Firms

	Active Product-Innovator Firms (N = 8)	Less Active Product-Innovator Firms (N = 8)	Level of Significance[b]
1. Percentage of current sales revenue accounted for by products introduced in the past five years	52%[a] (Range 80–20%)	21% (Range 40–5%)	0.01
2. Percentage of current sales revenue where the firm claims to have a clear technological lead with its products	52% (Range 80–25%)	12% (Range 25–0%)	0.01
3. Percentage of turnover being exported (1981–1982)	42% (Range 60–18%)	12% (Range 25–10%)	0.01
4. Current average annual growth rate of markets being addressed	20% (Range 40–7%)	1% (Range 10%–neg.)	0.01

Source: Field interviews and secondary sources including inspection of certain company documents.

[a]To be read as follows: for the eight active product innovator firms, 52 percent of current sales came from products introduced in the past five years, within a range of 80 and 20 percent. (An unweighted average is used.)

[b]Mann-Whitney U-test conducted on individual firms' figures embraced within the ranges shown.

mittees, (2) project teams, and (3) new-product or venture departments. All eight active product-innovator firms were found to use temporary project teams for managing product innovation, whereas all eight less active product-innovator firms normally use permanent or semipermanent new-product committees. The division between the two groups could not have been clearer as far as organizational trappings are concerned.

None of the active innovator firms possessed a permanent new-product or venture department, a finding that supports the critical view propounded by Dunn (1977) that such departments frequently fail to live long for reasons expressed by one top corporate officer as follows:

> If the rest of the company perceives that members of the venture group stand higher on the career-path ladder, they will do their best to cut off the legs of the venture group.

These findings suggest that all firms desiring to emulate the example of active product innovators should consider establishing temporary project teams. That much is likely to be easy, but it gives no guidance on how project teams might optimally be managed. In this connection Souder (1978) has made an interesting attempt to dig behind formal organizational trappings by highlighting nine apparently different systems for organizing product innovation:

1. New-product department
2. Product committee
3. Commercial-product manager
4. Technical-project manager
5. Commercial-line manager
6. Technical-line management
7. Commercial one-man show
8. Technical one-man show
9. Dyad

Each of these nine systems can, of course, be categorized into one of the three broad variants suggested by Randall. However, the merit of Souder's schema is its emphasis that a particular variant—such as a new-product committee—can have a formal power base that is predominantly technical or commercial. Likewise, a project team can be led by a person formally representing either the technical or commercial function. While this is a useful amplification for studying organizational arrangements, it still does not allow identification of how participants interact in terms other than formal power.

The fact that active product innovators place little reliance on permanent structures to handle complex decisions created a problem for analyzing their organizational mechanisms. At first it was thought that this problem arose because of their more organic structures, as had been found by Burns and Stalker (1961) in a number of lively electronics firms. This interpretation suggested that active product-innovator firms use organic structures, which are difficult to understand, while less active product-innovator firms use mechanistic structures where job titles more clearly reflect responsibilities. However, this was not a satisfactory explanation, because in the implementation phase all active product-innovator firms were found to exercise far greater control over tasks than they do over initiation activities, *but without an accompanying change in formal job titles on the part of those involved.*

Infrastructures

To gain deeper insight into the complexities of organizational decision making, particular in active product-innovator firms, use was made of the infrastructural attributes already described. Operationalizing these attributes in the form of scales aimed at capturing the actions required of those involved in initiating and in implementing product innovation allowed important differences to be identified between the two groups of firms.

Taking the *initiation* of product innovation first, it was found that active product innovators use predominantly loose structures, whereas less active product-innovator firms use more tightly structured organizational arrangements. This is what one would expect to find on the basis of previous research.

More specifically, in active product-innovator firms, there is high role specialization for initiating that is accompanied by medium functional specialization. Typically, in these firms the marketing and engineering (R&D) functions are intimately involved in idea generation, screening, and concept development because these business functions are most closely in touch with specialized market needs. Less active product-innovator firms, on the other hand, exercise low levels of specialization and sometimes even leave the task of suggesting new-product ideas solely to the production function, which is clearly less likely to produce new-product ideas that are both workable and marketable.

As has already been stated, the structural properties in active product-innovator firms are as broad as one would expect during the phase of initiation. Important exceptions are consistency in control (a measure of standardization) and centralization. This is because in the sample of active product-innovator firms, ideas for new products are typically encouraged for a specific market area delineated in the firm's overall market plan. Only in one firm were staff given what appeared to be complete freedom to explore all new-product ideas that might catch their imagination.

Remarkably different structures were in evidence for the purpose of *implementing* product innovation. What is of particular interest here is that, in both groups of firms, evidence was found of a shift in infrastructures between the initiation phase and the implementation phase. However, as is explained shortly, the shift in operating structures is functional in the case of active product-innovator firms but dysfunctional in firms with less experience with the activities involved.

In active product-innovator firms, high levels of specialization during implementation reflect the involvement of a wide range of functions in product development proper, test marketing, and launching. In these firms, measurement of infrastructures revealed a highly organized approach to tasks that are closely watched over and controlled by top management. Of particular importance is the use of development manuals for insuring that individual projects are monitored against a standard set of criteria. Overall, the methods of operation were found to be quite different from those used for initiating product innovation. This is in accordance with the analytical literature on innovation in organizations, in which it is stressed that idea generation and exploration require a certain freedom of thought and action, whereas the implementation of innovation requires a certain singleness of purpose.

What is of special interest is that the group of less active product-innovator firms also experience a shift in their infrastructures between initiation and implementation. In their case, however, as has already been mentioned, the shift in structures is dysfunctional for efficient product innovation. The reasons for this assertion are not difficult to appreciate once the infrastructures for the two phases of initiation and implementation are examined. It has already been explained why the structures found in less active firms are dysfunctional for initiating new-product ideas. What makes their structural arrangements unsuited for implementing is their very looseness. For example, only one less active product-innovator firm was found to possess a development manual spelling out (in the form of checklists) tasks required of specific functions. But, in that particular firm it was not mandatory to adhere, even in spirit, to the procedures laid down in the manual! A particularly depressing feature, again identified by the infrastructural attributes measured, was that while chief executive officers in this type of firm seek to retain tight control over development tasks, they manage to distance themselves from the consequences of new-product–development failures by ascribing responsibility for any failures to persons lower in the hierarchy.

A summary rating and a detailed analysis for each infrastructural attribute measured for the phase of *initiation* (idea generation, screening, concept testing, and development) and for the phase of *implementation* (product development proper, test marketing, launching) in the two groups of firms is given in tables 2–2 and 2–3.

Implications

The findings have revealed considerable differences in the way product innovation is organized in firms with varying levels of experience with the tasks involved. Important and statistically significant differences in both the formal and the infra- (or "hidden") structures were identified in these firms. Analysis of task-group infrastructures provided particularly meaningful insights into why certain organizational arrangements are better suited for efficiently initiating the implementing product innovation. Loose infrastructural arrangements were seen to be functional for initiation and tight infrastructural arrangements functional for implementation in experienced product-innovator firms. It was also shown that firms with less experience display important differences in their infrastructures that are less suited for efficient product innovation.

These findings are interesting and intuitively appealing, particularly because they accord with assertions made in the analytical literature on innovation. However, for the purposes of pinpointing implications of direct use to management, it is necessary to consider carefully the various subactivities embraced within each of the two main phases of initiation and implementation. Taking first the phase of implementation, which covers product development proper, test marketing, and launching, my findings show that active and experienced product-innovator firms attach great importance to

Table 2–2
Infrastructures for Initiating Product Innovation

Structural Variable	Active Product-Innovator Firms (N = 8)		Less Active Product-Innovator Firms (N = 8)		Level of Significance[2]
	Summary Rating	Scores	Summary Rating	Scores	
Specialization					
Functional	Medium	(–,8,–)[1]	Low	(–,4,4)	N.S.
Role	High	(6,2,–)	Low	(–,3,5)	>1%
Formalization					
Written guidance	a		a		
Written communication	Low	(–,–,8)	High	(6,2,–)	<1%
Standardization					
Consistency in control	Medium	(1,5,2)	High	(8,–,–)	<1%
Frequency of reviews	Low	(–,2,6)	Low	(2,1,5)	N.S.
Centralization					
Power retention by CEO	Medium	(–,8,–)	High	(7,1,–)	<1%
Stratification					
Seniority of dominant coalition	Low	(–,2,6)	High	(4,4,–)	<5%

Source: Field study data. See also scales in appendix 2A.

[1]To be read: of the eight active product-innovator firms, none were scored high, eight were scored medium, and none were scored low, in terms of functional specialization. These scores resulted in a summary rating of *medium*.

[2]The Fisher Exact Probability Test is used to examine the statistical significance of the structural differences between active and less active product-innovator firms. To enable the test to be carried out, it is necessary to dichotomize the data collected on three-point scales. This has been done by grouping the medium scores with high or low scores as appropriate. The test shows the degree to which the two groups of firms differ in the proportion with which they fall into this twofold structural classification. The level of significance indicates the probability of a particular set of frequencies (or of a more extreme set) occurring by chance. N.S. indicates that the probability is greater than 5 percent, meaning that no statistically significant differences can reasonably be claimed for that particular structural attribute.

[a]Unsatisfactory scale. The question was badly worded and caused confusion.

adhering to formal control mechanisms. In this way, progress can be checked and coordinated to insure efficient development. As has already been mentioned, four of the eight active product-innovator firms studied possessed a control manual for coordinating the subactivities involved in implementing. The remaining four all used various types of checklists for controlling and coordinating separate implementation subactivities.

Hence, as far as product development proper, test marketing, and launching is concerned, my findings lend support to Booz, Allen & Hamilton's (1982) assertion that there is now far more formality in the new-product–development process in successful firms. My findings do, however, conflict with those of Feldman and Page (1984), who state: "In the nine companies we observed there did not seem to be much order in the process.

Table 2–3
Infrastructures for Implementing Product Innovation

Structural Variable	Active Product-Innovator Firms (N = 8)		Less Active Product Innovator Firms (N = 8)		Level of Significance
	Summary Rating	Scores	Summary Rating	Scores	
Specialization					
Functional	High	(7,1,–)[1]	Low	(–,6,2)[1]	<1%
Role	High	(6,2,–)	Medium	(–,6,2)	<1%
Formalization					
Written guidance	High	(4,4,–)	Low	(1,1,6)	<1%
Written communication	High	(6,2,–)	Medium	(2,4,2)	N.S. (<7%)
Standardization					
Consistency in control	High	(4,4,–)	Low	(1,1,6)	<1%
Frequency of reviews	High	(5,2,1)	High	(3,4,1)	N.S.
Centralization					
Power retention by CEO	High	(7,1,–)	High	(4,4,–)	N.S.
Stratification					
Seniority of dominant coalition	High	(4,3,1)	Medium	(2,5,1)	N.S.

Source: Field study data. See also scales in Appendix.
[1]See note to table 2–2.

Few had documents spelling out the procedure, and if they had them, they were more often honored in the breach." One possible explanation for the conflict is that Feldman and Page's sample may have included a large number of firms that were not market leaders and that therefore may not be experienced in product-innovation procedures. Certainly all that I observed in case examples in active and experienced product-innovator firms leads me to believe that such firms have taken considerable trouble to streamline and closely control the subactivities involved in implementing product innovation.

The main implication of my findings for management is that firms with little or no experience with product innovation stand to benefit considerably by more tightly organizing implementation tasks, not only for the purpose of reducing development costs, but also to shorten the time needed to get new products to market successfully. This is likely to involve such firms in making changes to the levels of specialization, formalization, and standardization. Centralization is likely to be already high in less active product-innovator firms but important changes will almost certainly need to be made in terms of stratification—particularly in ascribing ultimate responsibility for implementation to top officers.

The managerial implications of our results for initiating product development (i.e., generating new ideas, screening, and testing and developing ideas) in concept are somewhat different from what we had anticipated. It will have been noticed that the findings concerning structural configurations are focused predominantly on how ideas for possible new products are generated. While in general terms, looser structures are undoubtedly functional for this purpose, case examples of recent product innovations revealed that active and experienced product-innovator firms temper looseness during initiation very carefully, as is explained shortly.

The generation of new ideas is generally not a problem in active product-innovator firms. Such firms are typically staffed with large numbers of bright, well-qualified persons who are well able to suggest how existing products might be improved on technological grounds and on how the latest advances in technology can be used for developing completely new products. A much more important problem in active product-innovator firms is how the creativity of well-qualified staff can be channeled so that ideas are suggested that fit in with a particular new-product strategy. The issue was well expressed by one senior manager:

> I don't want ideas on better toasters. I am sure we could make a super toaster, but we're not in that business. We're competing in a particular segment of the stand-alone instrument market—so it's better or completely new ways of meeting the test and measurement requirements of chosen customers that I am looking for.

It is relevant to note here that in a broadly based study, Booz, Allen & Hamilton (1982) found that a mere seven ideas are now required, on the average, to generate one successful new product. This led them to state: "Ideas generated today are more clearly defined and better focussed than they were 5 to 10 years ago."

From the results of my study, I would suggest that there is another reason why fewer ideas appear to be needed now, which is connected with the way such ideas are tested more rigorously in concept in many firms. Rockwell and Particelli (1982) of Booz, Allen & Hamilton have, in a separate publication, referred to this activity as "up-front analysis," during which ideas for new products are subjected to extensive and often expensive preliminary appraisal. Specifically, I suspect that the increased scrutiny given "up-front" to ideas for possible new products is responsible in many firms for far greater care being exercised over the quality of suggestions being made. That is to say, the emphasis during initiation is swinging away in many firms from sheer quantity of creative inputs to increased emphasis on meeting analytical targets qualitatively.

I regard the increased emphasis given to up-front analysis in many firms as a particularly important recent refinement of product-innovation–initiation procedures. Indeed, in several experienced product-innovator firms, the potential return of spending quite large sums of money on concept testing and development was stressed. As one R&D manager expressed it:

> At the concept stage we are testing the new-product idea. It's worth spending up to $100,000 on this—sometimes it's even more. The downside risk to the company is far less than letting the market test a fully developed new product costing say $5 million. And, even if the project is a flop, we will have learned something for next time.

In all eight active product-innovator firms, great importance was placed on up-front analysis. Typically, between $50,000 and $100,000 will be made available for developing and testing a new-product idea in concept under the leadership of a project engineer. This expenditure is committed expressly for the purpose of exploring the new-product idea further before making a decision on whether or not to engage in full-scale development work. Indeed, so clear is the division between initiation and implementation that it is accepted practice in many active product-innovator firms for a celebration to be held at the end of the initiation phase. Then, irrespective of whether an exploratory project is allocated further money for full-scale development or whether it is "killed" for technical and/or commercial reasons, a drinks party is held.

Case histories of product developments in less active product-innovator firms indicated no clear division between initiation-phase expenditures and implementation-phase expenditures. Indeed, there appears to be an implicit acceptance that all expenditure ought to be justified in terms of final commercial success. Consequently, once a new-product idea has been approved, a project often gains a momentum of its own that is only capable of being stopped by market forces *after* launch.

The main implication of my findings for management with respect to initiation activities is that firms with little or no experience of product innovation stand to benefit by separating initiation-related tasks from implementation-related tasks. There can be no doubt that technological product innovation is expensive and that it also requires leaps of faith on the part of top management in response to ideas put forward by often quite junior members of staff. As a safeguard against expensive and embarrassing mistakes, it would appear to be particularly advantageous to explore in concept as many new-product ideas as the resources of the firm will allow. To do so requires members of staff to be released from ongoing operational tasks and to be given freedom in exploring and developing their ideas in depth. For this purpose, a certain loosening in control and coordination is called for, along the lines practiced by active and experienced product-innovator firms.

Conclusion

Several writers have stressed that much decision taking in business fails to follow normative textbook models (Feldman and Page [1984], Mintzberg et al. [1976], Verhage et al. [1981]). The research reported in this chapter has identified a sample of active and experienced product-innovator firms that have taken positive steps to follow certain procedures in a textbook manner. The fact that most firms in an industry do not adhere to best current organizational practice is not really surprising. What is exciting and challenging is that a relatively small number of firms in one industry, in which product innovation is of great importance for competitive reasons, are pursuing organizational practices that have been shown to be functional for getting new technically advanced products to market efficiently.

Considerable problems do, of course, arise over the measurement of efficiency in product innovation. As has been explained, this can be measured in two main ways depending on whether an individual product or the firm as a whole is the focus of study. Individual product success is a limited measure because most firms can achieve it if they take low market-related and low technology-related risks. A better measure is success in terms of impact profit contribution. To achieve these corporate objectives in an industry afflicted by complex and turbulent changes in technology requires a firm to add new technically advanced products to its product range quickly and successfully. It is by using appropriate organizational mechanisms that this activity can be facilitated.

The actual organizational mechanisms that have been considered are those facilitating tactical or operational decisions. It was shown that while there are clear differences in the formal mechanisms used by active product-innovator firms compared with those used by less active product-innovator firms, it is infrastructures that reveal the most important differences in modes of operation. Whereas the scales used for this purpose have face validity (because they are meaningful to instrument-industry experts), no formal attempt has been made at this stage to test their internal validity. This is because the thrust of our exploratory study has so far concentrated on identifying the nature of the interactions between persons involved in product-innovation activities. This much has now been achieved. The next step in the research must be to test both the internal and external validity of scales to ascertain whether these can be used to analyze product-innovation procedures across a wider range of firms in different industries.

Lastly, it must be stressed that while important and statistically significant differences in infrastructures have been demonstrated between active product-innovator firms and those with less experience of the tasks involved, caution must be exercised in arriving at hasty conclusions concerning the directionality of particular structural attributes for efficient product-innovation purposes. The present findings are based on a limited sample and so suffer from the limitations inherent in any nonrandom-sample method. At this stage one can only speculate that it is likely that other high tech manufacturing industries are also likely to have a certain number of active and experienced product-innovator firms that will lead in terms of best current organizational practice.

Appendix 2A: Scales Used in the Interview Schedule

1. THE STRUCTURING OF PRODUCT-INNOVATION-INITIATION TASKS

1.1 Specialization

(i) Do ideas for possible new products stem predominantly from one department, or do several departments intimately involve themselves in this task? Check against case example.

    Low ☐ One function only
         ☐ Marketing and R&D
    High ☐ Marketing, R&D, and other(s)

(ii) By what means do those suggesting ideas get their inspiration? Are any specific activities engaged in—such as brainstorming sessions—to increase the potential number of ideas? Check against case example.

    Low ☐ Ad hoc
         ☐ Ad hoc and analytical techniques (e.g., lost orders, exhibitions, market surveys)
    High ☐ Ad hoc and analytical techniques, and regular and formal brainstorming, buzz sessions, and so on

1.2 Formalization

(i) To what extent are those who involve themselves in suggesting ideas for possible new products given guidance or guidelines on this task in writing? Check against case example.

    Low ☐ Not at all
         ☐ To some extent
    High ☐ Extensively

(ii) To what extent is information on ideas for possible new products exchanged in writing between those involved? Check against case example.

    Low ☐ Predominantly spoken
         ☐ More spoken than written
    High ☐ More written than spoken

1.3 Standardization

(i) What guidance is given on the sort of new-product ideas the company is seeking? <u>Check against case example.</u>

Low ☐ Business mission delineated
       ☐ Product market area delineated
High ☐ Product area delineated

(ii) How frequently are formal meetings held at which suggestions for possible new products are discussed? <u>Check against case example.</u>

Low ☐ Less frequently than every three months
       ☐ At between one-month and three-month intervals
High ☐ Monthly or more frequently

1.4 Centralization

How much influence does the CEO exert over the flow of ideas for possible new products? <u>Check against case example.</u>

Low ☐ CEO encourages as many ideas to be put forward as possible—the more the merrier.
       ☐ CEO encourages ideas within the confines of the delineated strategy.
High ☐ CEO seeks to keep tight control over the sort of ideas that are put forward.

1.5 Stratification

From what level in the organization are ideas typically taken up? <u>Check against case example.</u>

Low ☐ Departmental executive level
       ☐ H O D level
High ☐ Board level

2. THE STRUCTURING OF PRODUCT-INNOVATION-IMPLEMENTATION TASKS

2.1 Specialization

(i) Which department or departments are intimately involved in the development process? <u>Check against case example.</u>

Low ☐ R&D
       ☐ Marketing and R&D
High ☐ Marketing, R&D, and other(s)

(ii) Certain types of activities can be particularly important in the development process. Do you, for example, have persons who assume responsibility for the following roles? <u>Check against case example.</u>

    (1)   Business/project management (i.e., product championship)
    (2)   Entrepreneurial interpretation of market trends (market gate-keeping)

(3)   Analysis of scientific and engineering trends affecting the development (technical gatekeeping)

(4)   Manufacturing/quality gatekeeping

(5)   Godfathering (sponsorship by a senior member)

Low ☐ Two or fewer roles are specifically provided for.

☐ Three or four roles are specifically provided for.

High ☐ All roles are specifically provided for.

2.2 Formalization

(i) In what form are those involved in the development process given guidance or guidelines on their work? <u>Check against case example.</u>

Low ☐ The process is explained verbally.

☐ Some written guidelines are given.

High ☐ A control manual is provided.

(ii) In what way is progress on specific development tasks noted? <u>Check against case example.</u>

Low ☐ Informal notes are kept.

☐ Formal notes are issued as required.

High ☐ Formal minutes of meetings are issued.

2.3 Standardization

(i) Are the same development criteria applied to control each project? For example, has each project an equal chance of being stopped? <u>Check against case example.</u>

Low ☐ Totally different criteria

☐ Somewhat different criteria

High ☐ Essentially similar criteria

(ii) How frequently is progress on development work monitored formally? <u>Check against case example.</u>

Low ☐ Less frequently than every three months

☐ At between one-month and 3-month intervals

High ☐ Monthly or more frequently

2.4 Centralization

What control or influence does the CEO exert over the development work? <u>Check against case example.</u>

Low ☐ CEO expects others to get on with it independently.

☐ CEO is kept in touch with progress.

High ☐ CEO is informed of progress in detail.

2.5 Stratification

At what level is responsibility for the overall success of a project development assumed, i.e., at whom is the finger pointed if something goes wrong? <u>Check against case example.</u>

Low ☐ Department executive level
    ☐ H O D level
High ☐ Board level

References

Ansoff, H.I., R.P. Declerk, and R.L. Hayes (1976). "From Strategic Planning to Strategic Management," in *From Strategic Planning to Strategic Management*, Ansoff, Declerk, and Hayes, eds. London: Wiley, pp. 39–78.

Baldridge, J.V., and R.A. Burnham (1975). "Organizational Innovation: Individual, Organizational and Environmental Factors," *Administrative Science Quarterly* 20 (June): 165–76.

Booz, Allen & Hamilton (1982). *New Products Management for the 1980s*. New York: Booz, Allen & Hamilton.

Burns, T., and G.M. Stalker (1961). *The Management of Innovation*. London: Tavistock.

Chakrabarti, A.K., and A.H. Rubenstein (1976). "Interorganizational Transfer of Technology: A Study of Adoption of NASA Innovations," *IEEE Transactions on Engineering Management*. EM 23, no. 1 (February): 20–34.

Cooper, R.G. (1979A). "The Dimensions of Industrial New Product Success and Failure," *Journal of Marketing* 43 (summer): 93–103.

——— (1979B). Identifying Industrial New Product Success: Project New-Prod," *Industrial Marketing Management* 8 (May): 123–35.

——— (1982). "New Product Success in Industrial Firms," *Industrial Marketing Management* 11 (July): 215–23.

——— (1983). The Impact of New Product Strategies," *Industrial Marketing Management* 12: 243–56.

Crawford, C.M. (1979). "New Product Failure Rates—Facts and Fallacies," *Research Management* 22 (September): 9–13.

Cummings, L.L., and M.J. O'Connell (1978). "Organizational Innovation: A Model and Needed Research," *Journal of Business Research* 6 (January): 33–50.

Dewar, R.D., and R.B. Duncan (1977). "Implications for Organizational Design of Structural Alteration as a Consequence of Growth and Innovation," *Organization & Administrative Sciences* 8 (summer-fall): 203–22.

Dunn, D.T. (1977). "The Rise and Fall of Ten Venture Groups," *Business Horizons* (October): 32–41.

Feldman, L.P., and A.L. Page (1984). "Principles vs Practice in New Product Planning," *Journal of Product Innovation Management* 1 (January): 43–44.

Freeman, C. (1974). *The Economics of Industrial Innovation*. Harmondsworth, Middlesex: Penguin.

Hage, J., and M. Aiken (1970). *Social Change in Complex Organizations*. New York: Random House.

Hopkins, D.S. (1981). "New Product Winners and Losers," *R & D Management* (May): 12–17.

Khandwalla, P.N. (1977). *The Design of Organizations.* New York: Harcourt Brace Jovanovich.

Lawrence, P.R., and J.W. Lorsch (1967). *Organization and Environment: Managing Differentiation and Integration.* Boston: Division of Research, Harvard Graduate School of Business Administration.

Miles, R.E., and C.C. Snow (1978). *Organizational Strategy, Structure & Process.* New York: McGraw-Hill.

Miller, E., and P.H. Friesen (1982). "Innovation in Conservative and Entrepreneurial Firms: Two Models of Strategic Momentum," *Strategic Management Journal* 3: 1–25.

Mintzberg, H. (1979). *The Structuring of Organizations.* Englewood Cliffs, N.J.: Prentice Hall.

Mintzberg, H., D. Raisinghani, and A. Thoret (1976). "The Structure of 'Unstructured' Decision Processes," *Administrative Science Quarterly* 21: 246–75.

Nyström, H. (1979). *Creativity and Innovation.* Chichester: Wiley.

Peters, T.J., and R.H. Waterman (1982). *In Search of Excellence: Lessons from America's Best-run Companies.* New York: Harper & Row.

Pugh, D., et al. (1963). "A Schema for Organization Analysis," *Administrative Science Quarterly* 8: 289–315.

Randall, G. (1980). *Managing New Products.* London: BIM Survey Report 47.

Rockwell, J.R., and M.C. Particelli (1982). "New Product Strategy: How the Pros Do It," *Industrial Marketing* (May): 49–60.

Rothwell, R. (1977). "The Characteristics of Successful Innovations and Technically Progressive Firms," *R & D Management* 7: 191–206.

Rothwell et al. (1974). "Sappho Updated—Project Sappho Phase II," *Research Policy* 3: 258–91.

Shepard, H.A. (1967). "Innovation Resisting and Innovation Producing Organizations," *Journal of Business* 40 (October): 470–77.

Souder, W.E. (1978). "Effectiveness of Product Development Methods," *Industrial Marketing Management* 7: 299–307.

Utterback, J.M., and W.J. Abernathy (1975). "A Dynamic Model of Process and Product Innovation," *Omega* 3: 639–56.

Verhage, B., P. Waalewijn, and A.J. van Weele (1981). "New Product Development in Dutch Companies: The Idea Generation Stage," *European Journal of Marketing* 15: 73–85.

Weber, M. (1921/1947). *The Theory of Social and Economic Organization,* translated by A.M. Henderson and T. Parsons. New York: Free Press.

Zaltman, G., R. Duncan, and J. Holbek (1973). *Innovations and Organizations.* New York: Wiley.

Part II
Design as an Integral Part of Product Development

Design all too often enters the new-product–development process too late and with too little consumer perspective for the full potential of this critical aspect of product development to be realized. Parsons, in chapter 3, quotes Caplan's (1982) comment that design is "the artful arrangement of materials or circumstances into a planned form."

What considerations drive this planned form and how design is integrated within the process were the subjects of one of the more interesting workshop sessions from which this book evolved. Parson's discussion is supplemented by chapter 4 by Kotler and Rath (which first appeared in *Journal of Business Strategy* in 1984) with its focus on the strategic and managerial aspects of design. Both chapters stress the importance of including product design along with marketing and engineering inputs from the beginning of idea generation and concept testing. With market information and technology so widely available, product design may be one of the few characteristics of an innovation that can clearly differentiate a new-product introduction and provide a sustainable competitive advantage.

Chapter 3 discusses what product design is, addresses what "good" design should be, and provides a framework for evaluating design concepts. Chapter 4 stresses how the interface between designers and marketers can be improved and provides the reader with a design-sensitivity audit and a design-management-effectiveness audit to assist companies in evaluating the role of design in the new-product–development process.

References

Caplan, Ralph (1982). *By Design*. New York: St. Martin's.

3
Product Design

Leonard J. Parsons

Why Design?

Design excellence when used as a strong marketing force can provide corporations with a competitive edge. For example, Thomas Watson of IBM (1975, p. 79) stated:

> We do not think that good design can make a poor product good, whether the product be a machine, a building, or a promotional brochure, or a businessman. But we are convinced that good design can materially help a product realize its full potential. In short, we think good design is good business.

Thus, the reason a company pursues a policy of design excellence is that it can profit from it.

The major areas where design decisions come into play are corporate identity, product design, and brand identity. *Corporate identity* is a statement a corporation makes about itself through its architecture, interior design, products, logos, slogans, and advertising. Case histories for Citibank (New York), P&O Group (Great Britain), Deloitte Haskins & Sells (New York), Whatney, Mann, Truman Brewers (Great Britain), Trio-Kenwood (Tokyo), Cummins Engine (Columbus, Indiana), The Clarks Group (England), Citizens National Bank (Seoul, Korea), and the National Zoological Park (Washington, D.C.) are given in Nakanishi (1985). Other case histories are presented in White (1973). Maintaining a consistent corporate identity has become increasingly complex as firms expand internationally as well as domestically.

Product design involves the selection of a combination of functional, structural, and aesthetic characteristics (Reynolds [1969, p. 72], Wind [1982, pp. 341–42]). Functional characteristics are those connected to the benefits expected from a product. An umbrella, for example, should shelter the user from the rain. A stowaway bicycle provides another illustration (White [1973, p. 29]). It should be usable for any member of the family by instant adaptation, be capable of carrying shopping parcels steadily front and back, and be able to be put into the trunk of a car for availability away from home. Structural characteristics are those associated with the delivery of the functional product characteristics. These characteristics include size, shape, form, color, material, odor, and tacile qualities. An umbrella may be small enough to fit inside a suitcase and may be made with a clear fabric that can be seen through. The stowaway bicycle may require a new physical structure for the frame, a tire suitable for a small wheel, and appropriate systems of suspension, breaking, and gear changing. Aesthetic characteristics are those that combine to yield a sensual impression. This impression may involve a visual perception of style or thoughtful design.

Companies that accept the arguments of Levitt (1983) and pursue a global marketing strategy must minimize language barriers. This requires that these companies develop and use international symbols on their products. Graphic symbology is becoming an increasingly important aspect of product design (Bowers and Witt [1984]).

Brand identity includes all names, terms, signs, symbols, or designs that are used to differentiate the goods of one seller from those of competitors. Brand identities facilitate the development of permanent price and quality images for products. Family branding occurs when a group of products is sold under one label by a single firm. Family branding puts a premium on consistent design excellence.

The increasing intensity of domestic and foreign competition requires companies to place more emphasis on design as part of corporate strategy; especially crucial is the design of the product. Thompson (1987) makes the following argument:

> What makes design a strategic discipline is that it's the only visible definition available to the public of the corporation, its culture, and its philosophy. Design affects every aspect of the corporation, from the first perception of the logo to the packaging and, most important, the product, which remains with consumers long after the brochures and packages have been discarded.

and concludes: "Your product is your corporate identity."

Perhaps the most glaring weakness of Peters and Waterman's (1982) eight principles of corporate excellence is that the attributes are all people-oriented. This people-orientation must be balanced with product/service orientation. (We, of course, understand that at the heart of marketing are the people—customers.) A commitment to product/service quality cannot be ignored. While poor quality may result from a slipshod production process, it could be inherent in the design of the product. Design is a candidate for the ninth principle of excellence (Holt [1985]).

How much will design excellence cost? Hanks (1975) agreed that this is a valid question, but only if not divorced from the basic issue of design excellence itself. She (p. 102) argued:

> Design is not an add-on. It is a matter of doing what you do, but doing it better. It is a part of the essence of the thing. The appropriate question would be: How much will it cost if we don't incorporate the design factor?

Indeed, any product having an outdated design is quite vulnerable to attack by competitors.

Distinctive design provides a basis for product differentiation—and corporate identity. To achieve a competitive edge through superior design requires that a company have what Kotler and Rath (1984) termed a "design touch." In the following sections, I shall try to define what a design touch is by addressing a series of questions: What is design? What is "good" design? How can design be evaluated? How can design be improved? Is a design advantage sustainable? How might design activities be organized?

What is Design?

When Charles Eames was asked for his definition of design, he replied, "a plan for arranging elements in such a way as to best accomplish a particular purpose" (Amic and Eames [1983]). Caplan (1982, p. 26) describes design as "the artful arrangement of materials or circumstances into a planned form." The emphasis is on the selection and organization of constituent elements according to aesthetic principles to achieve a unified totality for a specific purpose. The whole should be more than the sum of the parts.

Design is driven by the function the object or situation is intended to fulfill. This has given rise to the saying that "form follows function." At the extreme, one school of design asserts that the form of a product must be conceived in terms of what the product is intended to do. While it is true that one functional characteristic of a product is to look like what it is, a product designer had better make sure a product works before worrying about its appearance. On the other hand, if a product works, it does not necessarily follow that it must possess an attractive appearance. Function does not specify one particular form; rather, it imposes a constraint on the set of possible designs.

Design is said to take place within a triangle of constraints: the end use of a product, the materials of which it is made, and the tools and processes by which it is made. This triangle forces the marketing researcher, the industrial engineer, and the industrial designer to collaborate. The marketing researcher and industrial engineer tend to focus on technical details and usually work from the inside out, whereas the industrial designer tends to conceive of the product concept as a whole or thereby works from the outside in.

Designers are skilled in the spatial organization of matter. They are adept in giving visual form to something through the basic elements of the visual arts: line, space, light, color, transparency, motion, and texture. Principles they use include proportion, harmony, balance, emphasis, rhythm, variety, scale, and unity (Evans and Dumesnil [1982]). With their obsession with visual literacy, their abilities to create products that appeal to the other senses are somewhat suspect.

Finally, it should be noted that the emphasis in design is moving from the design of things to the design of the circumstances in which things are used. Marketing has long had an interest in store designs. Examples of award-winning store interior designs are shown in NRMA/ISP (1986). As economies become more service-oriented, this shift to "situation design" will become more pronounced.

Walter Hoving of Tiffany & Co. has said: "The basic problem is that corporate management does not know what good design is." We now turn our attention to this issue.

What is Good Design?

Answering the question "Does this product have the capabilities to successfully compete in the marketplace?" requires that more than the functional aspects of the product be examined. The design of a single product must address usability, ergonomic tractability, technical/economic viability, aesthetic sensibility, and image congruity. (I am not analyzing the intrinsic desirability for the product itself, which is a much broader issue. For an introduction to new-product evaluation, see Dalrymple and Parsons [1986].) I shall discuss each of these dimensions in turn. In judging a product's design, any criteria employed by customers must be respected. We shall consider these dimensions from the perspective of the firm as well as the customer.

A good practical design must be distinguished by its fitness for its purpose. An axehead on a broomstick is not a suitable substitute for an ordinary axe. The end user often does not know, understand, or care about how a product works, but the end user does expect things to work. Moreover, the product should continue to function under the most adverse conditions, if only for a time (Cullen [1984]). The product should also be convenient— easy to install, operate, maintain, and eventually dispose. For example, Massey Ferguson now fits the auxiliary hydraulic pump on its agricultural tractors to the side of the engine rather than burying it in the gearbox, where it was expensive to service.

The firm has a somewhat different perspective. It is interested in being able to extend the product's life and being able to bring out new variations of the product in the face of changing market conditions. Gardiner and Rothwell (1985) call a design that can lead to a family of products or design variants, a "robust design." The key requirement for a good design is *usability* (Brochmann [1970]).

To be usable, a product must be proportioned to people's physical and psychological needs. A good design should offer the user the greatest ease of use, comfort, hygiene, and safety possible. In addition, for durable products, a good design should strive to decrease operator learning time. For example, understanding the human factor—in keyboards, screens, accessories, chairs, and workstations—is critical in personal computing (Dickinson [1984], Edelhart [1984], Howard [1984], Kariya [1984], Porter [1984], Rosch [1984]). Poorly designed and placed video computer displays cause eyestrain, while noisy printers cause irritability. Another illustration is Syntex's Rumen Injector. Syntex needed a way to inject Synanthic, a drug that kills parasites in the digestive systems of range cattle, into the animal's rumen stomach. The ability to administer the drug by range hands, instead of by veterinarians, was desirable. The existing method of oral drenching was unsafe to both the animal and the person administering it. A syringe is not very suitable when working with frightened, perhaps resisting, animals in a muddy or dusty environment in the middle of the chaos of a roundup. The solution was a "gun." The gun had a safety mechanism that prevented it from firing if the animal pulled away suddenly. The shape was much easier to handle than a syringe. Productivity increased as much as fivefold (Abler [1986]).

In its persuasive communications with its customers, a firm would like to be able to convey information on those design characteristics that make a product usable. White (1973, p. 63) posed the following scenario:

> An office chair, for example, may be designed with particular attention to reduction in fatigue in the office worker. The height of the seat may have reduced substantially the obstruction which the front edge can cause the leg. The configuration of the back may give good support to the lumbar region when working at a desk. Its covering may be particularly easy to change for cleaning.

White concluded that "It is one thing to say to a customer 'See how comfortable it is.' and another to be able to explain what design characteristics make a chair comfortable." The second requirement for a good design is *ergonomic tractability* (Gasson [1974]).

To be affordable as well as usable, a good design must take into account economy, energy, and values. The customer is likely to focus on the cost per unit of use for a consumable product and the capital cost and operating costs for a durable good. Operating costs include power consumption and maintenance. The durability of the product may be important in some product categories. Durability is related to the suitability of the materials and the methods by which they are connected.

From the firm's point of view, not only must the materials in a product be suitable for its intended use, but also the least possible material should be used in meeting product requirements. The need to *make* and *distribute* products in an expedient manner must also be taken into account in a good design. In the case of Syntex's Rumen Injector discussed earlier, the casing was painted gray to create a strong metallic impression; however, it was made of plastic for durability and lower manufacturing cost. Since Syntex is in the business of selling medication, not devices, the gun had to be inexpensive enough to be given away with significant orders. The plastic employed was not compatible with competitive drugs so the gun would jam if one of the competitive products were used (Abler [1986]).

Designing for makeability and ease of distribution makes it necessary to define the physical requirements of a product design (Witt [1986]). The physical dimensions of a product, including its weight, need to be established. The number of variations in the product, such as selective or optional features, need to be considered. Selective features are those for which the buyer must select one of the options—for example, the color of a new car. Optional features are those that the buyer may or may not choose—for example, cruise control for a new car. The component contents of a new product need to be identified. New parts must be designed whereas common parts are available in existing products or as standard forms from suppliers. The source of each part should be anticipated. Consideration for how the product will be put together is mandatory. (Redford [1983] and Melloan [1987] have discussed design for assembly.) Any special conditions in the manufacturing process need to be identified. These might include supply conditions such as just-in-time delivery, environmental conditions such as clean rooms and temperature/humidity-controlled storage, or control conditions such as precious metal usage. Similarly, any special conditions in the distribution process need to be identified. These might include fragility and stability in transportation, shelf life, and store-display considerations. A selection of physical-design guidelines is given in table 3–1. All these physical product factors impinge on the cost structure of the product. Thus, recognition must be given to material availability and suitability, construction or processing capability, and logistics (Gasson [1974], Constable [1983], Witt [1986]). The third requirement for a good design is *technical/economic viability*.

The characteristics of materials and the methods of manipulating them must be related to what the marketplace will take. The appearance of products is formed primarily, but not solely, by utilitarian considerations. People respond emotionally to things presented to the senses. The holistic perception of a product that arises from these sensory qualities is called the *presence* of the product (Gilles [1985]). Sensory responses are influenced by

Table 3–1
Physical-Design Guidelines

Sourcing

Use existing parts and common parts when possible.

Specify cheapest materials consistent with quality.

Avoid single-source parts that are patented or proprietary.

Minimize the number of parts that must go to multiple suppliers to be produced.

Be aware of any import/export restrictions.

Manufacturing and assembly

Minimize the number of parts.

Be sure that options, including language panels for international markets, can be installed as late and as easily as possible. If possible, do the same for high-cost parts.

Take skill out of each operation and eliminate the possibility of errors during production. Allow for realistic tolerances. Provide positive location aids to facilitate assembly. Structure parts to "nest" during assembly. Avoid color-match problem. Make adjacent covers of contrasting color or texture.

Service

Do not "bury" parts that have a high probability of early life failure or are preventative-maintenance parts.

Physical distribution

Supply the means for efficient handling and movement, e.g., casters or places for lifting. Take into account lifting restrictions, stability requirements, and applicability for automated equipment.

Prepare for efficient use of common carriers. Match product size to common pallet size. Use standard container size. Give product the ability to stack.

Regulation

Incorporate requirements of all countries where the product may be marketed.

Source: Drawn from Oakley (1984) and Witt (1986).

experience. As Caplan (1982) said: "The public is not unready to accept the superior; it is unready to accept the unfamiliar."

On the other hand, novelty is an important aspect of the appeal of a design. One director of industrial design has pointed out that in many purchase situations: "A person is drawn [to a product] first by design. If product features match up to the design, and the price is right, you've got a sale" (Skolnik [1985, p. 46]). The ability of a product to arouse and sustain the interest of customers is driven by the novelty of its design (Abler [1986]).

A good design will convey a pleasant impression. The more technical products become, the greater the need to make them comprehensible and desirable. Abler (1986) noted that a "design pleasing to the eye and evocative to the emotions favorably affects perceived value . . . for products." He gave the example of Mindset home computers. Market research on the target market indicated desirable properties for the appearance of a home computer were low profile, less bulk, and a "soft" look. The soft look was achieved by using semicircular cutouts for its floppy drives. As a by-product, the cutouts made it easier to change disks and connoted "friendliness." This is an example where an appealing form contributed to function. (The home market was an illusionary one; the professional-graphic-design market was pursued by Mindset instead.) The fourth requirement for a good design is *aesthetic sensibility*.

Consumers may prefer a product design whose image is similar to their own self-concept—whether the self that the individual wants to be or the self that the individual is. This preference is influenced by membership in various social groups. Consumers frequently select product designs that will indicate their social status to others. The widespread appeal of clothing and other accessories with designers' names or initials prominently displayed is but one manifestation of this.

In addition, the connection between an individual product design and the firm needs to be taken into account. The character of a corporation is communicated through its product designs, advertising, promotions, instructional materials, displays, letterheads, and designs on trucks. John Sainbury of J. Sainbury, a British food retailer, placed this in the context of situation design:

> I believe . . . that one should look at these problems of design not as individual items but how each fits with the other in the wider sense. However good a single item may be, its importance and value is lost, or at least diminished, if not related to the whole. If careful attention is paid to the way in which each item—the shop front, interior decor, design of fittings, packaging, display material—fits into the whole, then providing each is well and tastefully produced, the overall effect and impact can be tremendous. (White [1973, p. 140])

The design of a single product should interact synergistically with a firm's overall design program.

A product design must be recognizable as the "visible incarnation of a company's personality" (MacDonald [1987a]). For example, the personality Sainbury's wanted to portray was one of honest trading, good quality, and cleanliness. Thus, products should be designed to complement a company's idea of itself (Olins [1985]). The fifth requirement for a good design is *image congruity*.

These dimensions are not independent of one another. As an illustration, Nissan, lacking a strong corporate image, has attempted to create a personality for its cars by stressing "human engineering" in its advertising through the slogan "Built for the human race." Its commercials have discussed the role of designing cars that fit individuals' driving habits (Alsop [1987]).

Design, in general, entails some form of compromise among conflicting requirements arising from the various dimensions. For example, even with the help of computers, modern designers have been unable to make the perfect chair. The best way to combine comfort with beauty has eluded them (Stewart [1987]; for another twist, see MacDonald [1987c]). In the case of automatic coffeemakers, one trade-off is between appearance and assembly requirements. Coffeemakers made by Braun of West Germany have clean and minimal lines. Their parts are precision-matched and require careful assembly, but, as a result, the lines where the parts come together, known as separation lines, barely show. In contrast, coffeemakers from Mr. Coffee are designed so that separation lines as wide as an eighth of an inch can be tolerated; consequently, their manufacture will generate a low product-rejection rate even with "bash-and-fit" (or, more colorfully, "bash-and-bang") assembly. Overhangs and deep recesses in the product's design provide dark, shadowy areas for hiding the bad joining of misaligned parts. A consumer's attention is diverted from these areas by flashy chromium strips and extra buttons (Papanek [1983, pp. 59–61]).

An important marketing consideration is how much variation to offer within each product line. One approach is to maximize customer satisfaction by carrying a full line of sizes, shapes, grades, and colors. An alternative strategy would be to market only the most profitable items within each product line. Other product-line strategies that could be followed would be to concentrate on the highest-volume products or emphasize items that can be most easily manufactured with the skills and equipment of the firm. Although a strategy of supplying a maximum of product variation might seem desirable from a customer-oriented marketing standpoint, there is no assurance that this is the most profitable approach for all, indeed perhaps most, firms. Witt (1986, pp. 45ff.) pointed out a product with many options may make impossible a build-for-shelf manufacturing-and-inventory policy. If customers demand off-the-shelf delivery, then there are limits on the number of options or on the way items are designed. His rule of thumb is to make standard any option forecasted to be selected by over 80 percent of buyers and to drop any option forecasted to be selected by fewer than 20 percent of buyers, although this last stricture may be waived for new options with favorable long-term prospects. For example, General Motors made many of its most popular automobile options standard equipment. The cost savings allowed G.M. to charge consumers less than what comparably equipped cars went for the previous year. Options that are forecasted to be selected by more than 20 percent, but fewer than 80 percent, of buyers must be justified individually.

The conflict between standardization (cost containment) and flexibility (variety) has been ameliorated by drawing on the intrinsic adaptability of component systems. (Oxman [1986] has discussed design for variety.) Massey Ferguson (United Kingdom) seeks to gain the benefits of volume production in agricultural machinery by supplying its global markets from only a few locations. However, significant product variation is necessary to meet very different customer preferences and government regulations. Massey Ferguson has met this challenge by stressing flexibility in assembly. Tractors are designed so that customer-specified items are, to the greatest extent possible, add-ons. Subsystem builds are emphasized. For instance, the optional cab, one of a limited number of types, is designed to be dropped in as a complete unit at the end of the tractor assembly line (*Engineer's Digest* [1987]).

Perhaps the options can be designed to be added to the basic product at a distribution center rather than integrated during the manufacturing process. For example, Kitchen Aid meets customer desires for different decorator colors by having a dishwasher with a front panel that can easily be changed by the installer. Two panels are provided with different colors front and back. The customer picks the color side desired and the other panel is discarded. The cost of providing the extra panel is less than the costs of manufacturing and inventorying four separate models. There is no need to forecast the demand for color.

Appropriate design may be a better aim than good design inasmuch as meaningful criteria exist for determining what an appropriate design is; furthermore, appropriate design takes into account the reality of change and circumstance (Caplan [1982]). Examples of award-winning designs can be found in Busch et al. (1984) and Edwards et al. (1986).

How Can a Design be Evaluated?

A checklist for evaluating product designs can be developed based upon the five dimensions of a good design just discussed. Specific factors that describe the characteristics of each dimension can be identified. These factors may general– or product-class–specific depending the nature of the design-evaluation problem. Customer-specific factors will be grouped under the heading "value analysis" and firm-specific factors under "suitability analysis." Each factor can then be assessed on a rating scale. For example, a five-point scale might include very poor (1), poor (2), average (3), good (4), and very good (5). Other descriptive adjectives might be used; however, no matter which adjectives are chosen, they should yield a scale that can be regarded as an interval scale (Myers and Warner [1968]). The factors in any checklist must be modified to take into account their relative importance. Buck and Butler (1970) gave a product-specific example for value analysis. Six models of baby strollers were evaluated in terms of, in order of importance, inside size (.29), appearance (.15), safety (.13), size when folded (.13), comfort (.10), durability (.08), ease of folding (.06), and ease of cleaning (.06). Individual-value-rating and suitability-rating indices are obtained by multiplying the rating scores by their weights and summing. The value factors and suitability factors are weighted separately. The value-rating index and suitability-rating index are combined by weighting them by their relative importances to yield an overall design-rating index. The resulting index numbers range in size from 1.0 for the poorest designs to 5.0 for the most attractive. A prototypical design evaluation form is shown in appendix 3A.

An alternative to rating each design individually would be to rank competing designs on the same dimensions. The dimensions would again be weighted by importance. This approach was proposed by Oakley (1984, pp. 132–33). The problem is that rank is an ordinal scale. We do not know whether a design ranked better than another design is a lot better or only a little better. Consequently, weighting and summing rank scores is mathematically meaningless. More importantly, ranking only tells us the relative performance of a design on a dimension. The best-ranked brand may still be bad or the worst-ranked brand may be good. Absolute performance ratings provide more diagnostic information.

Design evaluation forms are usually filled out by a cross-section of employees within the firm. Given that designers may not have a good grasp of what the customer desires or, more importantly, will pay for, current and potential purchasers of the product should be surveyed. The importance of doing this was highlighted by a study conducted by JC Penney (Hanna [1986]). For each of fifteen products, a representative sample of consumers was shown randomly ordered pairs of color photographs of JC Penney's current best-seller and an alternative that designers considered a markedly better-designed version. For example, in 22-inch soft-sided luggage, a $19.95 plastic import from Taiwan is JC Penney's best-seller and it was paired with a $350 leather case made by Gucci. Consumers were told that price and performance within each pair were identical. No brand names were shown and the consumers were told that all items were sold by JC Penney. For eleven of the fifteen products (leather recliner chair, microwave oven, acrylic warm-up suit, food processor, 26-inch hard-side luggage, queen-size sofa bed, 22-inch soft-side luggage, pharmacy lamp, stoneware, athletic/leisure shoes, and ceramic table lamp), consumers preferred JC Penney's current best-seller—often by a wide margin. For example, the current leather recliner chair was preferred by a ratio of more than 7:1; 22-inch soft-side luggage, 2:1. Only for four products (stemware goblet, wide-angle binoculars, stereo receiver, and remote 19-inch color television) did consumers prefer the "better designed" product and, even then, it was usually only by a small margin.

Aesthetic sensibility is only one aspect of a good design. In the case of 22-inch soft-sided luggage, consumers surveyed acknowledged that the Gucci item was better looking; however, they felt that the thick, wide straps, heavy buckles, double stitching, and corner reinforcements of the Taiwan import were cues that it was more durable. On the other hand, aesthetic sensibility led consumers to choose the better-looking selections in the high tech categories (binoculars, stereos, and color televisions). They felt the "better-designed" products had to perform better. In both situations, consumers inferred usability differences among products from the designs despite having been told that within each comparable pair of products, price and performance were identical. Designs must possess "design appeal" and be market-tested!

Several possibilities exist for probing the aesthetic dimensions in more depth. One is the *focus-group interview*. Kotler and Roth (1984, p. 19) related how one firm used focus groups to develop designs for a bank's retail area environments:

> The designers . . . construct settings of bank interiors and test them on small focus groups of bank customers. Customer responses to different layout arrangements, textures, furnitures, etc., help [the designers] gain insight into customer perceptions and preferences. Based on customer responses, the designers then develop a design proposal for the bank. The design package is tested with another focus group to refine and verify the effectiveness of the design. The final version is presented to management with evidence of the degree of interest and satisfaction of the bank's customers in the proposed design.

Another is the *semantic differential survey*. Respondents react to designs by means of a series of contrasting word pairs. These adjectives relate to design attributes such as color, shape, configuration, size, texture, and detail. The semantic differential method was used in the development of the Mindset Computer (Abler [1986]).

How Can a Design be Improved?

The problem of identifying at an early stage those products that are beginning to lose their attractiveness to customers is most serious in multiproduct firms. In a small company, declining products are known, and there may be no need for a formal review procedure. With a broad product line, a product-and-design—review committee would seem to be the ideal form of organizational structure for responding to this problem because it allows for representation of several departments within a firm. The composition of such a committee will vary among firms but might include executives from marketing, manufacturing, purchasing, control, human resource management, and research and development. The committee must include someone from the design department or a design consultant.

Formal criteria and procedures for evaluating product performance must be developed. Eckles (1971) proposed a four-level product-review system.

The first stage is a regular periodic scan of the product line to find items that are performing poorly in terms of sales, profits, inventory, competitive activity, and total generic demand. The factors reviewed should include measures of product performance as well as financial performance. For example, Oakley (1984, p. 124) suggested that an index of "product quality relative to other companies" might be one measure of product performance. In the second stage, weak products are matched against company objectives, and those that pass are programmed for formula or package changes, extra promotion, cost reduction, or new market development. Unsuitable products move to the third stage of the system in which a detailed analysis is made of such factors as scope of the line, company new-product research, customer satisfaction, utilization of facilities, and marketing problems. This step gives weak items another chance to redeem themselves, and those that are salvaged are recycled through the corrective-action phase of the program. The losers proceed to the last stage, where the time of burial is determined from the stock on hand, holdover demand, effects on profits, and status of replacement parts. Our interest is in what to do about those products in stages two and three that are designated for redesign. Ideas for redesign can come from many sources. I shall mention two: value analysis and search for visual inconsistencies.

Design improvements may be suggested by *value analysis,* an exercise to reduce cost without reducing value. Cost is the measure of the difficulty in manufacture and distribution, whereas value is the measure of worth to the customers (Buck and Butler [1970, p. 11]). Value analysis is a creative brainstorming activity involving a team drawn from marketing, design, production, buying, and cost accounting. Value analysis challenges the whole concept of how and why a product is made the way it is (*Research Management* [1982, p. 20]).

Information is collected on labor cost, material cost, and value or function of each part or subassembly. Next, the desirability of each part is questioned. For those deemed desirable, ways of making them less costly are probed. The physical guidelines in table 3–1 can be a starting place. The stricture "Minimize the number of parts" yields the questions "Can it be eliminated?" and "Can it be combined with other components?" A series of these questions are given by Buck and Butler [1970, p. 47]. Answering the value and cost questions requires team input.

The effect of changing one component on the other components must be recognized. Cost savings may be offset by implementation costs. Because of implementation problems, incremental design improvement of a product is very difficult unless planned for in the initial design. Redesign of the entire product and the introduction of a new model may yield superior results.

Whirlpool is striving to drive the service incidence of its appliances down to virtually zero. It has completely redesigned its laundry equipment. In the process, it switched to a plastic tub and replaced wear-prone belts with direct-drive systems. The result was reduced metal-machining operations, simplified assembly, and the elimination of 20 percent of the appliance's parts (Schiller [1987]).

A good visual design will convey a sense of order and organization. One way to identify possibilities for design improvement is to search for *visual inconsistencies*. This is just an extension of the childhood activity, "What is wrong with this picture?" For example, consider the drawing of a motorcycle in figure 3–1. Some of the visual contradictions detected are curvature of the mudguards that do not follow the wheels, the vertical alignment of the cylinder (despite the inclined alignment of most other parts), and the wasted space under the fuel tank. Functional inconsistencies may also be inferred. The most obvious, and well-known, problem is the placement of the rider's legs close to moving and hot parts (Jones [1970]).

Rather than wait until a product is in obvious trouble, a firm is usually better off to prepare for any eventuality by conducting regular redesign exercises. (Continuous design and redesign as a design strategy has been discussed by Jones [1983].) Customers will have accumulated expertise regarding the product, its performance, and usage, so they should be consulted (Gardiner and Rothwell [1985]). The redesign exercise can take advantage of the latest emerging technologies and shifts in customers' wants and tastes. The new design need not be implemented immediately, but may be put on the shelf for contingencies.

Figure 3–1. Looking for Visual Inconsistencies

Source: Jones (1970, p. 210).

Is a Design Advantage Sustainable?

Too often, organizations lose sight of the value of sustained design excellence. Greiner (1972) found that of the five chronological stages of an organization's evolution, design is most integrally a part of the first (or creative) stage of growth. However, as a company matures, less emphasis is placed on design, and more is put on general management policy and practice.

Inevitably, innovative designs will be imitated. If a firm has stressed economy of design, the imitators may face difficulties in operating profitably. Nonetheless, a strategy of design excellence would seem to require a policy of regular innovation. This is especially true in the United States, which is one of the few industrialized nations without laws protecting design. American Tourister introduced a line of side-pleated soft luggage. Within only a few months, no less than six other companies were marketing copycat versions (Lehrer [1985]). Design falls between the protection offered by patents to functional innovations and by copyrights to original works of art. The only recourse is to argue that one's "trade dress" has been violated:

> If the manufacturer can demonstrate that the "look" of the article is well known and that consumers buy the product not only because they like it but because they associate it with a specific source, then copyists can be prevented from making an identical or closely similar item, so that there will not be confusion among the public. (MacDonald [1987d])

Trade dress is related to a trademark and has usually been applied to package labeling.

For a corporation to successfully pursue a strategy based on design excellence, design quality must be embedded in its corporate culture. The keystone of any corporation is its set of shared values (Peters and Waterman [1982]). While a company can gain a temporary advantage from an occasional quality design, consistent performance requires that a striving for design excellence permeate the organization. Holt (1985) aptly describes this as "integrating the design process into the fabric of the company." He cites the examples of Precor in rowing machines, ADS in stereo equipment, Esprit, Benetton, Commes de Garcons in clothes and life-style, Swatch in watches, and Eclipse, Cannondale, and Rhode Gear in bicycle accessories. Esprit, as an illustration, is a life-style company that markets accessories, shoes, kids' wear, clothing collections, bed and bath accessories, and eyewear. Michael Vanderbyl, a noted San Francisco graphic designer, created a line of bed linens and towels for it (Anderson [1987]). Esprit has won design awards for its exuberant store interiors, packaging, graphics, and even store fixtures. Since the actual role of a chief executive is to manage the values of the organization, a stress on design quality must start at the top of the organization.

How Might Design Activities be Organized?

Design activities are located in different places in different companies (Dann [1982], Oakley [1984]). The location depends on the nature of these activities and the size of the organization. Small companies by necessity tend to consolidate design personnel into a central staff. Many larger companies decentralize design groups to where needs exist in operating units. I shall relate the nature of design activities to where they might be located in an organization.

If design activities relate primarily to corporate identity, graphics, and communications, the design staff reports to corporate communications or public relations, as shown in figure 3–2. Exhibit and tradeshow design may take place here. Corning Glass, for instance, has a corporate design group that is organized in this manner. Corning also has four design centers located in operating units.

If design activities relate to development and marketing of a technical product, the design staff will usually report to an R&D, engineering, or product-development function, as represented in figure 3–3. A problem with housing design within operations is that designers may fail to relate the product to market requirements. Moreover, creativity and innovation may be suppressed.

To protect against production considerations taking priority over customer satisfaction, especially if design activities relate to the development and marketing of a nontechnical product, the design staff may report to a

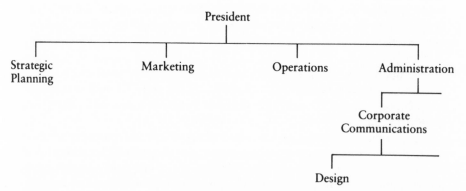

Figure 3–2. Design as a Component of Corporate Communications

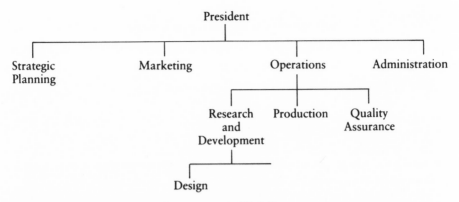

Figure 3–3. Design as a Component of R&D

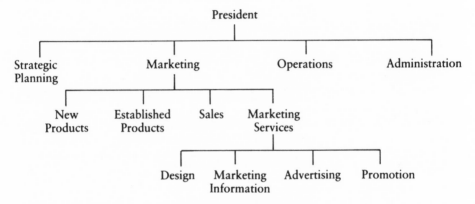

Figure 3–4. Design as a Component of Marketing

new-product–marketing or marketing-services function, as shown in figure 3–4. Packaging, exhibits, and graphics design are often the responsibility of marketing services.

Design may be too important to be left to any single functional area of the firm. If design plays a crucial strategic role in the marketing of a product, it might be placed under strategic planning, as figure 3–5 depicts. Placement in strategic planning would give emphasis to the concept that design is a long-run activity.

Achieving quality design may be difficult when designers report to a manager who has not been trained in design. Maintaining consistency in design may be affected by the normal rotation of functional managers. Improved performance might result from establishing design as an independent department equal in importance to the other major functional areas. (See,

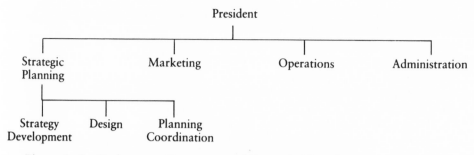

Figure 3–5. Design as a Component of Strategic Planning

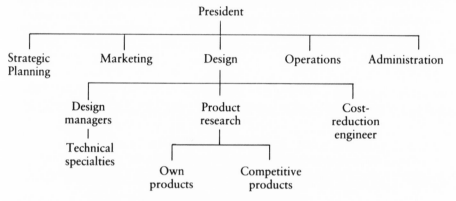

Figure 3–6. Design as an Independent Department

for instance, White [1973, pp. 24–25].) Figure 3–6 provides an example. The independent design department is a way to make sure any new product is imaginative. The design center for Corning Glass's Stueben Glass reports directly to top management. Dann (1982) notes that the quality of everything designed expresses the image, philosophy, and position of Stueben to the public. As a consequence, the design center is involved with strategic directions and decisions in all aspects of design: product, communications, exhibits, and identity.

The problem with having design under strategic planning or as an independent entity usually manifests itself when the design of the new product is complete and the new product is placed under line management. Line management may not be committed to the new success of the new product because of the "not-invented-here" syndrome. One way to overcome this implementation problem is to use a temporary team composed of the staff and line personnel from various levels of the organization. The temporary team may be either a "task force" or "venture team." The distinction between these two forms is that members of a task force continue to have other responsibilities while members of a venture team concentrate solely on the new-product project. The venture team (see figure 3–7) is regarded as the most effective method of R&D–marketing integration (von Hippel [1979], Gupta et al. [1987]). The venture team is a way of cutting across formal definitions of authority, breaking down interdepartmental jealousies, and insuring marketing's influence on the design process. The venture team encourages an efficient exchange of information on design matters.

Design consultants may be used by firms either in addition to or in place of their own designers. Design consultants offer the advantages of any temporary service. They fill gaps when a company's own resources are lacking or stretched thin. Design consultants can provide new insights and are often used for concept generation.

Discussion

We have been discussing *design management.* Design management has been defined as follows:

> Design management consists of establishing corporate design policy, organizing design policy and procedures within the firm, and determining and evaluating the design concept of the firm. (Hoving and O'Brien [1975, p. 1])

Managing design begins with identifying the key area for design within the company. In a product-led company, it is the product (Olins [1985]). My premise is that:

1. Design is an integral part of management strategy.
2. Strategy incorporating design will yield better corporate performance.

A key corollary is that:

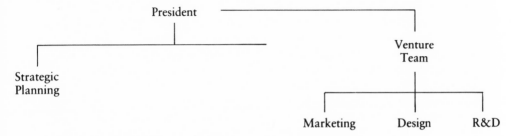

Figure 3–7. Design as a Component of a Venture Team

Sustained use of design requires that design be embedded in the corporate culture.

Norms should exist that encourage and expect creative contributions in design.

Research on the design/strategy relationship is needed to provide answers to questions such as:

1. Which corporations are using design as a part of their corporate strategy?
2. Under what environmental or economic conditions is design an important element of strategy?
3. How are design issues communicated in the corporate world?

As part of this process, Kotler and Rath's proposed design-sensitivity audit and design-management-effectiveness audit could be elaborated upon and tested.

Change in the marketplace and developments in technology interact with each other. Effective coordination among marketing, design, and production can exploit opportunities created by emerging trends—even those not yet fully grasped by the customers themselves. I strongly subscribe to the statement:

If products are designed for use and affection, sales and acceptance will result.

Appendix 3A: Design-Evaluation Form

Part I: Value Analysis

Factors	Weight (B)	Very Good (5)	Good (4)	Average (3)	Poor (2)	Very Poor (1)	Factor Score (A × B)
Usability							
Fitness for purpose							
Versatility							
Convenience							
Ease of installation							
Ease of operation							
Ease of maintenance							
Ease of disposal							

The column group "Very Good (5) Good (4) Average (3) Poor (2) Very Poor (1)" falls under the heading *Rating (A)*.

Factors	Weight (B)	Rating (A)					Factor Score (A × B)
		Very Good (5)	Good (4)	Average (3)	Poor (2)	Very Poor (1)	
Ergonomic tractability							
Comfort							
Hygiene							
Safety							
Technical/economic viability							
Material suitability							
Cost per unit of use							
Capital costs							
Maintenance costs							
Energy efficiency							
Durability							
Reliability							
Aesthetic sensibility							
Pleasant impression							
Well-styled							
Image projectability							
Congruence with self-image							
Status							
Total	1.00			Value-rating index			x.xx

Part II: Suitability Analysis

Factors	Weight (B)	Rating (A)					Factor Score (A × B)
		Very Good (5)	Good (4)	Average (3)	Poor (2)	Very Poor (1)	
Usability							
Adaptability to changed conditions							
Ease of product extension							
Ergonomic tractability							
Ease of explaining what design characteristics make product usable							
No product liability							

Factors	Weight (B)	Rating (A)					Factor Score (A × B)
		Very Good (5)	Good (4)	Average (3)	Poor (2)	Very Poor (1)	
Technical/economic viability							
Cost							
Material availability							
Manufacturing capability							
Energy efficiency							
Transportability							
Storability							
Patentability							
No patent infringement							
No pollution							
Safe reuse or recycling							
Regulations met							
Aesthetic sensibility							
Simplicity							
Novelty							
Visual clues to functional features							
Image projectability							
Congruence with company image							
Total	1.00		Suitability-rating index				y.yy

Part III: Overall Analysis

Index	Weight (B)	Index Score (A)	Relative Index Score (A × B)
Value		x.xx	
Suitability		y.yy	
Total	1.00	Design-rating index	z.zz

References

Abler, Robert A. (1986). "The Value-Added of Design," *Business Marketing* (September): 96–103.

Alexander, Harold H. (1976). *Design: Criteria for Decisions*. New York: Macmillan.

Alsop, Ronald (1987). "What's a Nissan? New Ads Give Car a Brand Personality," *Wall Street Journal* (October 15): 35.

Amic, L., and Charles Eames (1983). "Q & A," *Innovation* 2 (spring): 6–7.

Anderson, Kurt (1987). "Nouvelle Cuisine for the Eyes," *Time* (June 8): 88–89.

Bevlin, Majorie Elliott (1984). *Design through Discovery*. New York: Holt, Rinehart and Winston.

Black, Misha (1975). "The Designer and Manager Syndrome," in *The Uneasy Coalition*, Thomas F. Schutte, ed. Philadelphia: University of Pennsylvania Press, pp. 41–55.

Bonnent, Didier C.L. (1986). "Nature of the R&D Marketing Cooperation in the Design of Technologically Advanced New Industrial Products," *R&D Management* 16 (April): 117–26.

Bowers, William D., and David Witt (1984). "International Symbols, A Strategy for Global Marketing," *Innovation* 3 (fall): 12–14.

Brochmann, Odd (1970). *Good or Bad Design?* New York: Van Nostrand Reinhold.

Buck, C. Hearn, and D.M. Butler (1970). *Economic Product Design*. London: Collins.

Busch, Akiko, and the editors of *ID* (1984). *Product Design*. New York: PBC International.

Caplan, Ralph (1982). *By Design*. New York: St. Martin's.

Constable, Geoffrey (1983). "Design for Economic Manufacture," *Engineer's Digest* 44 (November): 3–4.

Cullum, Roy D. (1984). "The Essence of Good Design," *Engineer's Digest* 45 (February): 3.

Dalrymple, Douglas J., and Leonard J. Parsons (1986). *Marketing Management*. New York: Wiley.

Dann, Herbert I., Jr. (1982). "Using the Corporate Structure to Build a Strong Design Department," 1 (spring): 18–22.

Dickinson, John (1984). "Straining to See the Screen," *PC* 3 (October 2): 127–36.

Eckles, Robert W. (1971). "Product Line Deletion and Simplification," *Business Horizons* 14 (October): 71–74.

Edelhart, Mike (1984). "Workplaces That Fit," *PC* 3 (October 2): 169–71.

Edwards, Sandra, and editors of *ID* (1986). *Product Design 2*. New York: PBC International.

Engineer's Digest (1985). "Customer Needs Drive Technology" 46 (October): 12–16.

———— (1986). "Intimate Partners—Fastening and Design" 47 (June): 31–35.

———— (1987). "Engineering Reacts to World Markets" 48 (February): 12–14.

Evans, Bill (1985). "Japanese-Style Management, Product Design, and Corporate Strategy," *Design Studies* 6 (January): 25–33.

Evans, Helen Marie, and Carla Davis Dumesnil (1982). *An Invitation to Design*. New York: Macmillan.

Gardiner, Paul, and Roy Rothwell (1985). "Tough Customers: Good Designs," *Design Studies* 6 (January): 7–17.

Gasson, Peter (1974). *Theory of Design*. London: BT Batsford.

Gilles, Wim (1985). "The Presence of Products: A Question of Perspective," *Innovation* 4 (spring): 5–8.

Greiner, Larry E. (1972). "Evolution and Revolution as Organizations Grow," *Harvard Business Review* 50 (July-August): 27–36.

Gupta, Ashok K., S.P. Raj, and David Wilemon (1987). "Managing the R&D–Marketing Interface," *Research Management* 30 (March-April): 38–43.

Hanks, Nancy (1975). "Design for America's Third Century," *The Uneasy Coalition,* Thomas F. Schutte, ed. Philadelphia: University of Pennsylvania Press, pp. 91–105.

Hanna, Annetta (1986). "Design Quiz," *ID* 33 (January/February): 58–62.

Holt, Steven (1985). "Design, the Ninth Principle of Excellence: The Product Half of the Business Equation," *Innovation* 4 (fall): 2–4.

Hoving, Walter, and George O'Brien (1975). "The Crisis of Design and Aesthetics in American Management," in *The Uneasy Coalition,* Thomas F. Schutte, ed. Philadelphia: University of Pennsylvania Press, pp. 1–16.

Howard, William K. (1984). "Bio Tech Add-Ons," *PC* 3 (October): 153–58.

Jones, J. Christopher (1970). *Design Methods.* New York: Wiley-Interscience.

—— (1983). "Continuous Design and Redesign," *Design Studies* 4 (January): 53–60.

Kariya, Scott (1984). "Seeking a Perfect Chair," *PC* 3 (October 2): 139–48.

Kotler, Philip, and G. Alexander Rath (1984). "Design: A Powerful but Neglected Strategic Tool," *Journal of Business Strategy* 5 (fall): 16–21.

Lehrer, Linda (1985). "Designers Want Protection from Imitators," *Wall Street Journal* (October 1): 35.

Levitt, Theodore (1983). "The Globalization of Markets," in *The Marketing Imagination,* Theodore Levitt, ed. New York: Free Press, pp. 20–49.

Little, S.E. (1987). "Incremental and Systematic Innovation Strategies: Reflections of Technical Choice," *Design Studies* 8 (January): 41–54.

MacDonald, Stephen (1987a). "Looking Good: More Firms Place Higher Priority on Product Design," *Wall Street Journal* (January 22): 33.

—— (1987b). "Awareness of Industrial Design Grows, Firms Start to Use It as a Marketing Tool," *Wall Street Journal* (February 23): 29.

—— (1987c). "Form + Function," *Wall Street Journal* (August 6): 27.

—— (1987d). "Form + Function," *Wall Street Journal* (October 29): 27.

Melloan, George (1987). "Robots Talk Back to Product Designers," *Wall Street Journal (May 26): 33.*

Moody, S. (1980). "The Role of Industrial Design in Technological Innovation," *Design Studies* 1 (October).

Myers, James H., and W. Gregory Warner (1968). "Semantic Properties of Selected Adjectives," *Journal of Marketing Research* 5 (November): 409–12.

Nakanishi, Motoo (1985). *Corporate Design Systems 2.* New York: PBC International.

National Retail Merchants Association (NRMA) and Institute for Store Planners (ISP), eds. (1986). *The Best of Store Designs.* New York: PBC International.

Oakley, Mark (1984). *Managing Product Design.* New York: Wiley.

Olins, Wally (1985). "Management by Design," *Management Today* (February): 62–69.

Oxman, Robert M. (1986). "Designing Variations," *Design Studies* 7 (October): 185–91.

Papanek, Victor (1971). *Design for the Real World*. New York: Pantheon.

——— (1983). *Design on a Human Scale*. New York: Van Nostrand Reinhold.

Peters, Thomas J., and Robert H. Waterman, Jr. (1982). *In Search of Excellence*. New York: Harper & Row.

Pilditch, James (1981). "Product Planning—We're Still Getting It Upside Down," *Long Range Planning* 14 (October): 20–26.

Pile, John F. (1979). *design*. Amherst, Mass. University of Massachusetts Press.

Porter, Martin (1984). "Factoring in the Human Element," *PC* 3 (October 2): 160–65.

Redford, A.H. (1983). "Design for Assembly," *Design Studies:* 170–76.

Research Management (1982). "R&D and New Products" 25 (July): 16–22.

Reynolds, William H. (1969). *Products and Markets*. New York: Appleton-Century-Crofts.

Rosch, Winn L. (1984). "Keyboard Ergonomics for IBMs," *PC* 3 (October 2): 110–22.

Rothwell, Roy, and Paul Gardiner (1983). "The Role of Design in Product and Process Change," *Design Studies* 4 (July): 161–68.

——— (1984). "Design and Competition in Engineering, *Long Range Planning* 17 (June): 78–91.

Schiller, Zachary (1987). "Appliance Repairmen Are Getting Lonelier," *Business Week* (June 8): 139–40.

Skolink, Rayna (1985). "The Rise and Rise of Product Design," *Sales & Marketing Management* (October) 46–48.

Stewart, Doug (1987). "Modern Designers Still Can't Make the Perfect Chair," *Smithsonian:* 97–105.

Thompson, Carl (1987). "Quality Sells Itself," *Sales & Marketing Management* (June): 13.

von Hippel, Eric (1979). "Successful and Failing Internal Corporate Ventures: An Empirical Analysis," *Industrial Marketing Management* 6 (June): 163–74.

Wagner, Walter (1982). "Products Are an Important Part of Design," *Architectural Record* (December): 19.

Watson, Thomas (1975). "Good Design Is Good Business," in *The Uneasy Coalition,* Thomas F. Schutte, ed. Philadelphia: University of Pennsylvania Press, pp. 57–79.

White, James Noel (1973). The Management of Design Services. Allen & Unwin: London.

Wind, Yoram J. (1982). *Product Policy*. Reading, Mass.: Addison-Wesley, pp. 341–42.

Witt, Philip R. (1986). *Cost Competitive Products*. Reston, Va.: Reston.

4

Design: A Powerful but Neglected Strategic Tool

Philip Kotler
G. Alexander Rath

I n this era of intensifying global competition, companies are searching
for ways to gain a sustainable competitive advantage in the hope of
protecting or improving their market positions. A great many industries
are characterized by intense service and/or price competition that only suc-
ceeds in driving down everyone's profits to an unhealthy level. One of the
few hopes companies have to stand out from the crowd is to produce su-
periorly designed products for their target markets.

A few companies stand out for their design distinctiveness, notably IBM
in computers, Herman Miller in modern furniture, and Olivetti in office
machines. But most companies lack a "design touch." Their products are
prosaically styled, their packaging is unexciting, and their information bro-
chures are tedious. Their marketers pay considerable attention to product
functioning, pricing, distribution, personal selling, and advertising, and much
less attention to product, environment, information, and corporate-identity
design. Many companies have staff designers or buy design services, but the
design often fails to achieve identity in the marketplace.

The following real (though disguised) example is typical of many managers' attitudes toward design:

> Steven Grant, an entrepreneur, visited one of the authors and described a
> device he was developing called the Fuel Brain, which monitors room tem-
> perature and controls the heating and air-circulation functions of oil fur-
> naces. When asked whether he would use professional design services to
> assist in this venture, he said there was no need. His engineer was designing
> the logo. His marketing officer was designing a four-page brochure. The
> Fuel Brain would not need any fancy packaging, advertising, or general
> design work, because he felt that the product would sell itself. Grant be-
> lieved that anyone with an oil-burning furnace and a desire to save money
> would buy one. A year later, upon being recontacted, he sadly explained
> his disappointment in the sales of the Fuel Brain.

Reprinted with minor alterations with permission from *Journal of Business Strategy,* Fall 1984,
Vol. 5, No. 2. Copyright © 1984, 210 South Street, Boston, MA 02111. All rights reserved.

One only has to look at current U.S. products in many product categories—kitchen appliances, office supplies, air conditioners, bicycles, automobiles, and so on—to acknowledge the lack of good design. Yet its potential rewards are great. Consider the dramatic breakthroughs that some companies have achieved with outstanding design:

- In the stereo-equipment market, where several hundred companies battle for market share, the small Danish company of Bang & Olufsen won an important niche in the high end of the market through designing a superbly handsome stereo system noted for its clean lines and heat-sensitive volume controls.

- In the sports-car market, Datsun endeared itself by designing the handsome 240Z. For most buyers before 1976, the 240Z was a dream car at an affordable price, around $4–6,000. A copy is by Mazda, which coupled innovative pricing with the 240Z design, capturing a large share of the sports-car market with its first offering, the RX7.

- In the hosiery market, Hanes achieved a dramatic breakthrough in a mature market by using creative packaging design and modern packaged-goods marketing techniques, catapulting the L'eggs division to the position of market leader. The L'eggs boutique (in-store display) used information design effectively, pulling consumers from other stores and brands. Design was a key component in the marketing strategy and created instant product recognition for the brand.

- In the kitchen-furnishings market, Crate & Barrel selects products for its retail stores that meet good standards of material, finish, form, and color. Most of the products are Italian and Finnish. The look has become so well entrenched that many consider it to be the standard in kitchen furnishings. Crate & Barrel also designed environments to promote traffic and used seconds of expensive products as loss leaders. Once again, good design is used as an element in a marketing strategy.

Well-managed, high-quality design offers the company several benefits. It can create corporate distinctiveness in an otherwise product- and image-surfeited marketplace. It can create a personality for a newly launched product so that it stands out from its more prosaic competitors. It can be used to reinvigorate product interest for products in the mature stage of its life cycle. It communicates value to the consumer, makes selection easier, informs, and entertains. Design management can lead to heightened visual impact, greater information efficiency, and considerable consumer satisfaction.

This chapter aims to help company strategists think more consciously and creatively about design leadership and to help company marketers work more effectively with designers. It addresses the following questions:

- What constitutes effective design?
- What keeps executives from becoming more effective design managers?
- How can a corporation's design-sensitivity be measured?
- How can the interface between marketers and designers be improved?

What Constitutes Effective Design?

The term *design* has several usages. People talk about nuclear-plant design and wallpaper design even though the two emphasize different design skills: those of functional versus visual design. Design also appears in the description of higher-priced products, such as designer jeans and designer furniture.

Certain countries—notably Italy, Finland, Denmark, and Germany—are often described as being outstanding in design. These countries use design as a major marketing tool to compete in world markets. Even here, design connotes different qualities depending on the country: Italian design is artistic, Finnish design is elegant, Danish design is clean, and German design is functional.

Design is also used to describe a process. Pentagram, the noted British design firm, sees design as a planning and decision-making process to determine the *functions* and *characteristics* of a finished product, which they define as something one "can see, hold, or walk into" (Gorb [1979]). Our definition of design is as follows:

> Design is the process of seeking to optimize consumer satisfaction and company profitability through the creative use of major design elements (performance, quality, durability, appearance, and cost) in connection with products, environments, information, and corporate identities.

Thus, the objective of design is to create high satisfaction for the target consumers and profits for the enterprise. In order to succeed, the designers seek to blend creatively the major elements of the design mix, namely performance, quality, durability, appearance, and cost. These elements can be illustrated in the problem of designing, for example, a new toaster:

- *Performance*. First, the designer must get a clear sense of the functions that the target consumers want in the new product. Here is where marketing research comes in. If target consumers want a toaster that heats up rapidly and cleans easily, then the designer's job is to arrange the features of the toaster in a way that facilitates the achievement of these customer objectives.

- *Quality*. The designer faces many choices in the quality of materials and workmanship. The materials and workmanship will be visible to the consumers and communicate to them a certain quality level. The designer does not aim for optimal quality but for affordable quality for that target market.

- *Durability*. Buyers will expect the toaster to perform well over a certain time period, with a minimum number of breakdowns. Durability will be affected by the product's performance and quality characteristics. Many buyers also want some degree of visual durability, in that the product does not start looking "old hat" or "out-of-date" long before its physical wearout.

- *Appearance*. Many buyers want the product to exhibit a distinctive or pleasing "look." Achieving distinctive style or form is a major way in which designed products, environment, and information can stand out from competition. At the same time, design is much more than style. Some well-styled products fail to satisfy the owners because they are deficient in performance characteristics. Most designers honor the principle that "form follows function." They seek forms that facilitate and enhance the functioning of the object rather than form for its own sake.

- *Cost*. Designers must work within budget constraints. The final product must carry a price within a certain range (depending on whether it is aimed at the high or low end of the market) and designers must limit themselves to what is possible in this cost range.

Consumers will form an image of the product's design value in relation to its price and favor those products offering the highest value for the money. Effective design calls for a creative balancing of performance, quality, durability, and appearance variables at a price that the target market can afford. Design work needs to be done by a company in connection with its products, environments, information, and identity.

What Keeps Executives from Becoming More Effective Design Managers?

According to one estimate, over five thousand U.S. companies have internal design departments and many others use outside design consultants. There are eight industrial-design consulting firms in 1982 with over ten employees, as well as numerous smaller ones (Siegal [1982]). In spite of the availability of design services, many companies neglect or mismanage their design capabilities. The reasons are design-illiteracy, cost constraints, tradition-bound behavior, and politics.

Design Illiteracy. Some designers charge that U.S. managers are largely illiterate when it comes to design. According to Rita Sue Siegal (1982):

> For the past 20 years American industry has been run by managers. They are trained in business schools to be numbers-oriented, to minimize risks and to use analytical, detached plans—not insights gained from hands-on experience. They are devoted to short-term returns and cost reduction, rather than developing long-term technological competitiveness. They prefer servicing existing markets rather than taking risks and developing new ones.

Although this is stereotyped thinking, it represents a widespread view that many designers have of the people who run U.S. corporations.

Cost Constraints. Many managers think that good design will cost a lot of money, more than they can afford. Using Skidmore, Owings & Merrill to design a new warehouse will be expensive. But bad design can cost even more money. Actually, good design does not have to be expensive. Many companies have found that having an internal designer or outside design consultant on retainer pays for itself many times, not only in avoiding costly errors but in creating a positive image for the company too.

Tradition-bound Behavior. Tradition-bound behavior is also a barrier to effective design management. A catalog format is very hard to change; and a product design or a company name is even harder to change. Salespeople will argue that their customers will be confused by name, product, and catalog changes. Managers prefer to stick with the original design instead of exposing their tastes to critical judgment.

For example, after Pillsbury bought Green Giant Foods, several suggestions were made that a facelift was in order. Pillsbury asked Leo Burnett, the Green Giant's agency, to look into this, but after initial creative development, the agency gave up because no one would commit to backing the new designs.

Politics. Company politics play a role in every firm. Some executives might oppose a proposed design simply because they want to block another group. Politics surface in creative reviews, budget meetings, and strategy-planning sessions.

How Can a Corporation's Design-Sensitivity and Design-Management Effectiveness be Measured?

Companies need to review periodically the role that design plays in their marketing program. At any point in time, company management will have a certain degree of design-sensitivity. A design-sensitivity audit (table 4–1) consists of five questions that will indicate the role design plays in the company's marketing decision making. A design-management audit (table 4–2) asks five more questions that rank how well management uses design. Each question is scored 0, 1, or 2. A corporation's design-sensitivity will range from 0 to 10, and its design management will also range from 0 to 10. Companies with a combined design-sensitivity and design-management-effectiveness rating of anywhere from 14 to 20 are in fairly good shape. Those scoring less than 8 should examine whether they are missing a major opportunity by not making more use of design thinking in their marketing strategy.

How Can the Interface between Marketers and Designers be Improved?

If a company recognizes the need for more and better design work, then a two-way process of education must occur. Marketers must acquire a better

Table 4–1
Design-Sensitivity Audit

1. What role does the company assign to design in the marketing-decision process?
   (0) Design is almost completely neglected as a marketing tool.
   (1) Design is viewed and used as a minor tactical tool.
   (2) Design is used as a major strategic tool in the marketing mix.
2. To what extent is design thinking utilized in product-development work?
   (0) Little or no design thinking goes into product-development work.
   (1) Occasionally good design thinking goes into product-development work.
   (2) Consistently good design thinking goes into product-development work.
3. To what extent is design thinking utilized in environmental-design work?
   (0) Little or no design thinking goes into environmental-design work.
   (1) Occasionally good design thinking goes into environmental-design work.
   (2) Consistently good design thinking goes into environmental-design work.
4. To what extent is design thinking utilized in information-design work?
   (0) Little or no design thinking goes into information-design work.
   (1) Occasionally good design thinking goes into information-design work.
   (2) Consistently good design thinking goes into information-design work.
5. To what extent is design thinking utilized in corporate-identity–design work?
   (0) Little or no design thinking goes into corporate-identity–design work.
   (1) Occasionally good design thinking goes into corporate-identity–design work.
   (2) Consistently good design thinking goes into corporate-identity–design work.

Table 4–2
Design-Management-Effectiveness Audit

1. What orientation does the design staff follow?

    (0) The design staff aims for high aesthetic ideals without any surveying of the needs and wants of the marketplace.

    (1) The design staff designs what marketing or consumers ask for with little or no modification.

    (2) The design staff aims for design solutions that start with an awareness of consumer needs and preferences and adds a creative touch.

2. Does the design staff have an adequate budget to carry out design analysis, planning, and implementation?

    (0) The budget is insufficient even for production materials.

    (1) The budget is adequate but typically cut back during hard times.

    (2) The design staff is well budgeted, especially on new-product–development projects.

3. Do managers encourage creative experimentation and design?

    (0) Creative experimentation and design are discouraged.

    (1) Designers are occasionally allowed creative freedom, but more typically they have to design within tight specifications.

    (2) Designers have creative freedom within the limits of the project parameters.

4. Do designers have a close working relationship with people in marketing, sales, engineering, and research?

    (0) No.

    (1) Somewhat.

    (2) Yes.

5. Are designers held accountable for their work through postevaluation measurement and feedback?

    (0) No.

    (1) Designers are accountable for cost overruns in the production process.

    (2) Design work is evaluated and full feedback is given to the designers.

understanding of the design process and designers must acquire a better understanding of the marketing process.

Marketers need to be aware of the split in the design community between the functionalists and the stylists. The orientation of the functionalists is based on putting good functional performance, quality, and durability into the design. The orientation of the stylists is to put good outer form into the design. Functional designers are normally responsive to marketing research and technical research, while stylists often resist a marketing orientation. The stylists prefer to work by inspiration and tend to pay less attention to cost. Fortunately, few designers are at the extremes, and most are willing to pay some attention to market data and feedback in developing their designs.

Marketers also often split into the same two camps. Some marketers, notably those in the salesforce, often plead with the designers to add "bells and whistles" to the product to catch the buyer's attention and win the sale. They press for features and styling that are eye-catching, even though they might not contribute to good design and performance. Other marketers hold that the key to customer satisfaction and repeat sales is not simply attracting initial purchase but providing long-term product-use satisfaction. These marketers are more interested in supporting the incorporation of good performance, quality, and durability characteristics into the product. They point to the success of Japanese automobiles as based not on style leadership so much as the consumer belief that Japanese automobiles offer better quality, durability, and useful features. So marketers also need to get their act together when they work with designers and make recommendations as to what counts most in the consumers' mind.

A common management mistake is to bring designers into the new-product–development process too late or to bring in the wrong type of designer. There are eight stages in the new-product–development process:

1. Idea generation
2. Screening
3. Concept development and testing
4. Marketing strategy
5. Business analysis
6. Product development
7. Market testing
8. Commercialization

Typically, the designer is invited in at stage 6, product development, when the prototype product is to be developed. Designers, however, should be brought in earlier, preferably in the idea-generation stage or at least the concept-development–and–testing stage. Designers are capable of producing ideas that no customers would come up with in the normal course of researching customers for ideas. And, during the concept-development–and–testing stage, designers might propose intriguing features that deserve investigation before the final concept is chosen.

Design Philosophy

Each company has to decide on how to incorporate design into the marketing-planning process. There are three alternative philosophies. At one extreme are design-dominated companies that allow their designers to design out of their heads without any marketing data. The company looks for great designers who have an instinct for what will turn on customers. This philosophy is usually found in such industries as apparel, furniture, perfumes, and tableware.

At the other extreme are marketer-dominated companies that require their designers to adhere closely to market-research reports describing what customers want in the product. These companies believe designs should be market-sourced and market-tested. This philosophy is usually found in such industries as packaged foods and small appliances.

An intermediate philosophy—one espoused by most companies—holds that designs need not be market-sourced but at least should be market-tested. Consumers should be asked to react to any proposed design because often consumers have ways of seeing that are not apparent to designers and marketers.

Here is how one firm, Atmospheres, develops its designs for bank retail environments:

> The designers at Atmospheres construct settings of bank interiors and test them on small focus groups of bank customers. Customer responses to different layout arrangements, textures, furniture, etc., help Atmospheres gain insight into customer perceptions and preferences. Based on customer responses, the designers then develop a design proposal for the bank. The design package is tested with another focus group to refine and verify the effectiveness of the design. The final version is presented to management with evidence of the degree of interest and satisfaction of the bank's customers in the proposed design.

This rhythm between the visual conceptions of the designer and the consumers' reactions to proposed designs represents the essence of market-oriented design thinking. It neither inhibits the designer from coming up with great ideas nor allows bad design ideas to be accepted without testing.

Conclusion

While every corporation buys and uses product, environmental, information, and identity design, very few have developed a sophisticated understanding of how to manage design as a strategic marketing tool. Design has been defined as a process that seeks to optimize consumer satisfaction and company profitability through creating performance, form, durability, and value in connection with products, environments, information, and identities. Strong design can help a company stand out from its competitors. The best results can be achieved by training general managers, marketers, salespeople, and engineers to understand design and by training designers to be aware of and understand the functions of these people. Design ideas should at least be market-tested and preferably market-sourced or stimulated by market survey data. As other strategic marketing tools become increasingly expensive, design is likely to play a growing role in the firm's unending search for a sustainable competitive advantage in the marketplace.

References

Business Week (1982). "Architecture as a Corporate Asset" (October 4): 124–26.

Gorb, P., ed. (1979). *Living by Design.* L. Humphries: London, pp. 7–8.

King, J.P. (1982). "Robots Will Never Be Practical Unless Products Are Designed for Them," *Industrial Design* (January/February): 24–29.

Kotler, P. (1973–74). "Atmospheres as a Marketing Tool," *Journal of Retailing* (winter): 48–64.

Siegal, R.S. (1982). "The USA: Free to Choose," *Design* (January): 24.

Part III
Attribute Analysis as Part of Concept Evaluation

A critical early need in the development of a new-product concept is the design of the optimum bundle of benefits. Which attributes are important to the consumer and the relative attractiveness of different levels of each attribute are critical questions that need to be answered in order to develop successful new-product concepts. When benefit bundles have identifiable incremental costs associated with their delivery, as well as incremental worth to the consumer, profit trade-offs can also be estimated. Conjoint analysis is a broad-based methodology for estimating attribute importance and the consumer's perceived worth of various levels of different attributes. Conjoint analysis technology has matured considerably since its introduction to the field of new-product development by Green and Wind (1975) in their now classic *Harvard Business Review* article.

Chapters 5 and 6 offer new extensions to the "classic" conjoint approach. In chapter 5, Srinivasan and Wyner discuss a two-stage approach that addresses a fundamental concern with the underlying choice-process assumption, implicit in conjoint analysis, and provide an alternative to the very real respondent-overload issue recognized by research practitioners. In chapter 6, Green and Krieger present an extension of the "hybrid" conjoint model featuring a novel method for estimating individual respondent intercepts, and they provide an empirical Bayes procedure for estimating individual price utilities in the analysis of residuals. Some readers may not wish to delve deeply into the technical details of the proposed hybrid conjoint model for price-demand estimation and can skim it lightly. Those readers who are concerned with carrying out price-demand estimation during the concept-testing phase will find that the chapter presents an innovative application of hybrid conjoint to problems illustrated with an industrial-service concept with emphasis on competitive price relationships.

Chapter 7 moves further from traditional conjoint procedures. In it, Friedmann and French discuss the measurement of a product concept's psychological meaning as an alternative to standard attribute-importance analysis.

A review of the assumptions underlying "classical" conjoint analysis along with a description of how to carry out the analysis in its most basic form are provided for the reader unfamiliar with the technique. Others may wish to skip the following discussion of classic conjoint analysis and go directly to the chapters of this part.

Underlying classical conjoint analysis techniques is a fundamental consumer-choice–process assumption. Consumers are assumed to be rational in that their choice preference among alternative benefit bundles (new-product concepts) will lead to choosing the concept offering the highest level of total utility or worth. It is further assumed that each level of each attribute making up the benefit bundle has a partial worth or "part-worth" associated with it. A simple additive model allows a total-worth figure to be estimated for all possible attribute bundles, so that the full range of alternative concept-configuration trade-offs may be examined.

Conjoint analysis techniques provide the methodology by which the part-worths of attribute levels may be estimated in an efficient manner and the relative importance of the attributes over the range of levels presented may be examined. In the most basic form of classical conjoint analysis, respondents are shown verbal and or pictorial descriptions of a sufficient number of simulated product concepts to allow the part-worths associated with the various levels of each attribute to be estimated using ordinary least squares (OLS) dummy-variable regression analysis. Respondents are requested to review a set of new-product–concept descriptions and provide their relative preferences. The preference information may be a simple rank ordering of the described concepts or some form of a preference ratings.

A particularly important practical consideration is the number of product concepts that the respondent is asked to judge. Experience has shown that when more than twenty concepts are used, the respondents may become overwhelmed by the task and resort to some alternative ranking behavior not congruent with their underlying choice-behavior assumptions. The number twenty is only a guide and the critical number can be affected by the level of interest on the part of the respondent and on the design of the research instrument itself. Also affecting the number-of-concepts issue is the minimum number of observations required in order to carry out the OLS estimating procedure.

The total number of concept combinations possible is the product of the levels of the attributes under examination. For a new-product concept composed of four attributes with two levels each, the total number of combinations is 16. In this case, the respondent might reasonably be shown all possible concepts providing 16 observations for OLS regression. When more complex concepts are to be investigated (for example, 6 factors with 3 levels), a total of 729 combinations become available. The sorting task quickly becomes beyond what can be expected from a respondent.

Key to the efficiency of classical conjoint analysis is its ability to estimate the part-worths of the various levels of the attributes without requiring the respondent to examine all possible concept combinations. An operational rule of thumb is that the minimum number of concepts that must be preference-ordered is 1.5 times the number of dummy variables used to describe the combinations possible in the product concept.

Each attribute included in the concept study can be represented by one or more dummy variables taking on the values of 0 or 1. The number of dummy variables required for each attribute is one less than the number of levels in that attribute. The total number of dummy variables used in the regression model is then the sum of the dummy variables required by each attribute across all the attributes included in the new-product concept. For the preceding example, each attribute can be represented by two dummy variables. Since there are 6 attributes, the total number of dummy variables required to sort the main effects would be 12. Respondents in this case are only required therefore to provide preference information among 18 concepts out of the 729 available.

Which reduced set of concepts to use in the research instrument is the final critical decision. What is required is a subset of the total number of combinations that are representative of all of the concepts available, while at the same time maintaining independence among the dummy variables describing the subset. Without going into great detail, this is what is called a fractional factorial design providing an orthogonal main-effects plan. Green (1974) provides a comprehensive discussion of this approach. Also, a number of orthogonal plans are catalogued by Addelman (1962), from which the user of classical conjoint analysis can select the appropriate subset of new-product concepts to be used in the data-collection phase of the research. The concepts presented to the respondent are taken directly from the basic plan with the appropriate substitution of attribute-level descriptions.

Respondent-preference rankings of each concept described in the instrument will provide the dependent variable data in the OLS regression-analysis procedure. The 0's and 1's assigned to the dummy variables describing the concepts are the independent variable for the regression model. Individual regression analysis is performed on the set of concepts presented to each respondent. Estimated regression coefficients found are the relative part-worth estimates for each attribute level examined. In our example, this would be the utility increment associated with the two levels of each attribute with respect to a null level, usually the high or low extreme. The overall worth of any benefit-bundle combination can then be calculated by using a simple additive model. Trade-offs, such as a high-price/high-quality concept and a lower-price/lower-quality concept, may be examined. A measure of the relative importance of the attributes included in the new-product concept can also be found by ranking the attributes by the magnitude of the range in part-worths observed across all levels of the attribute.

In interpreting the results of a classical conjoint analysis, the basic assumptions underlying the approach must be kept in mind. The consumer is assumed to use a single-stage additive-choice model, which may not be the case when inappropriate attributes are used or inappropriate ranges of attribute levels are included in the concepts to be tested. Also, there is always the danger of respondent overload when dealing with large numbers of attributes and/or attribute levels. Chapters 5 and 6 will deal with some of these issues as well as introducing the reader to hybrid conjoint approaches. The psychological-meaning approach to attribute-importance evaluation is described in chapter 7.

References

Addelman, Sidney (1962). "Orthogonal Main-Effect Plans for Asymmetrical Factorial Experiments," *Technometrics* 4 (February).

Green, Paul (1974). "On the Design of Choice Experiments Involving Multifactor Alternatives," *Journal of Consumer Research* 1 (September).

Green, Paul, and Jerry Wind (1975). "New Way to Measure Consumers' Judgements," *Harvard Business Review* 53 (July-August); 107–17.

5

CASEMAP:
Computer-Assisted Self-Explication of Multiattributed Preferences

V. Srinivasan
Gordon A. Wyner

onjoint analysis has evolved since 1970 to a position of prominence in applied marketing research. It is widely accepted by practitioners as a useful way to approach certain kinds of preference-measurement problems (Cattin and Wittink [1982]). At the same time, considerable developmental and validation research has been conducted by academic researchers as well as practitioners (Green and Srinivasan [1978]). Major modifications of the technique have been made to reduce the data-collection burden on respondents associated with the traditional conjoint techniques. Unfortunately, the results of these "self-explicated" and "hybrid" approaches have only been partially successful. There is still a need to develop simplified preference-measurement procedures that reduce the respondent burden without sacrificing the conceptual advantages of traditional techniques.

This chapter presents CASEMAP, a computer-assisted self-explication of multiattributed preferences, a new approach that addresses the difficulties associated with the traditional conjoint techniques. It is unique among conjoint-type techniques in several respects:

- It extends the conceptual model used in conjoint analysis to capture aspects of choice behavior that are ignored by the traditional model.

- It simplifies the questioning sequence sufficiently to enable the data collection to be conducted solely by telephone. At the same time, the method is flexible enough to permit data collection by other means such as personal interview or mail plus telephone interview.

- It utilizes computer technology to achieve these advantages unobtrusively. The interview is easy to administer and easy for respondents to participate in. The computer power, which is essential to the implementation, is transparent to the respondents.

We begin by reviewing some of the basic objectives, concepts, and uses of conjoint analysis. This serves as background for considering some of the theoretical and practical problems in implementing the technique. Next, we describe the CASEMAP method, both from a theoretical perspective and in terms of implementation. Finally, we provide illustrations of the analysis and validation work on CASEMAP.

Background on Conjoint Analysis

Conjoint analysis is a methodology for measuring preferences for alternative products, services, or other types of choice alternatives (Green and Wind [1975]). In a marketing context, it answers the question, "Why do consumers buy the products they do?" Conjoint analysis gets to the answer by first defining the product in terms of the relevant attributes that characterize all products in the category. Product attributes might include such things as price, features, packaging, and brand name. The attributes are usually defined in terms of discrete levels; for example, price may be defined as $3, 4, or 5, and packaging may be defined as a cardboard box, a paper bag, or a plastic carton. Hypothetical product concepts are then put together by combining the different levels of the multiple attributes, e.g., brand B in a plastic carton at $5. The respondent is then asked, for instance, to rank order by overall preference a subset of all possible hypothetical options. Such a comparison might show, for instance, that a consumer prefers a plastic carton at $4 to a cardboard box at $3. Thus, the plastic carton is "worth" at least an extra $1 to that consumer. The rank-order overall-preference data are usually analyzed by computerized estimation procedures to yield the relative appeals or "worths" of the product components. When a representative sample of consumers is selected and so analyzed, a picture of the market's preference structures emerges. Thus, at the most basic level, conjoint analysis provides an understanding of the values consumers place on the different components of the product. Furthermore, benefit segments can be constructed by grouping consumers based on the similarity of their preference structures.

In addition to furthering understanding of preference structures, the results of conjoint analysis also provide managerial direction. They suggest the changes to make in the product (e.g., lower price, different packaging) to enhance its overall appeal to different groups of consumers.

An important objective of conjoint analysis is to predict the likely market response to changes in products in terms of their attribute components. Changes can be made in the features, in prices, or in any combination of attributes. One can simulate changes made by competitors as well as by one's own firm. Furthermore, changes may include the addition of an entirely new product concept or the elimination of an existing one. The conjoint data base, for a representative sample, can be used to simulate numerous competitive scenarios in order to find the "best" strategy for the firm. A simulation might show, for example, that a new high-priced product in a plastic carton will capture a substantial market share.

Conjoint analysis uses several basic concepts. Traditionally, the approach assumes a simple additive model that relates overall preference for a brand to its component attributes. The specific attribute levels each have a *utility value* or *part-worth* that represents the appeal of that level to the consumer. Overall preference for a product is equal to the sum of the part-worths for the attribute levels that comprise that particular product. In the example considered earlier, the product class is characterized by three attributes: price, package, and brand name. Overall preference for any particular product would be defined as:

$$\begin{matrix} \text{overall} \\ \text{brand} \\ \text{preference} \end{matrix} = \begin{matrix} \text{part-worth for price} \\ + \\ \text{part-worth for package} \\ + \\ \text{part-worth for brand name} \end{matrix}$$

Other more complex models (such as those with interaction effects) are possible, but the additive model is robust enough for many applied problems.

The measurement of the part-worths for these attributes yields a series of part-worth functions for each person as illustrated in figure 5–1. The vertical axis is the part-worth or utility scale, common to all three attributes. The horizontal axes are the particular levels of each attribute. Note that attributes can be conceptualized as continuous variables, as in the case of price, or as discrete categories, as in the case of package or brand.

A useful concept in conjoint analysis is *attribute importance*. Intuitively, it captures the salience of each attribute compared to the others. Operationally, it is defined as the difference in part-worths between the most preferred level and least preferred level for a given attribute. In figure 5–1, the most

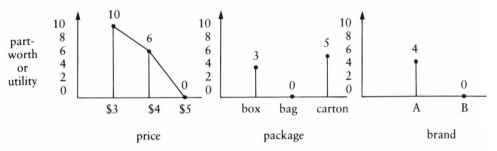

Figure 5–1. Part-Worth Functions

preferred price, $3, has a part-worth of 10, while the least preferred price, $5, has a part-worth of 0. The difference, 10, indicates the relative impact on overall utility of a change in price from the worst to best option. For package, the comparable difference is 5 (carton minus bag). For brand, the difference is 4 (brand A minus brand B). In this sense, price is the most important or critical attribute. It is twice as important as package and 2½ times as important as brand name. The importance rating of the critical attribute can be given any arbitrary positive number. In this example, it has been set equal to 10. The other attribute importances have been scaled relative to the critical attribute.

Choice simulations are conducted by specifying two or more products in terms of the attributes. The part-worths are added across the attributes. A simple decision rule is that the consumer will choose the product for which he or she has the greatest overall preference score. In the example displayed in figure 5–2, the consumer would choose product 1 despite its higher price because of its brand name and, to a lesser extent, its packaging.

This simplified example illustrates the beginnings of the simulation process. When aggregated across a sample of consumers, this approach leads to market-level predictions of the share of choices each product would receive. It can be run repeatedly by changing the product definitions and product mix to assess any hypothetical scenario. More complex models can be developed to capture the influence of other variables outside the product itself (e.g., distribution, advertising, consumer segmentation) and other choice processes (e.g., probabilistic models, multiple choices).

Some Theoretical and Practical Problems in Using Conjoint Analysis

Both conceptual and operational problems have limited the usefulness of conjoint analysis. This section discusses the difficulties with the "classical" conjoint approach.

	Product 1		Product 2	
Attribute	Level	Part-worth	Level	Part-worth
Price	$4	6	$3	10
Package	Carton	5	Box	3
Brand	A	4	B	0
Overall utility = sum of part-worths		15		13

Choice

Figure 5–2. Choice Simulation

Two-Stage Decisions

Traditional conjoint analysis holds that consumers evaluate multiattribute choice alternatives in one cognitive step. The consumer is assumed to actively consider all product attributes and form the overall preference as the sum of the part-worths of the multiple attributes. He or she may assign a lower part-worth to some levels than others, but implicitly the consumer is willing to make trade-offs among *any* attribute levels. No unattractive attribute levels are ever totally ruled out.

Published literature (e.g., Payne [1976], Lussier and Olshavsky [1979]) as well as everyday experience argue against this one-step view of choice behavior. Consumers often do judge choice alternatives according to whether they meet their own standards of minimal acceptability *before* they consider trade-offs among particular attribute levels. For example, in the process of buying a new family car, a family with three children may rule out subcompact cars from any consideration. The decision as to whether a particular attribute meets a consumer's threshold of acceptability reflects a very different cognitive process than the trade-offs implicit in the classical conjoint model. This alternative model, known as the conjunctive model (Coombs [1964], Wright [1975]), is characterized by a screening process in which each attribute of the product is evaluated to determine its acceptability. Products that contain one or more (totally) unacceptable attribute levels are excluded from further consideration. Thus, to be chosen, a choice alternative must contain attribute levels that are all acceptable. One unacceptable level results in rejection of the whole product as unacceptable.

Empirical results (Payne [1976], Lussier and Olshavsky [1979]) suggest that first-stage product evaluations are frequently conjunctive. A consumer may have a price threshold in mind, which dictates a rejection of any product above that price level. He or she may have a quality standard that effectively rules out certain types of lesser-quality products. The consumer may exhibit very strong brand preferences and aversions. Perhaps previous experience with a brand may lead to the judgment that a particular brand is unacceptable. The consumer may be very loyal to just one or perhaps more than one brand and declare others to be unacceptable. These kinds of judgments, common in our experience, exhibit a conjunctive decision model.

Once the consumer has isolated a reduced set of choice alternatives with attribute levels that are acceptable, he or she may go on to use a compensatory decision process, i.e., make trade-offs among alternatives based on their part-worths. For example, within the prices, quality levels, and brands that the consumer will actively consider, he or she may be willing to sacrifice some quality for a lower price. The consumer will not, however, accept quality below a particular threshold in any situation.

If we accept this two-stage decision-making process—first conjunctive, then trade-off—there are some major implications for standard conjoint practice. How are the survey responses, estimated part-worths, and predicted choices from conjoint analysis to be interpreted when the underlying process is conjunctive/trade-off? The answer is that each of these outputs from traditional conjoint will be distorted in a way that is not directly observable by the researcher. Conclusions will therefore be biased to an unknown degree.

The measurement of attribute-level part-worths will be affected by the two-stage process. An unacceptable level will be given a utility value, when in reality it has been categorically rejected. For example, a price level at the high end of the range for the category might be $5, as in the example. If the consumer would never consider paying that price, any estimate of the part-worth for that price is too high. In fact, the consumer is "not in the market" at that price. Under these conditions, traditional conjoint inevitably overstates some part-worth values.

Second, attribute importance is improperly represented. Importance will be derived from the difference between the most preferred and least preferred attribute levels, without regard for whether these levels passed the acceptability threshold. The "least preferred" end of the scale may have a meaningless part-worth value if that level is judged unacceptable. The resulting importance weight would, of course, be distorted.

Under a conjunctive/trade-off model, it is apparent that attribute importance is a complex, multidimensional concept itself. It is a function of both the attribute levels that have been rejected as unacceptable and the range of the part-worth values for the acceptable levels. Rejection of certain product features is clearly a key measure of the importance of an attribute in product choice. The range of part-worths is still a key concept too, but now it varies depending upon the consumer's unique selection of acceptable attribute levels. For example, outright rejection of the highest price level, $5, conveys that price is important in the first sense. Among the remaining price levels, $3 and $4, price-sensitivity may not be great. Thus, over the trade-off end of the price continuum, price may be relatively unimportant.

The implications for choice simulation follow directly. If biased part-worths are added together, the net result must be distorted. Traditional conjoint analysis does not identify simulated products that are truly unacceptable. While an unacceptable attribute level will likely get a relatively low part-worth, there simply is no provision for a low enough scale value to insure a product's sure rejection.

An additional implication of the two-stage process is the effect on data collection. Suppose that traditional "full-profile" conjoint data are gathered for a product category with three attributes, one at two levels and two each at three levels. This generates 18 possible product combinations in a full factorial experimental design. Respondents would normally be asked to rank these 18 products. This full rank ordering contains information about 153 pairs of the products (18 products taken 2 at a time = $18 \times 17/2$ pairs).

Suppose further that one level of the two-level attribute is actually unacceptable to the consumer. This means that every time one of the products with the unacceptable level is compared to one with the acceptable level, information is lost about all the other differences between products. Since half the 18 combinations (i.e., 9) would have the unacceptable level, the number of combinations in which information is lost is 81 (9 times 9). The degradation of the data quality is substantial; over half the paired comparisons are of limited value. Clearly the problem is compounded for each additional unacceptable level.

Respondent Overload

Practitioners of conjoint analysis are well aware of the data-collection burden the technique imposes. In its original formulation, factorial experimental designs were used such that each attribute was represented as a factor and each level or feature option was represented as a factor level. Unfortunately, as the number of attributes increases, the number of factorial combinations to be evaluated increases dramatically. Fractional factorial experimental designs have been used effectively to reduce the number required. However, to get reliable part-worth estimates, the least-complex problems (4–5 attributes) typically require as many as 16–18 combinations, and moderately complex problems (6–7 attributes) often require about 25–30 combinations to be evaluated by each respondent.

Previous research (e.g., Wright [1974]) has suggested that when faced with rating tasks of this magnitude, respondents engage in simplifying strategies designed to cope with the task. Their objective becomes one of extricating themselves as easily as possible from the research task. They do this by focusing on a small number of attributes and levels and ignoring the others. The respondent's answers are suspect since the research task does not simulate actual choice behavior. Rather, they represent a response to a formidable ranking/rating task that exceeds their patience and tolerance levels.

Recognizing this kind of problem with full-profile data collection, a number of alternative methods have been developed. The pairwise or trade-off table method utilizes matrices for a pair of attributes at a time (Johnson [1974]). Each level of one attribute is crossed with each level of the other. The task is to rank order by overall preference the cells of each matrix. This method achieves simplifications in the sense that each individual table is less complex. Even so, the number of matrices expands quickly as the number of attributes increases, adding burden to the respondent. Also, this method is subject to respondent simplifying strategies as well. Consumers adopt a row-by-row or column-by-column approach to cope with the task rather than give an accurate response.

Another approach to reducing respondent burden is the self-explicated method (e.g., Huber [1974]). Part-worth values and attribute importances are elicited by direct self-report from the respondents (e.g., Green [1984, figures 1 and 3]). Clearly, this reduces respondent burden since the number of judgments required increases additively with the number of attributes and levels rather than multiplicatively, as with the full-profile and pairwise methods. The chief drawback of this method is that attribute importance is generally not well defined. It is generally based on an attitudinal measure (e.g., "How important are the attributes?" or "Allocate one hundred points across the attributes on the basis of importance."). The meaning of *importance* is unclear. The resulting importance scale cannot be thought of as especially sensitive or precise.

Finally, hybrid models have been proposed as a compromise between self-explicated and full-profile methods (e.g., Green [1984]). Self-explicated attribute importances and part-worths are gathered at the individual-respondent level. Subsets of full-profile descriptions are evaluated by individuals so that aggregate-level adjustments to self-explicated utilities can be made. A model that combines the two kinds of information is fitted to allow each to contribute to the estimation of preferences. Research on the performance of these methods has shown them to be sometimes better than the traditional conjoint methods and in some cases worse (Green [1984, table 2]).

No Telephone-Only Method

Among all the attempts at improving conjoint models and reducing respondent burden, no method has been proposed that utilizes the telephone alone as the data-collection device. The telephone method has several advantages over other alternatives. First, telephone sampling is more likely to yield a random sample than is sampling for in-person research. A geographically dispersed, equal-probability-of-selection sample can easily be drawn. Only nontelephone households (about 3 percent of the United States) are excluded. In-person methods are geographically clustered, either by neighborhood (as in area-probability sampling) or by interviewing site (as in central-location studies). Clustering results in a loss of sampling efficiency. Mail surveys can reach any geographic area, but response rates are generally so low that any sampling advantage is lost. Telephone-mail-telephone surveys produce a higher response rate than mail surveys, but the attrition from the three-step process leads to a net reduction in the response rate in comparison to the telephone-only method.

Telephone interviewing also provides a quality advantage over in-person and mail methods. Interviewing is under constant supervision, thus reducing interviewer errors. In door-to-door personal interviewing, the interviewer is free to operate more independently, thus increasing the chances of interviewer errors. In group or self-administered questionnaires, the respondent is left free to make errors and omissions. When computer-assisted telephone interviewing is done, quality control is enhanced even further. The skip logic, sequences, and valid-response codes are strictly enforced. Invalid answers are not accepted.

There are, in addition, practical advantages to telephone interviewing. It generally costs less than in-person and telephone-mail-telephone methods and the research can be completed faster. Computer-assisted interviewing reduces data-collection and -tabulation time.

CASEMAP Methodology

The limitations of conjoint methods discussed to this point suggest a need for a conceptually improved, telephone-based method that would minimize respondent overload. In this section, we describe the CASEMAP approach and its implementation by computer-assisted telephone interviewing.

Approach

CASEMAP integrates the conjunctive—trade-off decision sequence into the data-collection process. The respondent is first queried about attribute levels that he or she considers to be totally unacceptable, i.e., a product with one or more unacceptable attribute levels would never be chosen no matter how attractive the product might be on other attributes. The second phase of the questioning determines the part-worths that are relevant to the trade-offs. The part-worths are determined only for the attribute levels that are considered acceptable, i.e., have not been eliminated as unacceptable.

CASEMAP determines the part-worths using the self-explicated process. Unlike the earlier self-explicated approaches, it clarifies the concept of attribute importance using the conjoint philosophy, i.e., importance of an attribute is the range of the part-worth function from the least preferred but acceptable level to the most preferred level of that attribute.

There are other approaches that have also questioned respondents regarding unacceptable levels (e.g., the SIMALTO method referenced in Green [1984, p. 158]). However, these approaches suffer from the conceptual problem discussed earlier regarding the meaning of attribute importance when unacceptable levels are involved. To illustrate, consider an example with two attributes, each of which has an unacceptable level. Since the part-worth for the unacceptable level is not even defined, the range of the part-worth function from the unacceptable to the most preferred level has no real meaning. Thus, it is not clear what meaning can be attached to the relative-importance ratings provided by the respondent. By separating the conjunctive stage from the trade-off stage and by defining importance as the range of the part-worth function only over acceptable levels, CASEMAP gets around the conceptual difficulty present in other methods. In addition, CASEMAP explicitly utilizes the concept of importance from conjoint rather than a vague question such as "How important is each attribute?"

As will become clear subsequently, CASEMAP takes advantage of the computer to minimize the information overload on the respondent. Since the list of acceptable attribute levels varies over respondents, the computer keeps track of this information at the respondent level so that subsequent questions are tailor-made to the respondent, thereby considerably simplifying the respondent's task.

Finally, CASEMAP provides output similar to conjoint analysis so that understanding consumer-preference structures and doing market simulations are just as easy. Also, CASEMAP provides additional information on the percentage of respondents considering each attribute level to be unacceptable. The market simulations incorporate the consumer's conjunctive—trade-off decision process.

Data Collection

Table 5–1 provides CASEMAP's questionnaire sequence.

Step 1: Identification of Unacceptable Levels and Rating the Relative Desirability of Acceptable Levels. The first step captures the conjunctive decision-making process in which the unacceptable levels of product attributes are screened out. The respondent determines which, if any, of the levels are not acceptable to him or her and then excludes them from further consideration. The technique is flexible in allowing each person to choose as many or as few unacceptable levels as he or she deems appropriate. Some individuals may choose none. Others may choose several. The mix of acceptable and unacceptable levels will vary across consumers.

Once the acceptable set of attribute levels has been isolated, the con-

Table 5–1
CASEMAP's Questioning Sequence

Step	Description
0	Introduction; explain usage occasion (choice situation), attributes, and levels.
1	For each attribute, identify unacceptable levels; determine the most and least preferred levels (within acceptable levels); and rate the relative desirability of acceptable levels.
2	Identify critical attribute.
3	Rate attribute importances for all but the critical attribute.

sumer is led through a questioning sequence to measure the relative desirability of the acceptable levels within each attribute. This is done by identifying for each attribute the most preferred and least preferred levels from within the set of attribute levels considered acceptable by the respondent. By anchoring the scale values of the most preferred level at 10 and the least preferred level at 0, the relative desirability of the remaining acceptable levels is provided by the respondent on the 0–10 scale. This questioning process is then repeated for the remaining attributes. The approach to measuring relative desirability is similar to previous self-explication procedures with the important distinction that the 0–10 scale is applicable only over acceptable levels.

Step 2: Identifying the Critical Attribute. Next, an important weight for each attribute is obtained. As stated earlier, CASEMAP defines the importance of an attribute as the range of the part-worth function from the least preferred level to the most preferred level. (Note that by construction in step 1, both these levels are acceptable levels.) Thus, the most important or *critical attribute* is the one for which the range of the part-worth function over the acceptable levels is maximal.

Consider two attributes, A and B. Let the subscripts L and M denote the least and most preferred levels and let U denote the utility or part-worths. Then attribute A is more important than B if and only if

$$U(A_M) - U(A_L) > U(B_M) - U(B_L).$$

Rearranging terms,

$$U(A_M) + U(B_L) > U(B_M) + U(A_L).$$

In other words, the combination (A_M, B_L) is preferred to the combination (A_L, B_M). Thus, a simple paired-comparison question comparing the two options (A_M, B_L) and (A_L, B_M) would identify whether attribute A or B is more important. If there are K attributes, $(K-1)$ paired comparisons are needed in this process. (For example, if there are three attributes, we need to first compare attributes 1 and 2 and then pit the "winner" against attribute 3.)

The importance of the critical attribute is set arbitrarily equal to 10. By definition of the critical attribute, the importances of the remaining attributes will fall between 0 and 10.

Step 3: Rating Attribute Importances. Once the critical attribute is determined, the importance of the remaining attributes are scaled on the 0–10 scale by respondent self-report by using the critical attribute as the anchor.

(The wording of the question is provided later.) Importance is thus measured by magnitude estimation on a scale with ratio properties.

Computing Part-Worths

The importance weights are used to convert the within-attribute relative desirabilities into part-worths. This process is illustrated in figure 5–3 in the context of the same example as in figure 5–1. To facilitate the comparison with figure 5–1, we assume that there are no unacceptable levels. Figure 5–3A provides the relative-desirability data collected in step 1. In this example, price was identified to be the critical attribute (step 2) and the importance ratings for the attributes obtained in step 3 are provided in figure 5–3B. We note that the part-worths computed as shown in figure 5–3C are the same as in figure 5–1.

Implementation via Automated Custom Research System (ACRS)

Interviewing is customized for each CASEMAP study, but in general the questioning follows the sequence depicted in table 5–1. Computer control over the questioning is essential for several reasons. The unacceptable options vary for each person. Thus, the options that remain for further questioning are determined during the interview. The computer keeps track of these shifting sets of attribute levels.

The computer can insure that when subsequent questions appear on the interviewer's screen, irrelevant information is omitted. For example, once the most preferred and unacceptable levels are known, they can be eliminated from the next question about least preferred level. In some cases, the entire question can be eliminated. For instance, if there are three levels (A, B, and C), and A is most preferred and C is unacceptable, then B must be least preferred. For some attributes, the preference ordering of attribute levels is obvious so that the question on the most preferred and the least preferred levels need not be asked.

Similar kinds of efficiencies are obtained in the attribute-importance measurement. If level A of a three-level attribute is most preferred and both levels B and C are unacceptable, then this attribute is relevant only in the conjunctive phase and not in the trade-off phase. Thus, it would not appear in the critical-attribute selection or importance-rating section.

All of this complex skip logic is programmed into the questionnaire and is invisible to both the interviewer and respondent. The task for both parties is simple. It does not require computer knowledge on either side. It does not require taking a computer to the respondent's residence or business. Also, it does not require any printed materials be sent to the respondent. On the

A. *Relative Desirabilities*

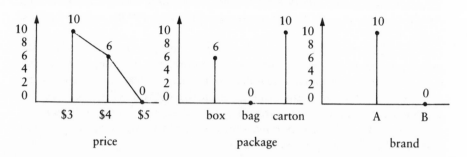

Note: For each attribute, the relative desirabilities for the most preferred level = 10, least preferred level = 0.

B. *Importances*

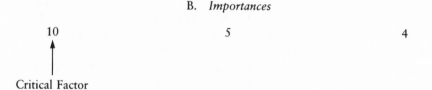

Critical Factor

C. *Part-Worths = (Relative Desirability × Importance)/10*

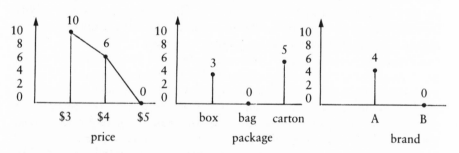

Figure 5–3. Computing Part-Worth

other hand, if the project requires the demonstration of a new product, CASEMAP can be adapted to a mall intercept or in-person computer-assisted interview.

Interviewing is done via Automated Custom Research System (ACRS) from a central location. ACRS is M/A/R/C Inc.'s integrated computer-assisted telephone-interviewing system for sampling, data collection, and processing.

It has been in use since 1976. It is available for WATS-line interviewing as well as in-person interviewing at central locations. Data can be tabulated at any point during the interviewing process. This can be useful for monitoring the production aspects of the study as well as to obtain early empirical results.

Computer control makes quality improvements at several phases of the study. Scheduled, systematic callbacks are enforced to maximize sample representativeness. Computer-controlled skip logic "locks out" invalid responses. The efficiencies that emerge from the CASEMAP procedures and computer control allow more attributes to be handled. As many as fourteen attributes have been incorporated into a CASEMAP study in an interview that lasted about thirty minutes, on average.

An Illustration

The first steps in a CASEMAP study are the same as those in traditional conjoint analysis. We need to specify the choice situation (or usage occasion), identify product attributes that are relevant to the product category, and determine the particular levels or options of those attributes that are to be investigated. Consider the hypothetical example of a household appliance such as toaster ovens. Suppose there were five attributes of interest: brand, price, toasting speed, a self-cleaning feature, and an automatic–shut-off feature. Suppose further that five brands were to be investigated: Sunbeam, Norelco, General Electric, Toastmaster, and Proctor-Silex. The range of prices for this category might be from $35 to $75. Three speed levels ranging from two minutes to six minutes would be possible. The self-cleaning and automatic–shut-off features may or may not be present.

In step 1 of CASEMAP, we determine the most preferred level for each attribute. We illustrate this process with the brand of the product. The interviewer would read the question as follows: "The brand name of this product could be Sunbeam, Norelco, General Electric, Toastmaster, or Proctor-Silex. Which of these do you prefer the most?" The respondent would give his or her most preferred brand—in this case, Toastmaster.

The next step is to identify any unacceptable levels on this attribute. The interviewer would ask: "Which, if any, of the following brands would you never consider under any circumstances: Sunbeam, Norelco, General Electric, or Proctor-Silex." This respondent says "Proctor-Silex." At this point, a series of probes are used to insure that when a respondent says that something is unacceptable, he or she truly means that the product would be rejected no matter how attractive the product is on other features.

Having determined the most-preferred level of the attribute and identified any unacceptable levels, the next step is to determine the least preferred level of this attribute. In the example, the interviewer asks: "Which of the following brands do you prefer the least: Sunbeam, Norelco, or General Electric?" (Note that the list of brand names is changing from five to four to three over the past three steps.)

In this case the respondent says "Norelco."

Up to this point, we have identified the most preferred level, an unacceptable level and the least preferred level. We now need to obtain relative-desirability ratings of the other two brands that remain. In the example, the interviewer says: "Suppose we give your most preferred brand, Toastmaster, a value of ten, and your least preferred brand, Norelco, a value of zero. What value between zero and ten would you give to Sunbeam?" The respondent says "Four points." The interviewer follows with: "What value would you give to General Electric?" The respondent says "Eight points." In sum, we have now obtained a relative-desirability measurement for each of the five different brand names that make up this attribute.

A similar series of questions is asked for each of the other attributes. At the conclusion of that series, we go on to steps 2 and 3 to obtain the relative importance of the attributes themselves in order to obtain the part-worths.

Step 2 of CASEMAP determines the critical product attribute. As explained earlier, a sufficient number of paired-comparison questions are asked until the most important attribute is revealed.

To illustrate, the interviewer might be asking a question that compares brand and price. The question is a paired-comparison question as follows: "Which of these do you prefer? A Toastmaster at $75 or a Norelco at $35?" (Note that this question compares the most preferred brand at the least preferred price with the least preferred—but acceptable—brand at the most preferred price.) And in this case the respondent says: "I would prefer a Toastmaster at $75." We know from this response that brand is more important than price and go on to compare brand with the next attribute. After completing this series of questions, we have identified the critical attribute. We shall now use that attribute as the anchor against which to measure the relative importance of all the other attributes.

This final step in the data collection is where we obtain ratings of attribute importance. For example, if brand were the critical attribute, the interviewer would say: "If the increased benefit to you of having a Toastmaster instead of a Norelco is ten points, how many points would you give to paying $35 instead of $75?" The respondent says "Eight points."

The interviewer would go on to ask the same kind of question for all the remaining attributes. At the conclusion of this series of questions, we have now obtained an importance weight for each of the attributes, which, when combined with the relative desirability values, produces the part-worths we need to conduct the analysis.

CASEMAP Analysis

There are a number of different analysis options depending upon the marketing objectives of the particular study. At the most basic level, CASEMAP allows us to *profile* the market's preferences in terms of the relative appeal/unacceptability of the different attribute levels and features. Second, the data collected using CASEMAP afford us the opportunity to conduct market-*segmentation* analyses based on the similarity in the pattern of unacceptables and/or the benefits that consumers seek in the category. Third, the data provide the input data base to build a *choice-simulation* model. The data base can be used to predict market choices under a variety of competitive scenarios. Each of these analyses will be described in the context of the toaster-oven illustration considered earlier.

Market Profile. Each of the five attributes in the study can be profiled according to the part-worth values associated with each level or option. In figure 5–4, the brand attribute is presented indicating that, on average, Toastmaster is preferred to General Electric, which is in turn preferred to Sunbeam, while Norelco and Proctor-Silex are rated relatively lower. In addition to these aggregate part-worth values, CASEMAP produces another useful statistic, the percentage of people who would reject each brand as being totally unacceptable to them. In the example, very few people rejected Toastmaster or General Electric, while a fairly significant percentage rejected Proctor-Silex as being totally unacceptable.

Market Segmentation. Benefit segmentation can be conducted using either the acceptable-versus-unacceptable responses, the part-worth values, or both. In table 5–2, there are three market segments based on the pattern of unacceptable attribute levels. The first segment perceives all brands to be acceptable. They exhibit a price threshold of $45, meaning that, in general, consumers in this segment reject products that are priced above this level. Finally, this group expresses no strong requirement for particular feature options. The second segment perceives Sunbeam and General Electric to be acceptable brands while rejecting Toastmaster, Proctor-Silex, and Norelco. Their price threshold is very high, meaning that this segment is willing to pay the high prices provided there are compensating benefits. This segment tends to have strong requirements for some of the feature enhancements such as self-cleaning and automatic shut-off. The third segment finds Toastmaster and General Electric to be acceptable while rejecting a different combination of brands: Sunbeam, Norelco, and Proctor-Silex. They exhibit a price threshold at $75 and exhibit strong requirement for only the fastest-speed option.

Segmentation analysis can be very useful in identifying attractive segments that are predisposed toward the firm's brand and exhibit strong re-

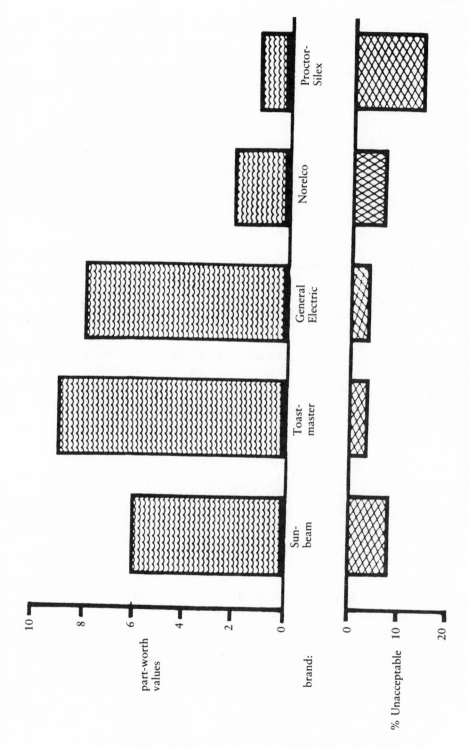

Figure 5–4. Hypothetical Market Profile

Table 5–2
Hypothetical Market Segmentation

	Segment 1	Segment 2	Segment 3
Acceptable brands	All	Sunbeam G.E.	Toastmaster G.E.
Unacceptable brands	None	Toastmaster Proctor-Silex Norelco	Sunbeam Norelco Proctor-Silex
Price threshold	$45	$75	$75
Strong requirements for feature options	None	Self-cleaning Automatic shut-off	Fastest speed

Table 5–3
Hypothetical Market Simulation

	Product			
Attribute	1	2	3	4
Brand	Sunbeam	G.E.	Toastmaster	Proctor-Silex
Price	$75	$75	$45	$35
Speed	4 mins.	4 mins.	2 mins.	6 mins.
Self-cleaning	Yes	No	No	No
Automatic shut-off	No	Yes	No	No
Share of choices	25%	20%	40%	15%

quirements for the features that the firm's products have to offer. It is also useful in identifying segments that reject the firm's brand or are attracted more strongly to competitive brands. Finally, it is possible to integrate the segmentation results with the simulation analyses. One can assess a product's likely success against particular segments, and using demographic and psychographic variables, to identify the types of individuals who would be most attracted to it.

Market Simulation. In the example illustrated in table 5–3, four products are being simulated: a Sunbeam product, General Electric product, Toastmaster product, and Proctor-Silex product. Each is defined in terms of a particular price, speed, self-cleaning, and automatic–shut-off configuration. The market-simulation model reveals the share of choices that would be obtained by each of these products using the unacceptable levels and the part-worth expressed by the consumers in the survey sample.

Pricing Effects. Repeated application of the market simulation approach leads to an in-depth pricing analysis. For example, figure 5–5 indicates the new-product share at various price levels, holding all other variables constant. Similar analyses can be conducted to evaluate the potential cannibalization effect and the potential gain in share from competitive brands.

CASEMAP Validation

To date, validation work has been carried out in a few applications.

Validation in Research on MBA Job Choices. Srinivasan (1985) conducted a CASEMAP study of MBA students' choices among job offers. The study was designed based on previous conjoint-analysis research done by Wittink and Montgomery (1979) using trade-off matrices. In order to maximize comparability, a self-administered paper questionnaire was used to collect the data from MBA students. The design consisted of eight attributes of jobs such as travel, salary, location, and company performance. The date were collected in February from a sample of MBAs prior to the MBAs receiving job offers. Additional data collected in June characterized the job offers received by the MBAs in terms of the same eight attributes. CASEMAP's prediction of the offer that the MBA would take was then compared with the actual job choice. CASEMAP predicted the job choice correctly for 69 percent of the forty-five students, which is slightly better than the predictive validity of 63 percent obtained in the earlier trade-off–analysis study done by Wittink and Montgomery. The CASEMAP predictive validity was also better than the predictive validity of 60 percent obtained with the traditional

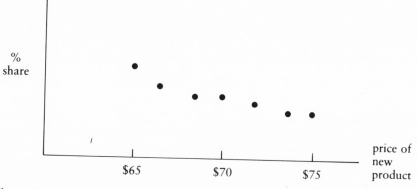

Figure 5–5. Hypothetical Pricing Analysis: New-Product Share at Various Price Levels

method of defining attribute importances (i.e., asking the respondent to rate the importance of the different attributes). Among the 27 percent students who classified a job offer's one or more attribute levels as unacceptable, *none* actually chose such an offer. At a minimum, the results of this specific study support the conclusion that the simpler CASEMAP procedure is at least as valid as conjoint analysis in doing what conjoint analysis does. In sum, the results are supportive of the CASEMAP methodology.

Applied Marketing Studies. We have conducted CASEMAP research in a variety of product categories including telecommunications for business and residential, televisions, deodorants, and potato chips. The wording and sequencing of questions vary somewhat by category, but the essential elements remain the same.

Based on our experience, which includes over 4,000 interviews, we can estimate the length of interviewing time CASEMAP requires to conduct a relatively small design. Four or five attributes will require about ten minutes for the CASEMAP portion of the interview. A moderately complex study with seven to ten attributes will take about fifteen minutes of interviewing time. The most complex study undertaken to date had fourteen attributes and required about thirty minutes.

The latter study, done for a commercial client, provided the opportunity to validate some of our results against other research the client had conducted. The basic point of comparison was a trade-off between the client's brand name and price. Repeated simulations were used to quantify the price premium customers were willing to pay to get this brand. Our analysis compared the client to its chief competitor while systematically varying price. A search program located the point on the price-attribute scale where an equal proportion of consumers would choose the client and competitor's brands. It was determined that if the competitor's price dropped to 20 percent below the client's price, the market would split evenly between the two.

The client's previous research, using conjoint methods, had generated estimates between 20 and 22 percent. Thus our estimate was within the narrow range of the previous work.

Conclusion

In conclusion, CASEMAP has proven to be an effective, practical, and valid method for doing conjoint-type analysis by collecting date in a single telephone interview. Conceptually, it extends the traditional conjoint model to capture complexities of choice behavior that the classical method ignores. Compared to other self-explicated preference-measurement methods, it uses a conceptually more appropriate definition of attribute importance. Using the power of the computer, it minimizes the information overload on the respondent. It allows researchers to conduct studies having larger number of attributes in situations where traditional techniques may break down. It also plays a role in small-scale studies. Rather than use imprecise attitude-measurement techniques, CASEMAP provides an alternative that does not necessarily add much to study costs. CASEMAP makes conjoint analysis accessible for many more market-research studies, where in the past conjoint analysis would not be used.

References

Cattin, Philippe, and Dick R. Wittink (1982). "Commercial Use of Conjoint Analysis: A Survey," *Journal of Marketing* 46 (summer): 44–53.

Coombs, Clyde (1964). *A Theory of Data.* New York: Wiley.

Green, Paul E. (1984). "Hybrid Models for Conjoint Analysis: An Expository Review," *Journal of Marketing Research* 21 (May): 155–69.

Green, Paul E., and V. Srinivasan (1978). "Conjoint Analysis in Consumer Research: Issues and Outlook," *Journal of Consumer Research* 5 (September): 103–23.

Green, Paul E., and Yoram Wind (1975). "New Way to Measure Consumers' Judgments," *Harvard Business Review* 53 (July-August): 107–17.

Huber, George P. (1974). "Multi-Attribute Utility Models: A Review of Field and Field-Like Studies," *Management Science* 20 (June): 1393–402.

Johnson, Richard M. (1974). "Trade-off Analysis of Consumer Values," *Journal of Marketing Research* 11 (May): 121–27.

Lussier, Denis A., and Richard W. Olshavsky (1979). "Task Complexity and Contingent Processing in Brand Choice," *Journal of Consumer Research* 6 (September): 154–65.

Payne, John W. (1976). "Task Complexity and Contingent Processing in Decision Making: An Information Search and Protocol Analysis," *Organizational Behavior and Human Performance* 16 (August): 366–87.

Srinivasan, V. (1985). "A Conjunctive-Compensatory Approach to the Self-Explication of Multi-Attributed Preferences." Research paper. Stanford, Calif.: Graduate School of Business, Stanford University.

Wittink, Dick R., and David B. Montgomery (1979). "Predictive Validity of Trade-off Analysis for Alternative Segmentation Schemes," in *1979 Educators' Conference Proceedings,* Neil Beckwith et al., eds. Chicago: American Marketing Association, pp. 69–73.

Wright, Peter (1974). "The Harassed Decision Maker: Time Pressures, Distractions, and the Use of Evidence," *Journal of Applied Psychology* 59 (October): 555–61.

——— (1975). "Consumer Choice Strategies: Simplifying vs. Optimizing," *Journal of Marketing Research* 12 (February): 60–67.

6

A Hybrid Conjoint Model for Price-Demand Estimation

Paul E. Green
Abba M. Krieger

The application of conjoint analysis to problems in price-demand analysis has received considerable attention recently. Mahajan et al. (1982) describe an adaptation of a data-collection procedure by Jones (1975) that uses a conditional logit model (Theil [1969]) to estimate competitive price-demand relationships at the group level. Wyner et al. (1984) apply a modification of the Majahan et al. procedure that substitutes units purchased of each item in a set of products for the constant-sum dependent variable and ordinary least squares (OLS) regression for the logit-based estimation. The Wyner et al. approach also fits the parameters at the total-group level. Both applications emphasize only product/supplier and price as the predictor variables. (However, Mahajan et al. briefly discuss the incorporation of other product-service attributes into the model, albeit with accompanying increased complexity in the design and respondent-evaluation task.)

Concomitant with the application of conjoint methods to price-demand estimation, increased attention has been given to the development and testing of hybrid models that combine self-explication data with conjoint-designed profile evaluations (Green et al. [1981], Akaah and Korgaonkar [1983], Cattin et al. [1982]). In a later expository paper, Green (1984) summarizes the status of hybrid conjoint models and discusses their limitations and future research needs.

The present chapter is concerned with the development of a hybrid conjoint model for price-demand estimation. Unlike earlier approaches, our extension maintains individual differences in utility estimation. In addition, the proposed model incorporates various product-service attributes (as well as price) and utilizes an empirical Bayes procedure to estimate individual price utilities from residuals computed in the first-stage analysis.

The Hybrid Price-Demand Model

The proposed model incorporates three steps in data collection. In the first (self-explicated) phase, the respondent evaluates the acceptability of various product-service–attribute levels (including price) on an equal-interval scale, ranging from "highly undesirable" to "highly desirable." This step is followed by the respondent's allocation of 100 points across the attributes (constant-sum procedure), so as to reflect their perceived relative importance in the overall decision process. The first set of (ratings) data are called "desirabilities" (normalized to vary between 0 and 1.0). The second set of data are called "importances" (also normalized to range between 0 and 1.0 and, in addition, to sum to 1.0).

In the third phase of the data-collection procedure, the respondent is shown a set of product-service profiles, constructed according to a fractional factorial design (Green and Srinivasan [1978]). Each profile card shows a description of each of S suppliers (or brands). For each profile, the respondent is asked to allocate 100 (or some other such total number) points across the options, so as to reflect the subjective likelihood of choosing each supplier on the next buying occasion. Each supplier differs from the others in one or more attributes, including price. In commercial studies, the total number of profiles evaluated by any one respondent generally ranges between eight and twelve.[1]

To anticipate the discussion to follow, we present a model that develops individual-respondent–utility functions for each of S suppliers. The approach consists of three stages:

1. Stage 1 obtains individual self-explicated utilities for each attribute level and computes regression parameters (including individual-respondent intercepts) so as to best fit the respondent's profile-evaluation data. In this step, the arguments of the regression model are (normalized) subjective utilities of attribute levels, rather than the levels themselves. Residuals from this first-stage regression are computed.

2. The first-stage residuals from the full-profile evaluations are then regressed on the actual price variable (expressed either in dollars or relative to a dollar base level, rather than in utilities). A single regression coefficient is estimated for each combination of individual and supplier via an empirical Bayes procedure.

3. The user is then free to enter one or more test profiles, consisting of attribute levels (including price) for each of the S suppliers. The program computes each respondent's likelihood of choice for each supplier for each test profile.

Note that the price variable enters twice, once as an attribute for which a self-explicated utility is obtained and once in "natural" units (e.g., dollars) as a single predictor, for each supplier in turn, in the analysis of each respondent's residuals.

Preliminary Notation. Prior to presenting the model, we consider the following notation:

s = the supplier (or brand); $s = 1,2,...,S$

k = the respondent; $k = 1,2,...,K$

i = a nonprice attribute; $i = 1,2,...,I$

j_i = the level of nonprice attribute i; $j_i = 1,2,...,J_i$

p = the level of the price attribute; $p = 1,2,...,P$

$h^{(k)}$ = the profile (drawn from the master design) received by respondent k; $h = 1,2,...,H$ (All respondents receive the same total number of profiles.)

$L_{sh}^{(k)}$ = a vector of length I, denoting the levels of the I nonprice attributes offered by supplier s to respondent k in profile $h^{(k)}$

$p_{sh}^{(k)}$ = the level of price of the product-service offered by supplier s to respondent k in profile $h^{(k)}$

$z_{sh}^{*(k)}$ = the actual (dollar-value) price offered by supplier s to respondent k in profile $h^{(k)}$

Self-Explicated Part-Worths. In the self-explicated data-collection step, we assume that attribute-level desirabilities and attribute importances are "supplier-neutral," i.e., they do not depend on which supplier is offering the particular levels. (This assumption is made primarily to reduce the data-collection burden on the respondent. The model can be extended to allow the self-explicated responses to vary by supplier.) The following notation is adopted:

$d_{ij}^{(k)}$ = desirability of level j of nonprice attribute i to respondent k

$e_p^{(k)}$ = desirability of level p of price to respondent k

$\lambda_i^{(k)}$ = importance of nonprice attribute i to respondent k

$\pi^{(k)}$ = importance of price to respondent k

We can then find the self-explicated utilities as shown next.

Product Score (Normalized)

$$t_{sh}^{(k)} = d_{iL_{sh}^{(k)}(i)} \bigg/ \sum_{s'=1}^{S} d_{iL_{s'h}^{(k)}(i)} \tag{1}$$

where $L_{s'h(i)}^{(k)}$ denotes the level of the ith nonprice attribute for person k in profile h, as offered by supplier s'; $s' = 1,2,...,S$. We then introduce the respondent's importance weights $\lambda_i^{(k)}$ to get

$$x_{sh}^{(k)} = \sum_{i=1}^{I} \lambda_i^{(k)} \, t_{shi}^{(k)} \tag{2}$$

where $x_{sh}^{(k)}$ denotes the (normalized) utility for the nonprice portion of the offering of supplier s in profile $h^{(k)}$ to respondent k.

Price-Score (Normalized)

$$v_{sh}^{(k)} = e_{p_{sh}^{(k)}} \Big/ \sum_{s'=1}^{S} e_{p_{s'h}^{(k)}} \tag{3}$$

where $p_{sh}^{(k)}$ denotes the level of price for person k in profile h as offered by supplier s'; $s' = 1,2,...,S$. We then introduce the importance weights $\pi^{(k)}$ to get

$$z_{sh}^{(k)} = \pi^{(k)} \, v_{sh}^{(k)} \tag{4}$$

where $z_{sh}^{(k)}$ denotes the (normalized) utility of the price component of supplier s in profile $h^{(k)}$ to respondent k. As just shown, $x_{sh}^{(k)}$ and $z_{sh}^{(k)}$ terms are "built up" from the self-explication ratings and attribute-importance weights, as collected at the individual level.

The First-Stage Model. As previously shown, the $x_{sh}^{(k)}$ and $z_{sh}^{(k)}$ represent (normalized) utility scores of supplier s in profile $h^{(k)}$ to respondent k. In the conjoint task, the respondent also provides an explicit evaluation of each of the S suppliers, via a likelihood-of-choice response. We let:

$y_{sh}^{(k)}$ = evaluative score of respondent k for the product-price offered by supplier s to respondent k in profile h(k),
  where scores are normalized so that

$$\sum_{s=1}^{S} y_{sh}^{(k)} = 1.0.$$

This score, $y_{sh}^{(k)}$, represents the dependent variable in an OLS regression that is implemented for each supplier, in turn.[2] Since we estimate parameters at the supplier-specific level, we can suppress the supplier index to get

$$y_h^{(k)} = \alpha^{(k)} + \gamma x_h^{(k)} + \delta z_h^{(k)} + \epsilon_h^{(k)} \tag{5}$$

which is the first stage of the hybrid price-demand model.

As noted, the regression coefficients γ and δ are estimated at the group level, but their arguments ($x_h^{(k)}$ and $z_h^{(k)}$, respectively) reflect *individual* differences in the self-explicated evaluation task. We also note that the proposed model allows for an individual-level intercept. Since this feature appears to be novel in hybrid conjoint models, some discussion of the estimation procedure is warranted.

Estimating the Individual Intercepts. Estimation of the $K+2$ parameters in equation (5) is by OLS regression, which is equal to maximum likelihood if $\epsilon_h^{(k)}$ is assumed to be normally distributed. We wish to find $\hat{\alpha}^{(k)}$, $\hat{\gamma}$, and $\hat{\delta}$ that minimize the sum of squared errors:

$$\min \psi = \sum_{k=1}^{K} \sum_{h=1}^{H} \left[y_h^{(k)} - \hat{\alpha}^{(k)} - \hat{\gamma} x_h^{(k)} - \hat{\delta} z_h^{(k)} \right]^2. \tag{6}$$

We first find the partial derivative of ψ with respect to $\hat{\alpha}^{(k)}$:

$$\frac{\partial \psi}{\partial \hat{\alpha}^{(k)}} = 0; \quad \sum_{h=1}^{H} y_h^{(k)} - \hat{\alpha}^{(k)} - \hat{\gamma} x_h^{(k)} = \hat{\delta} z_h^{(k)} = 0. \tag{7}$$

$$\hat{\alpha}^{(k)} = \bar{y}^{(k)} - \hat{\gamma} \bar{x}^{(k)} - \hat{\delta} \bar{z}^{(k)}. \tag{8}$$

Then, substituting (8) into (6), we get

$$\min \psi = \sum_{k=1}^{K} \sum_{h=1}^{H} \left[(y_h^{(k)} - \bar{y}^{(k)}) - \hat{\gamma}(x_h^{(k)} - \bar{x}^{(k)}) - \hat{\delta}(z_h^{(k)} - \bar{z}^{(k)}) \right]^2. \tag{9}$$

Hence, we run OLS on equation (9) to get $\hat{\gamma}$ and $\hat{\delta}$. Then we obtain the $\hat{\alpha}^{(k)}$s from equation (8).

Naturally, we expect that $\hat{\gamma}$ and $\hat{\delta}$ will be nonnegative since their arguments are utilities estimated from the self-explicated data. The individual intercepts $\hat{\alpha}^{(k)}$ may be positive or negative, depending upon the empirical context. Suitable summary statistics, such as R^2 for the total model, standard errors of $\hat{\gamma}$ and $\hat{\delta}$, correlations of each respondent's estimated $\hat{y}_h$ scores with the actual y_h scores, stimulus profile correlations (across–respondent-profile evaluations), and so on are also computed for diagnostic purposes.

It should be mentioned that, in principle, one could also obtain an individual intercept term via inclusion of a dummy variable for each respondent's data, in turn; this is the conventional procedure for finding individualized intercepts.

In the proposed method, however, we take advantage of the fact that the sum of the residuals, within an individual, is zero. Our procedure is considerably more parsimonious while producing the same results as the more traditional approach.

The Second-Stage (Residuals) Model. After the first-stage fitting of the model in equation (5) is obtained, the proposed approach finds residuals:

$$r_h^{(k)} = y_h^{(k)} - \hat{y}_h^{(k)} \tag{10}$$

for each supplier, in turn. If the first-stage model fits the data well, then the residuals may not have much "signal" left in them. Empirically, however, we have generally found in the fitting of hybrid conjoint models that the residuals may reflect additional sources of variation, measured at the stimulus level.[3]

In the present model, which emphasizes competitive pricing, we assume that the impact of price may not be completely taken care of in the self-explicated data-collection stage. Hence, we reintroduce price as a predictor variable that is represented in actual (e.g., dollar) terms, rather than as a set of dummy-coded variables. We now wish to estimate an additional regression parameter for each respondent k that reflects the actual price of the offering of each supplier s.[4] The proposed model employs empirical Bayes for this purpose. Standard Bayesian estimation is first briefly reviewed, followed by an introductory description of the empirical Bayes procedure.

Bayes' Procedures

From the preceding discussion, it follows that we want to consider the following model at stage 2:

$$r_h^{(k)} = \beta^{(k)} \left(\overset{*}{z}_h^{(k)} - \overset{=*}{z}{}^{(k)} \right) + \mu_h^{(k)} \tag{11}$$

where $\overset{*}{z}_h^{(k)}$ is the actual price level for the supplier of interest and

$$\overset{=*}{z}{}^{(k)} = \frac{\displaystyle\sum_{h=1}^{H} \overset{*}{z}_h^{(k)}}{H}.$$

We assume that the $\mu_h^{(k)}$s are independent and identically distributed according to $N(0, \sigma^2_{(k)})$.[5] Since the information remaining in regard to estimating

$\beta^{(k)}$ might be minimal, we adopt a Bayesian approach and assume that $\beta^{(k)}$ is a random variable, i.e.,

$$\beta^{(k)} \sim N(\beta, \sigma_\beta^2). \tag{12}$$

The likelihood of observing b_k, the least squares estimator of $\beta^{(k)}$, is

$$L(b_k) = \frac{1}{\sqrt{2\pi}\, c_k}\, e^{-1/2(b_k - \beta^{(k)})^2/c_k^2} \tag{13}$$

$$\text{where } c_k^2 = \frac{\sigma_{(k)}^2}{\sum_{h=1}^{H} (\overset{*}{z}_h^{(k)} - \overset{\ast}{\bar{z}}^{(k)})^2}.$$

Bayesian Estimates

It follows from equations (12) and (13) and standard decision theory (Raiffa and Schlaifer [1961], Pratt et al. [1965]) that the posterior distribution is

$$\tilde{\beta}^{(k)}|b^{(k)} \sim N\left(\frac{\beta c_k^2 + b_k \sigma_\beta^2}{c_k^2 + \sigma_\beta^2}, \frac{\sigma_\beta^2 c_k^2}{c_k^2 + \sigma_\beta^2}\right). \tag{14}$$

If we assume a squared-error loss function, then the estimator of $\beta^{(k)}$ is

$$\hat{\beta}^{(k)} = \frac{\beta c_k^2 + b_k \sigma_\beta^2}{c_k^2 + \sigma_\beta^2} \tag{15}$$

(i.e., we weight the two estimates of $\beta^{(k)}$, β, and b_k inversely proportional to their variances).

In order to operationalize equation (15) we need β, c_k^2, and σ_β^2:

c_k^2: an estimate of c_k^2 can be obtained from the regression on each individual. If we assume that the $\sigma_{(k)}^2$s are equal, we can pool the mean squared errors across the K regressions.

β and σ_β^2: an empirical Bayes approach is used to estimate β and σ_β^2 (Maritz [1970]).

An introductory discussion of empirical Bayes estimation is presented next. Technical details of the approach appear in the chapter appendix.

The Concept of Empirical Bayes Estimation

An empirical Bayes approach is used to estimate the slope coefficients in the second-stage analysis for two reasons. The reason for a Bayesian approach stems from Stein's paradox (Efron and Morris [1977]). For example, if we want to estimate the batting average of baseball players, and, in particular, a player had 100 hits in his first 200 times at bat, should the estimate be 0.500? Stein showed that this "obvious" estimator is inadmissible (i.e., there exist other estimators that perform at least as well with respect to mean squared error for all values of the parameters and better for some values of the parameters) and that the batting averages of the *other* players should be incorporated into the estimate.[6] In other words, since this player's batting average is so high relative to the rest of the players', it is likely that the person's batting average would fall and so the estimate should be lower than 0.500. The standard procedure for finding admissible estimators is to place a prior on the parameter space and use the posterior mean derived from Bayes' theorem to find the estimator that minimizes squared error loss. We choose a normal prior since it is the conjugate prior in our context (i.e., the posterior distribution is also normal).

The reason for using empirical Bayes is that we want to avoid having the estimator depend on our subjective choice of the prior mean and variance. Empirical Bayes is used to estimate the prior mean and variance from the data. For an interesting application and discussion of empirical Bayes, see Rubin (1980).

In sum, empirical Bayes is used to find estimates of β and σ_β^2. The numerical aspects of the task entail the application of a Newton-Raphson procedure to find $\hat{\sigma}_\beta^2$, followed by solving for $\hat{\beta}$. (Details of the model and computational techniques are shown in the appendix.)

Hence, at this point estimates of all three quantities (c_β^2, σ_β^2, and β) are obtained from the data. Equation (15) is then used to find the individual $\hat{\beta}^{(k)}$ slope coefficients.

A Pilot Application

The hybrid price-demand model is illustrated with a (disguised) data set drawn from industrial marketing. The product-service class consists of large and complex electropneumatic devices that are used by a wide range of business enterprises. The original study was motivated by the desire to design attractive and competitevely priced maintenance services for these devices. The current pilot study consists of a small data set, selected to serve as a demonstration of the methodology. Since the purpose is largely one of technique demonstration (rather than empirical interest), we do not consider such issues as split-half cross-validation and the like.

Currently, three types of suppliers—the original manufacturer, the distributor, and a third-party broker—offer maintenance contracts and service. In recent years, the less-expensive distributors and brokers had been gaining share, at the expense of the manufacturer-suppliers. Interest focused on those aspects of service and price that respondents valued most highly and how their choice of future suppliers of equipment maintenance might be affected by changes in the composition of the maintenance offerings and price.

One of the smaller manufacturers of such devices was the study's sponsor. The manufacturer was interested in the six major service attributes shown in table 6–1. Based on recent experience, it was believed that distributor or broker-type suppliers were considering either a small price increase and/or a change in their current way (level E-2) of replacing small spare parts. (However, even with a 10 percent price increase, the distributor/broker prices would be well below those of the manufacturer.) Hence, in the survey, the distributors' and brokers' profiles were set at current levels (as shown in table 6–1) for the first four attributes:

Distributor	*Broker*
A-3	A-2
B-2	B-3
C-3	C-2
D-3	D-3

Table 6–1
Maintenance-Service Attributes and Levels Used in Price-Demand Study (Disguised Data)

A. When service personnel typically arrive after call
1. Within 3 hours
2. Within 6 hours
3. Next business day

B. Your involvement in repair
1. Vendor handles everything.
2. You run diagnostics first; then vendor handles repair.
3. Your personnel assist vendor's personnel in repair.
4. You repair yourself.

C. Preventive maintenance
1. Routinely provided by vendor
2. Provided only after an initial breakdown
3. Not provided at all

D. Availability of large spare parts
1. Stored at vendor's central location
2. Stored on your premises
3. Stored at vendor's local depot

E. Replacement of small spare parts
1. All is done at your location by vendor.
2. You take defective part to vendor's local depot.
3. Vendor's messenger takes part to vendor for replacement.

F. Annual contract price
1. 10% more than current price
2. Current price
3. 10% less than current price
4. 20% less than current price

Attribute E was considered at all three levels, while attribute F (price) was considered at levels F-1 and F-2 only for both distributors and brokers.

The resulting master design consisted of a fractional factorial derived from the following full factorial:

Manufacturer	Distributor	Broker
[3 × 4 × 3 × 3 × 3 × 4]	[3 × 2]	[3 × 2].

An orthogonal main-effects plan was constructed that required only 64 profiles, with balanced levels maintained within sets of 8 profiles, each. Accordingly, in the conjoint–data-collection step, each respondent received 8 profiles, where each profile card provided a description of the 3 types of suppliers in terms of 6 attribute levels each.

Preprocessing of the Data

The first step in the method consists of preparing the respondent by creating an attribute-level self-explicated data file of desirabilities and importances. The sample consisted of 228 purchasing-agent respondents. Since there are 6 attributes (see table 6–1) with a total of 20 attribute levels for the self-explicated responses, the input matrix to the first-stage fitting procedure is 228×26 (where the first 20 columns denote attribute-level desirabilities and the last 6 columns are attribute importances, all appropriately normalized to vary between 0 and 1.0).

Next, a 64×18 design matrix was prepared, consisting of the attribute levels of each of the 6 attributes of table 6–1 appearing on the stimulus card for each of the 3 competitive suppliers. The third input file consisted of the 3-component dependent variable of point assignments across the 3 suppliers and the stimulus-card number associated with the specific 3-supplier profile. These input matrices, along with the respondent's ID number, are sufficient to determine the criterion and predictor variables of equation (5), given application of equations (1) through (4).

First-Stage Regression

The parameters of equation (5) were then estimated by OLS, for each of the three suppliers, separately. (The program also has an option for applying a logit transformation, prior to parameter estimation; for simplicity, this option was not utilized in the pilot application.) The first-stage results for each supplier are shown in the top portion of table 6–2. To conserve space, results for individual respondents—intercept, goodness of fit, mean likelihood scores across all eight stimuli, and standard deviation—are not shown.

The R^2s each indicate about 50 percent variance-accounted-for in the

Table 6–2
Results of Model Fitting, First and Second Stages

	Supplier		
	Manufacturer	*Distributor*	*Broker*
First stage			
R²	0.544	0.547	0.510
$\hat{\gamma}$ (nonprice)	0.405	0.297	0.271
$t(\hat{\gamma})$	8.385	6.241	9.216
$\hat{\delta}$ (price)	0.161	0.243	0.080
$t(\hat{\delta})$	0.839	2.022	0.593
Second stage (residuals)			
R²	0.115	0.134	0.102
Average slope (across all respondents)	−0.087	−0.029	0.119

self-explicated portion. In all three supplier types, the regression coefficient for the nonprice attributes overshadows that for the price attribute (expressed in self-explicated utility terms).[7] However, as would be expected, both coefficients—$\hat{\gamma}$ (nonprice) and $\hat{\delta}$ (price)—are positive, since their arguments pertain to the utility of the attribute levels.

Second-Stage Fitting

Residuals were then computed via equation (10) for each supplier separately. Empirical Bayes was used to determine the individual-respondent estimates of $\beta^{(k)}$ in equation (11). As described earlier, the argument $\overset{*}{z}^{(k)}_b$ is the actual price of a given supplier.

The lower portion of table 6–2 indicates that the R²s associated with fitting the residuals were 0.115, 0.134, and 0.102, respectively, for manufacturer, distributor, and broker. In the case of manufacturer and distributor, the regression coefficients were negative, while that for broker was positive.

Product-Profile Predictions

For illustrative purposes, five product profiles were prepared, ranging from a "good" profile from the manufacturer's standpoint to a "poor" profile. Each of the five product profiles was run through the program, and predicted "shares" for the three types of suppliers were obtained. The results are shown in table 6–3.

As noted from the table, profile C shows all three suppliers at parity (current) price; their shares are 0.65, 0.15, and 0.20 for manufacturer, distributor, and broker. As the manufacturer reduces its price to 10 and 20

Table 6–3

Average Likelihoods of Choosing Each of Three Types of Suppliers for Selected Supplier Profiles

	Profile Attribute Levels			Average Likelihoods			
	Manufacturer	*Distributor*	*Broker*	*Manufacturer*	*Distributor*	*Broker*	*Total*
A	111214	323312	323312	0.716	0.129	0.155	1.000
B	111213	323312	323312	0.673	0.144	0.183	1.000
C	111212	323312	323312	0.651	0.154	0.195	1.000
D	111211	323311	323311	0.640	0.159	0.201	1.000
E	343121	323311	323311	0.527	0.220	0.253	1.000

percent below its current levels, share increases to 0.67 and 0.72, respectively (profiles B and A). However, where all three supplier types increase price by 10 percent, the manufacturer loses share slightly (from 0.65 to 0.64), as noted in profile D. Finally, when the manufacturer degrades some service elements as well, his share decreases to 0.53 (profile E). Clearly, other substantive issues regarding pricing or service strategy could be entered into the predictive portion of the model as well.

Discussion

Now that the multisupplier hybrid model has been described and illustrated numerically, we return to some of the conceptual issues underlying the model and its parameter-estimation procedures. Possible extensions of the approach, including its potential use in simulation and product-line optimization, are then discussed briefly.

Market-Share Models

The model's use of normalized utilities in the first-stage regression estimation bears similarities to 1980s econometric work in market-share modeling (Naert and Weverbergh [1981], Ghosh et al. [1984], Leeflang and Reuyl [1984], Brodie and de Kluyver [1984]). In the terminology of Brodie and de Kluyver, our first-stage OLS regression model is a linear market-share model with normalized values for the predictor variables (which happen to be self-explicated utilities in the present case).

As Brodie and de Kluyver indicate, this model does not satisfy sum and range constraints when market-share predictions are made of new supplier profiles. Hence, we first find the prediction for each supplier separately and then adjust, on an ex post basis, so that the shares sum to 1.0. (Nonnegativity of each separate forecast is achieved by either employing a preliminary logit transformation or setting any negative estimate to zero.)

Brodie and de Kluyver found that linear (and multiplicative) share models fared as well as attraction-type models, which obey sum and range constraints. Ghosh et al. also found reasonably good results for the model employed here, as did Leeflang and Reuyl. Hence, from other researchers' empirical comparisons, it appears that an OLS-based approach applied to supplier-specific data with ex post forecast adjustments (to obey sum constraints) is not unreasonable.

The Empirical Bayes Step

Our use of empirical Bayes in estimating an additional parameter for price (expressed in actual versus utility units) is conceptually in keeping with hybrid conjoint models. In the second-stage estimation step, we assume that the residuals could reflect an additional signal that is assumed to be linearly related to price. The reason why price is singled out as a special variable for attention is that the multisupplier model is typically used in pricing studies in which interest focuses on cross-demand as well as self-demand/price relationships. As such, we assume that the absolute level of price (and its possible influence as a budget constraint) may be useful in its own right, after its relative effect in terms of self-explicated utility has been removed.

Empirical Bayes has potential uses in hybrid modeling beyond its present application. For example, it could be employed in the first-stage estimation step if idiosyncratic slope coefficients are desired. Other possible application areas include conjoint models in which the arguments are numerical values (e.g., sucrose concentration) of manipulable variables in a response surface type of model with multiple judges and multiple observations per respondent. To the extent that the heterogeneity across respondents is low and the variance within individual respondents is high, the individual's parameters can be "stabilized" through the amalgamation of group-based estimates with individual estimates.

Simulations and Product-Line Optimization

If the nonnormalization of self-explicated utilities option is adopted, each individual's part-worths can be obtained from each supplier, in turn, as input to a choice simulator; the dependent variable of interest is the likelihood of choosing the specific supplier whose profile is entered as input. Separate simulations can be run independently for each supplier, prior to applying an ex post normalization that satisfies the sum constraint.

Similarly, product-line–selection programs (Green and Krieger [1985]) that take individual preferences for alternative products/services can be set up as well, assuming that the competitive supplier offerings have been specified, so that share varies only with the offerings of one supplier. All that is needed to implement this approach is a printout of the individual-respondent predictions (which have been summarized in table 6–3). In sum, it should not be too difficult to adapt current simulators and line selection models to data obtained from the multisupplier model.

Conclusion

The multisupplier hybrid model represents a logical extension of the Mahajan et al. approach. It is still too soon to be able to say how applicable the multisupplier hybrid model is to large-scale industrial problems. Clearly, the increased data-collection demands will be more burdensome on the respondent, since suppliers may vary on several attributes (other than price) simultaneously. From a practical standpoint, we speculate that in most cases only one of the suppliers (the sponsor) would be designed to vary extensively on the nonprice attributes, while competitive suppliers would be constrained to vary primarily on price (with a more or less fixed service profile, otherwise).

Appendix 6A

As noted earlier, c_k^2 can be obtained from the data by pooling the mean squared errors across the individual regressions of equation (11). However, we still need to estimate β and σ_β^2. To this end, we first observe that

$$E(b^{(k)}) = E_{\beta^{(k)}} E(b^{(k)}|\beta^{(k)}) = \beta \qquad (16a)$$

and

$$V(b^{(k)}) = E_{\beta^{(k)}} V(b^{(k)}|\beta^{(k)}) + V_{\beta^{(k)}} E(b^{(k)}|\beta^{(k)}) =$$
$$E_{\beta^{(k)}} (c_k^2) + V_{\beta^{(k)}} (\beta^{(k)}) = c_k^2 + \sigma_\beta^2. \qquad (16b)$$

Since $b^{(k)}$ is normal, β and σ_β^2 can be estimated empirically using maximum-likelihood estimators. Formally,

$$f(b^{(1)},...,b^{(k)}) = \prod_{k=1}^{K} \frac{1}{\sqrt{2\pi}} \frac{1}{\sqrt{\sigma_\beta^2 + c_k^2}} e^{-1/2(b^{(k)}-\beta)^2/(\sigma_\beta^2 + c_k^2)}. \qquad (17)$$

This implies that

$$L = \log f = -\frac{K}{2} \log 2\pi \; -1/2 \sum_{k=1}^{K} \log (\sigma_\beta^2 + c_k^2)$$
$$-1/2 \sum_{k=1}^{K} (b^{(k)} - \beta)^2/[(\sigma_\beta^2 + c_k^2)]. \qquad (18)$$

Hence, finding the MLE for β and σ_β^2 involves solving simultaneously the following two equations:

$$\frac{\partial L}{\partial \beta} = 0 \Rightarrow \sum_{k=1}^{K} (b^{(k)} - \hat{\beta})/[(\sigma_\beta^2 + c_k^2)] = 0$$

or

$$\hat{\beta} = \left(\sum_{k=1}^{K} b^{(k)}/(\hat{\sigma}_{\beta}^2 + c_k^2)\right)\bigg/ \sum_{k=1}^{K} (\sigma_{\beta}^2 + c_k^2)^{-1} \tag{19}$$

and

$$\frac{\partial L}{\partial \sigma_{\beta}^2} = 0 \text{ implies}$$

$$\sum_{k=1}^{K} \frac{1}{\hat{\sigma}_{\beta}^2 + c_k^2} = \sum_{k=1}^{K} (b^{(k)} - \hat{\beta})^2 \bigg/ (\hat{\sigma}_{\beta}^2 + c_k^2)^2. \tag{20}$$

In order to solve these equations, we substitute equation (19) into (20) and use a Newton-Raphson procedure to find $\hat{\sigma}_{\beta}^2$. Once $\hat{\sigma}_{\beta}^2$ is determined, this value can be substituted back into equation (19) to obtain $\hat{\beta}$. The only remaining detail to be resolved is the starting value in the Newton-Raphson procedure.

It is likely that c_k^2 will be approximately equal across individuals. Hence, if we assume that $c^2 \equiv c_1^2 = c_2^2 = \ldots = c_K^2$, we obtain a reasonable starting point for $\hat{\beta}$ and $\hat{\sigma}_{\beta}^2$ in the Newton-Raphson procedure. This leads to

$$\hat{\beta} = \sum_{k=1}^{K} b_{\xi}^{(k)}/K \tag{21a}$$

from equation (19).

Substituting equation (21a) into equation (20) and using the assumption that the c_k^2s are equal implies that

$$\frac{K}{\hat{\sigma}_{\beta}^2 + c^2} = \frac{\sum_{k=1}^{K} (b^{(k)} - \hat{\beta})^2}{(\hat{\sigma}_{\beta}^2 + c^2)^2}.$$

Hence,

$$\hat{\sigma}_{\beta}^2 = \left[\sum_{k=1}^{K} (b^{(k)} - \hat{\beta})^2 \bigg/ K\right] - c^2. \tag{21b}$$

Note that if the right-hand side of (21b) is negative, then the maximum of $g(\sigma_{\beta}^2)$ over feasible values of σ_{β}^2 (i.e., $\sigma_{\beta}^2 \geq 0$) occurs when $\hat{\sigma}_{\beta}^2 = 0$. Also, since the c_k^2 will not necessarily be equal, we can let $c^2 = [c_1^2 + \ldots + c_K^2]/K$ in (21b).

In the empirical studies completed to date, the likelihood function has been unimodal and so the procedure just described has found the global maximum. If the c_k^2 are equal, then the likelihood function is necessarily unimodal. Since the likelihood function is not necessarily unimodal for all (c_k^2, b_k^2); $k = 1, ..., K$, the Newton-Raphson procedure, which finds a local maximum, might not find the global maximum of the likelihood function. It is easy to verify that σ_β^2 must be in a bounded interval $[O,B]$ (i.e., the derivative of the likelihood is negative for $\sigma_\beta^2 > B$). This suggests that we can employ the following approach:

1. Divide the domain $[O,B]$ into 100 (say) pieces by $x_1 < x_2 < ... < x_{100}$
2. Evaluate the likelihood at x_i; $i = 1,...,100$
3. Begin a Newton-Raphson search at the points $\sigma_\beta^2 = x_i$ for those x_i for which the likelihood at x_i is greater than the likelihood at x_{i-1} and x_{i+1}.

Also, it is possible that the maximum likelihood estimator of σ_β^2 is zero. This is not cause for alarm since it implies that $\hat{\beta}^{(k)} = \beta$ for all k, from equation (15). Furthermore, β is estimated by

$$\hat{\beta} = \sum_{k=1}^{K} b^{(k)} \Big/ c_k^2 \Big/ \sum_{k=1}^{K} c_k^{-2} \tag{22}$$

from equation (19), which is quite natural.

Notes

1. Blocking principles are applied within individual respondents so that, where possible, equal numbers of levels of each attribute appear within each respondent's block of profiles.
2. If desired, $y_{sb}^{(k)}$ may be transformed to a logit, prior to parameter fitting (so as to obey the range constraint that all individual-supplier predictions fall in the 0–1.0 interval). However, in this case we use the logit strictly as a convenient transformation rather than as a conceptual representation of the constant-sum evaluation task.
3. As examples, see equations (2), (4), and (5) of Green (1984).
4. Since the sum of residuals within each respondent is equal to 0 (from the stage-1 model), intercept estimation is not needed.
5. Since $r_j^{(k)}$ are the residuals in the regressions from the first stage, it follows that $r_b^{(k)}$ cannot be independent and identically distributed. In fact, it is well known that the covariance matrix for residuals in regression is $\sigma^2[I_n - X(X'X)^{-1}X']$ $[I_n - X(X'X)^{-1}X']'$ where I_n is an identity matrix. We have found in practice that the entries in the X matrix are not likely to vary by much. When the number of profiles

offered to an individual is relatively large, then the preceding equation is not too different from σ^2 multiplied by the identity matrix. This approximation, of course, simplifies the analysis for the second stage.

6. This statement assumes that at least three players' averages are involved.

7. Of additional interest is the fact that in the self-explicated stage, price was much more salient ($t = 2.022$) for the distributor than for either manufacturer or broker.

References

Akaah, Ismael P., and Pradeep K. Korgaonkar (1983). "An Empirical Comparison of the Predictive Validity of Compositional, Decompositional, and Hybrid Multiattribute Preference Models," *Journal of Marketing Research* 20 (May): 187–97.

Brodie, Roderick, and Cornelis A. de Kluyver (1984). "Attraction versus Linear and Multiplicative Market Share Models: An Empirical Evaluation," *Journal of Marketing Research* 21 (May): 194–201.

Cattin, Philippe, Gerard Hermet, and Alain Pioche (1982). "Alternative Hybrid Models for Conjoint Analysis: Some Empirical Results," in *Analytical Approaches to Product and Market Planning: The Second Conference*. Cambridge, Mass.: Marketing Science Institute, pp. 142–52.

Efron, Bradley, and Carl Morris (1977). "Stein's Paradox in Statistics," *Scientific American* 236: 119–27.

Ghosh, Avijit, Scott Neslin, and Robert Shoemaker (1984). "A Comparison of Market Share Models and Estimation Procedures," *Journal of Marketing Research* 21 (May): 202–10.

Green, Paul E. (1984). "Hybrid Models for Conjoint Analysis: An Expository Review," *Journal of Marketing Research* 21 (May): 155–69.

Green, Paul E., Stephen M. Goldberg, and Mila Montemayor (1981). "A Hybrid Utility Estimation Model for Conjoint Analysis," *Journal of Marketing* 45 (winter): 33–41.

Green, Paul E., and Abba M. Krieger (1985). "Models and Heuristics for Product Line Selection," *Marketing Science* 4 (winter): 1–19.

Green, Paul E., and V. Srinivasan (1978). "Conjoint Analysis in Consumer Research: Issues and Outlook," *Journal of Consumer Research* 5 (September): 103–23.

Jones, D. Frank (1975). "A Survey Technique to Measure Demand under Various Pricing Strategies," *Journal of Marketing* 39 (July): 75–77.

Leeflang, Peter S.H., and Jan C. Reuyl (1984). "On the Predictive Power of Market Share Attraction Models," *Journal of Marketing Research* 21 (May): 202–10.

Mahajan, Vijay, Paul E. Green, and Stephen M. Goldberg (1982). "A Conjoint Model for Measuring Self- and Cross-Price/Demand Relationships," *Journal of Marketing Research* 19 (August): 334–42.

Maritz, J.S. (1970). *Empirical Bayes Methods*. London: Methuen.

Naert, P.A., and M. Weverbergh (1981). "On the Prediction Power of the Market Share Attraction Models," *Journal of Marketing Research* 18 (May): 146–53.

Pratt, John W., Howard Raiffa, and Robert O. Schlaifer (1965). *Introduction to Statistical Decision Theory*. New York: McGraw-Hill.

Raiffa, Howard, and Robert O. Schlaifer (1961). *Applied Statistical Decision Theory*. Boston: Division of Research, Harvard Business School.

Rubin, Donald B. (1980). "Using Empirical Bayes Techniques in the Law School Validity Studies," *Journal of the American Statistical Association* 75 (December): 801–16.

Theil, Henri (1969). "A Multinomial Extension of the Linear Logit Model," *International Economics Review* 10 (October): 251–59.

Wyner, Gordon A., Lois H. Benedetti, and Bart M. Trapp (1984). "Measuring the Quantity and Mix of Product Demand," *Journal of Marketing* 48 (winter): 101–9.

7

Psychological Meaning of Products:
A Basis for Product Positioning

Roberto Friedmann
Warren French

Geneneral Foods has posited a series of principles to insure successful positioning of its portfolio of brands. Offering product benefits that are "believable," "important," and "consistent with the attitudes of the target market" are three of those principles. Borrowing from recent developments in consumer behavior, sociology, advertising theory, and cross-cultural psychology, this chapter presents a case for investigating the psychological meaning (PM) of products and a procedure for measuring that meaning as a means of abiding by those positioning principles of believability, importance, and consistency.

The Nature of Psychological Meaning

In the development of research on perception, one trend that stands out is the increasing importance attributed to the role of meaning within perceptual processes. Whereas early writings on perception saw meaning merely as a by-product of the perceptual process (e.g., Wundt [1896]), meaning has progressively evolved to a position of the "finishing touch" of the perceptual process (Forgus [1966]). Because meaning is a direct consequence of the outside stimuli patterns being perceived (Gibson [1951, 1966]), it is now considered a cornerstone of the perceptual experience (Valle and King [1978]).

Researchers in different fields (for example, Szalay and Deese [1978] in sociology, Hirschman [1980] in consumer behavior, and Friedmann and Jugenheimer [1985] in advertising research) advocate classifying meaning into three types: lexical meaning, philosophical meaning, and psychological meaning.

Lexical meaning addresses the relation between words such as *car* and their empirical referents (e.g., an enclosed box-like object sitting on four wheels); its base for determination is convention, i.e., a collective, generally accepted code of labeling (Bloomfield [1933]). Philosophical meaning, in turn, focuses on the concept-referent relationship (e.g., a self-moving carriage that is an enclosed box-like object sitting on four wheels); here meaning becomes synonymous with rational knowledge (Katz [1972]). Psychological meaning (PM), in contrast, characterizes those "things" that are most salient in the way an individual reacts to a given perceptual stimulus, as well as describing the direction and affectivity of these "things" (Szalay and Deese [1978]).

Given the purpose at hand, our interests lie with psychological meaning—specifically, with the psychological meaning of products. The reason is that the nature of buying behavior is not fully conventional or rational. (If it were, concepts such as market segmentation and impulse-buying would not exist.) Furthermore, consumers' conceptualization of applicable product meaning is composed of elements that are beyond the framework of linguistic/lexical or logical meaning-type analysis.

Szalay and Deese (1978, p. 2) define psychological meaning as "a person's subjective perception and affective reactions" to stimuli. They argue that PM characterizes those things most salient in an individual's reaction while describing the degree and direction of affectivity. (As a comparison, lexical meaning describes the relationships between words and referents, while psychological meaning describes the abstract characteristics of the referent and its relation to other referents.) According to Szalay and Deese, what little theory there is about PM arises from the work of Osgood (1952). A major contribution that Osgood's work provides in explaining PM is his idea of meaning being a "bundle of components."

Components of Psychological Meaning

Regarding PM as a bundle of components allows one to visualize these components as the basic structural elements of a product concept to be tested. These components of PM may represent a person's understanding and evaluation of the concept/product stimulus formed by direct and/or vicarious experiences, images, feelings, and associated behavioral responses that have been accumulated over time.

This bundle of components is strongly affected by the context upon which they are derived. Olson (1983) and Peter and Olson (1983) state that meaning always needs to be defined in terms of a given context. As an illustration, if the meaning associated with a particular product (e.g., a car) is partially determined by the person's daily use of that product, that meaning comes to life within the context of that use. A natural interdependence exists whereby the evaluation is partially a determinant of the context, while at the same time the context (or the situation) can affect the evaluation. Thus, it is unrealistic to think of a one-way causal relation between context and PM. This relationship was formalized by Friedmann and Lessig (1986), who suggest that context can be conceptualized as being determined by the interaction of individual, social, and situational variables.

Component Characteristics of Psychological Meaning

Although PM is the sum of the consumer's understanding and evaluation resulting from the perceptual process, certain elements of this understanding could be vague, ambiguous, and not really communicable (Szalay and Deese [1978]). Components of that meaning may also include some vaguely defined, ambiguous, or even contradictory elements. For instance, the concept of car might evoke ideas of safety as well as speed. This is not an obstacle, for this phenomenon substantiates the role of PM in tapping elements beyond the scope of logical or even lexical meaning. Furthermore, these vague or contradictory elements are easily captured in the measurement technique proposed in the next section.

A second characteristic of the components of meaning is the issue of their relative importance. In goal-oriented human behavior, the components of meaning involving anticipated behavioral consequences are of particular concern. This notion that anticipated consequences affect a person's perceptual process and subsequent behavior is accepted in all expectancy-value–type models of decision making.

This being the case, some components of meaning will be more important than others, as characterized by their salience. This salience of the components of PM needs to be emphasized because neither the lexical nor the philosophical approach to meaning adequately explains an individual's reactions to product stimuli, since both approaches tend to ignore the "centrality" of components—those at the core of the perceived product (Hirschman [1980]).

In order to finalize the description of PM's structural components, there are two important conditions that need to be addressed: commonality and tangibility. *Commonality* relates to the relative uniqueness or degree to which particular components of PM are shared by a given group of consumers who would compose a market segment. *Tangibility* relates to components of PM in terms of whether they are objectively verifiable components of the product stimulus toward which PM is developed (tangible), such as a car's color, or whether they are cognitively ascribed by the consumer (intangible), for example, the car's social status.

Measurement of Psychological Meaning

For managerial reasons, the interest in PM relates to particular market segments. Therefore, the need is to identify the shared meaning that a product, a brand, or a particular attribute has within and across different market segments.

One-word associations elicited within a seventy-second time limit are appropriate to measure PM (Szalay and Deese [1978], Friedmann and Jugenheimer [1985]). Respondents are asked to state whatever issues, features, or ideas come to mind when they think about a stimulus cue such as a car, make of car, or attribute of a car. Respondents are also asked not to repeat any one-word association when responding to the stimulus.

These associations should be continuous, free, and stimulus-bound. *Continuous* means that respondents provide as many one-word associations as desired within the allowed time. *Free* means that subjects are asked to provide any idea or feature that comes to mind. Some of the earlier uses of associations in consumer research have required supportive, positive (something liked), or counterargument types of associations. In the PM procedure, these constraints are not required.

Stimulus-bound associations, the final methodological criterion, are such that respondents are "forced" to consider the original stimulus provided before every new association they provide. This can be simply done by making the stimulus cue as obtrusive as possible. This is to prevent chain-format associations in which the previous association the individual provides becomes the dominating stimulus cue for the next one word. For instance, if the original stimulus cue is the Korean car, the Excel, and the second association provided happens to be "mother," then "mother" may trigger or elicit "cook," which could elicit "calories," which clearly have very little to do with the research purpose at hand. Though a chain-format is the preferred style for the use of associations in other research (e.g., a possible tracing of cognitive schemas), it appears inappropriate for the purpose of tapping into the PM of a product/brand stimulus.

Once the associations for a given sample are rank-ordered in terms of frequency (number of times the same word was provided by a given sample group), the second step of the procedure, actually a twofold step, takes place.

First, idiosyncratic associations (those provided by just one individual in the sample) are eliminated, for we are interested in the shared meaning a given stimulus has for a particular group of respondents. Second, the data are reduced through semantic clustering. For instance, given our car example, associations such as "cost," "price," "money," "expensive," "maintenance," and "payments" could all be semantically factored by expert judges into a "cost" cluster. These clusters represent the components of PM we have been referring to. The reliability of the semantic clustering in an associative data set can be assessed with a variety of measures, such as Cohen's kappa, to reduce researcher bias and effect. The merits of association techniques in capturing the essence of perceptual thoughts have been thoroughly documented in psychology (Cramer [1968], Creelman [1966], Deese [1965]).

Furthermore, because one-word associations are not encumbered by the constraints of organized language (e.g., self-censoring, rationalization, selectivity), they have been proposed as extremely strong and uncluttered representations of thoughts (e.g., Szalay and Deese [1978]). As such, the PM procedure enables a closer approximation to the "real" components of meaning that a consumer derives when perceiving a product than other more traditional and commonly used measurement tools.

PM Methodology versus Traditional Measurements

Even though recent literature supports the methodology just described as the appropriate vehicle to measure PM (Friedmann and Jugenheimer [1985], Friedmann [1986]), inquiry should be made as to the relative merits of the PM method versus more traditional measurements of perceptual processes.

There are a variety of methodologies applicable for measuring consumers' perception. Among the most popular ones are Likert scales, semantic differential scales, perceptual mapping techniques such as discriminant analysis, multidimensional scaling (MDS), factor analysis maps, correspondence analysis, and conjoint analysis.

The PM method just described allows for the identification of as many components as the semantic clustering of one-word associations will develop. It is, therefore, a multidimensional approach as opposed to the Likert scale and semantic differential scale techniques. In terms of dimensionality, the PM methods appears then equally proficient to conjoint analysis and the perceptual mapping techniques, given their multidimensional nature.

Accepting the procedure for identifying PM just described, the traditional techniques are likely to have higher degrees of experimenter-induced bias than the PM method:

- Likert scales require the research to provide a priori attributes and categories for rating.
- Semantic differential scales require that categories and scales anchors be provided a priori.
- MDS requires that similarity/dissimilarity scales be provided to respondents.
- Factor analysis maps require that attributes be defined.
- Correspondence analysis requires that attributes be defined.
- Conjoint analysis requires that dimensions be selected.

With the PM procedure, though, the researcher is at no point in time providing the respondent with evaluative dimensions for the product/brand stimulus of interest. The components of PM that the procedure identifies can be thought of as the relevant evaluative criteria for the stimulus being studied. This is basically what the procedure sets out to find out in the first place. Even though the criteria, attributes, or dimensions that the traditional measurements use may be identified through generally accepted techniques such as focus-group interviews or factor-analyzing initial data sets—and therefore are usually thought of as "valid" dimensions—the PM procedure should be seen as less cumbersome and equally if not less artificial in terms of researcher intervention than the traditional measurement techniques.

Considering Conjoint Analysis

Conjoint analysis (Green and Rao [1971]) is a measurement technique applicable to psychological judgments (e.g., perceptual preferences) that has received widespread attention from both practitioners and academicians (Green and Srinivasan [1978]) in the study of consumers' multiattribute decision making (e.g., Fenwick [1978], Green and Srinivasan [1978], Green and Wind [1973]). Basically, the procedure's purpose is to decompose a set of overall preference responses to previously designed product stimuli, so that the utility of each stimulus's component (e.g., product attributes) can be inferred from the respondent's overall evaluations of the stimuli (Green and Tull [1978]). An extension of ANOVA—though with less restrictive assumptions about the scaling of the dependent variable (Jackson [1983])—conjoint analysis views respondent's overall preference judgments as criterion variables and the factorial levels making up each stimulus as predictor variables.

There are several procedural issues/problems affecting conjoint analysis that are not present in the PM procedure suggested in this chapter. Some of these are discussed next.

- In conjoint analysis, the stimuli must be designed beforehand by the researcher. This in itself introduces a priori bias, assumptions and expectations that will affect the results. If one is interested in the specific attributes associated with the product—particularly at the generic level— PM is thought to bring about "cleaner" attributes around which one may position a product.

- In assuming additivity of effects, the basic conjoint model does not allow for balance among such effects. Such a restriction is not present in the PM procedure.

- The conjoint-analysis procedure cues respondents—in relation to their evaluative criteria—to the point that they are asked to divorce from their minds those product attributes not included in the provided product profiles. One must regard this as inducing further artificiality on the respondent's selection task.

- The multiple factor evaluations of conjoint analysis are subject to the natural limitations of human information-processing skills with regard to how many bits of data we can efficiently process.

- In the case of large sets of product-attribute combinations, conjoint analysis uses fractional designs. Such designs are effective in reducing input data for the respondent's task, but they also have an impact on the meaningfulness of results.

- If we combine these last two points, another issue appears. The greater the number of product attributes and levels of product attributes presented to a consumer evaluator, the more likely that the correct bundle of utilities for a given market segment can be estimated with conjoint analysis. Two problems arise though. One problem is that in rank ordering a set of alternatives, the greater the number of alternatives, the greater the potential for poor test-retest reliability. Specifically, the most attractive and least attractive alternatives in a large set are easy to identify. The middle-ground alternatives are likely to elicit the greatest amount of indifference and result in a noticeably different rank ordering in a subsequent retest. The second problem is that for many products, the most important attributes are self-evident to the point where trade-offs at diminished levels of these attributes are not acceptable to the market, irrespective of utility calculations.

The purpose of the preceding comparisons is not to negate the traditional methods for investigating perceptual processes, but to present an alternative approach that is sound in terms of its theoretical and methodological basis and can be used—as illustrated in the next section—in the development of product positioning. Nevertheless, the PM procedure can further be seen as a complement—as opposed to an alternative—to conjoint analysis. In effect, PM can be thought of as acting as a two-stage filter through its ability to identify the appropriate product attributes to be included in trade-off analysis.

The first step in the filtering procedure would be to identify any attribute that is extremely important (given relative PM frequency scores and current positioning strategy) to the market segment. Diminishing that attribute, even while enhancing other attributes, would, according to common wisdom in the market, curtail demand.

The second step in the filtering process would then be to offer a limited number of attributes and levels so as to preclude confusion in the middle ranges of conjoint ranking. The appropriate attributes to choose would be ones on which the firm could build a difficult-to-duplicate positioning strategy. Those attributes would also be ones whose PM frequency scores were close to the scores of other attributes upon which trade-offs in levels could be made. The result of this filtering process might give more marketing credibility to the conjoint results.

Applicability of Psychological Meaning to Positioning Strategies

The procedure described can be applied to as many different groups of individuals as the decisionmaker might need to address. For each group (comprising a potential market segment), the method allows for a bundle of components of PM to be identified. Furthermore, each of the bundle of components is characterized by a frequency score per component (the aggregate frequency of all one-word associations clustered into that component) that allows for comparisons within and between groups. For the purposes of illustration, table 7–1 shows the components of PM derived from a sample of 107 young automobile drivers using "car" as the product stimulus. Table 7–2 presents the individual elements of the "pleasure functions/images" component.

The procedure permits two major types of information to be obtained. First, the qualitative nature of the data is directly observable from the elements present in each of the components as well as in the overall component clusters themselves. Second, structuring PM into components allows for quantitative comparisons between potential market segments in a manner

Table 7–1
Components of PM Associated with "Car"
($N = 107$)

Components	Frequency Score
1. Economic/financial considerations	133
2. Features/options	122
3. Make and model	121
4. Car image/appearance	81
5. Performance	77
6. Utility function	75
7. Style of car	71
8. Pleasure functions/images	69
9. Problems/potential problems	65
10. Color	63
11. Music	44
12. Size	20
13. Country of origin	14

Table 7–2
Elements Clustered into the "Pleasure Functions/
Images" Component in Table 7–1

Elements	Frequency
Vacation	2
Friend	2
Fun	8
Prestige	2
Travel	10
Mine	3
Florida	3
Status	7
Freedom	2
Mountain	2
Trip	4
Date	4
Cruising	2
Road Trip	3
Comfort	15
Total	69

compatible with traditional nonparametric tests (e.g., chi-square analysis, Mann Whitney U-tests).

One may, therefore, consider a positioning-strategy continuum with end points of standardization between markets versus adaptation to particular markets. The middle range of the continuum is characterized by differences in the magnitude and areas (e.g., pricing, promotion) where either of the previously mentioned strategies might take place. This midrange may be labeled a hybrid strategy.

As a purely arbitrary example, the procedure could prove beneficial to a firm such as the Korean automaker Hyundai. Hyundai's Excel model, which had been successfully marketed in Canada, and is now introduced into the United States. A question facing Hyundai at the time was whether the price and service appeals used in Canada are "standardized" appropriate appeals for all of English-speaking North America—specifically for the educated, under–age-30 market.

Assume that the resulting rank-ordered components of PM of the Excel in that market are status, style, performance, and cost in the United States, and cost, performance, style, and status in Canada. The PM of the American consumers might suggest possible strategic actions such as premium pricing given the status appeal, the stressing of style in promoting the car, and the overall positioning of the car as a symbol of social achievement. In Canada, the components of PM for the Excel would suggest such strategic marketing avenues as promoting the car as a good value and downplaying the status appeal. With the same physical product being marketed across national borders, even with the same overall components of PM, specific adaptations can be derived through their relative salience. In the case of entirely different components of PM, or only some of the same components appearing in the PM obtained in all of the markets investigated, even clearer strategic-positioning options would be derived.

It should be noted that an important benefit of the PM procedure just suggested is that it can be applied at the product, product-brand (make), or product-attribute level. If the preceding components had been obtained by Hyundai studying the PM of car at the generic level, the differences observed in the salience of components could have supported the argument for adaptations in terms of product-design features (e.g., engine horsepower, extras such as a sunroof or electric windows, aerodynamics, type of seats, and type of brakes).

PM helps the decisionmaker identify the correct range on the strategy continuum by identifying the degree of similarity or congruence between Americans' and Canadians' bundles of PM components. If the degree of similarity is high, the argument of standardization is enhanced. At the other extreme, if the PM associated with a given product is significantly different for the given markets, the argument for standardization becomes a moot point. What sense would there be in using similar procedures such as positioning, promotion, or pricing strategies if the Excel product is—as reflected in the derived PM—perceived very differently by Americans than Canadians?

A particular strength of the procedure is that the international marketer such as Hyundai can use both qualitative and quantitative information to guide its decision-making process. This is particularly important in the case where both similarities and differences are reflected in comparing the bundle of PM components for the different markets. The hybrid strategies this situation would call for can be settled from a higher vantage position than would be the case if only one type of data were available. For instance, even in the case of quantitative similarities (e.g., frequency score, relative salience) for a component of PM shared by different markets, observing qualitative differences would allow for the fine-tuning of marketing efforts. This would be reflected by a slight repositioning of the product or by the stressing of one product attribute versus another in the different markets.

Conclusion

The working goal of this chapter has been to discuss the concept of psychological meaning, show its theoretical underpinnings and support, and suggest its application to product positioning. A methodology for measuring PM has also been presented and compared with traditional measurements of consumer's perception to support the merits of this conceptual tool. Identifying the PM of products offers a procedure that can help in determining the degree of standardization, if any, marketers can incorporate into their strategies across market segments.

In brief, the procedure outlined in this chapter can provide marketers with a useful diagnostic tool from which strategic decisions can be derived for different markets. This implies that, upon identification and interpretation of cross-segment PM data, general "prescriptions" for positioning-strategies guidelines (i.e., standardize, adapt, create a hybrid strategy) are obtained. This PM procedure, as in the case with all tools, is not fully prescriptive, for the task of interpreting the data still rests with the marketers.

In effect, the components of PM can be used for brand positioning. Aside from the "believability, importance, and consistency" principles mentioned previously, General Foods has posited an additional principle for successful positioning—"uniqueness." The PM derived for a brand as well as the competing brands allows for the identification of common shared, salient components. These components are elements on or, perhaps, away from which the marketer can anchor a positioning strategy for his or her product. If the intent were to further strengthen the positioning of the brand, the components with the highest salience would serve as the positioning anchors. If the intent were to reposition the product being investigated, the marketing manager could know: (1) which elements of his or her product's PM to stress or not stress and (2) from the competing brand's most salient component(s) of PM, which can be selected for a head-on positioning, avoided for a differentiated positioning, or used as a secondary positioning element should that be the strategic option desired.

As a logical corollary of product positioning, the components of PM can allow the marketer to empirically determine issues, attributes, or ideas associated with his or her product or brand, upon which a differentiation strategy would be feasible. This reasoning follows from the fact that the components identified are shared by members of a market segment. Using the procedure just proposed, whichever component(s) of PM the marketer chooses to focus on for a differentiation strategy, they can be found in the consumer's evaluative criteria of the product or brand.

The brand/product manager can research the PM associated with his or her brand as well as major competitors', so if, for example, two other competitors are being addressed, the PM methodology provides the practitioner with three sets of rank-ordered components. Comparing and contrasting similarities in the structural components of PM associated with all three brands/products allows for a differentiation strategy based on ideas, features, and issues the manager will know are relevant to his or her target group of consumers.

References

Bloomfield, L. (1933). *Language*. New York: Holt.

Cramer, P. (1968). *Word Associations*. New York, Academic Press.

Creelman, M.B. (1966). *The Experimental Investigation of Meaning: A Review of the Literature*. New York: Springer.

Deese, J. (1965). *The Structure of Associations in Language and Thought*. Baltimore, Md.: Johns Hopkins University Press.

Fenwick, I. (1978). "A User's Guide to Conjoint Measurement in Marketing," *European Journal of Marketing* 12: 203–11.

Forgus, R. (1966). *Perception*. New York: McGraw-Hill.

Friedmann, R. (1986). "Psychological Meaning of Products: Identification and Marketing Applications," in *Psychology and Marketing* vol. III, no. 1.

Friedmann, R., and D. Jugenheimer (1985). "Copytesting through Psychological Meaning," *Proceedings of the American Academy of Advertising* (Charleston, N.C.).

Friedmann, R., and V.P. Lessig (1986). "A Framework of Psychological Meaning of Products," in *Advances in Consumer Research*, vol. XIII, Richard Lutz, ed.

Gibson, J.J. (1951). "Theories of Perception," in *Current Trends in Psychological Theory*, W. Dennis et al., eds. Pittsburgh: University of Pittsburgh Press.

———— (1966). *The Senses Considered as Perceptual Systems*. Boston: Houghton-Mifflin.

Green, P., and F. Carmone (1970). *Multidimensional Scaling and Related Techniques*. Boston, Mass.: Allyn & Bacon.

Green, P., and V. Rao (1971). "Conjoint Measurement of Quantifying Judgemental Data," *Journal of Marketing Research* 8: 355–62.

Green, P., and V. Srinivasan (1978). "Conjoint Analysis in Consumer Research: Issues and Outlook," *Journal of Consumer Research* 5: 103–23.

Green, P., and D.S. Tull (1978). *Research for Marketing Decisions*, 4th ed. Englewood Cliffs, N.J.: Prentice-Hall.

Green, P., and Y. Wind (1973). *Multiattribute Decisions in Marketing: A Measurement Approach*. Hinsdale, Ill.: Dryden.

Hirschmann, E. (1980). "Attributes of Attributes and Layers of Meaning" in *Advances in Consumer Research*, vol. VIII, J. Olson, ed.

Jackson, B. Bund (1983). "Multivariate Data Analysis: An Introduction." Homewood, Ill.: Irwin.

Johnson, R.M. (1974). "Trade-Off Analysis of Consumer Values," *Journal of Marketing Research* 11: 121–27.

Katz, J.J. (1972). *Semantic Theory*. New York: Harper & Row.

Nunnally, J. (1978). *Psychometric Theory*, 2nd ed. New York: McGraw-Hill.

Olson, J. (1983). Presentation at American Marketing Association Doctoral Symposium, Ann Arbor, Mich.

Osgood, C. (1952). "The Nature and Measurement of Meaning," *Psychological Bulletin* 49.

Peter, J.P., and J. Olson (1983). "Is Science Marketing?" *Journal of Marketing* 47, no. 4.

Szalay, L., and J. Deese (1978). *Subjective Meaning and Culture: An Assessment through Word Associations*. Hillsdale, N.J.: LEA Publishers.

Valle, R., and M. King (1978). *Existential-Phenomenological Alternatives for Psychology*. New York: Oxford University Press.

Wundt, W. (1901). *Lectures on Human and Animal Psychology*, translated from the 2nd German edition (1896) by J.E. Creighton and E.B. Titchever. London: Sonnenschein.

Part IV
New-Product–Evaluation Models

I n this part two chapters present comparative evaluations of pre–test-market (PTM) models. The reader may be familiar with one represen-tative model, ASSESSOR, as presented by Urban and Hauser (1980) in their book *Design and Marketing of New Products* and by Urban and Katz (1983) in *Journal of Marketing Research*. Although ASSESSOR has been replaced by ASSESSOR-FT, a number of other well-known models fit the category of PTMs (e.g., BASES, LITMUS, NEWS). Each of these models has its advantages and disadvantages (as discussed in each of the following two chapters). Experience with PTMs indicates that successful pre–test-market testing can provide the firm with large dollar savings by eliminating likely failures and predicting successful entrants. Pretests are considerably cheaper than full-fledged market tests, and they allow management to assess the effects of marketing inputs (advertising, price, promotion) on forecasted market share prior to actual market testing or market introduction.

The two chapters presented here are written with the practitioner in mind. Chapter 8, by Allan Shocker and William Hall, was first published in *Journal of Product Innovation Management*. It was selected for inclusion in this book because it presents an excellent and most recent evaluation and comparison of four popular PTM models. Potential users should find the chapter helpful in acquiring a working knowledge of pretest models within the framework of new-product evaluation and in selecting among the four models presented. The structure and conduct of each PTM model is pre-sented and comparative advantages and disadvantages are discussed. Where published validation data exist, the authors also summarize the comparative performance of the four models.

Chapter 9, "Advances and Issues in New-Product–Introduction Models" by R. Dale Wilson and David K. Smith, Jr., was presented at the workshop that inspired this book. The first part of the chapter presents a general overview of new-product models to include full test-market models. The contributing literature to the area of new-product models is also presented and a guide to these published studies and their contributions is summarized in appendix 9A. The second part of the chapter discusses extensions of new-product evaluation to personal-computer–(PC-) based models. A specific example is cited and described for the New-Product–Buyer Model developed by W.M. Luther. According to Wilson and Smith, the Luther model is one of about two dozen PC-based models relating to a variety of marketing inputs and forecasting.

As emphasized by Wilson and Smith, the Luther model is used primarily as a management aid for understanding the impact of key inputs on the forecasted sales of new products. The authors present an evaluation of the model using input to forecasted market share of a product previously evaluated by NEWS. Comparisons to actual achieved market share by both models are noted, with the PC-based model underpredicting actual share. Although the authors admit to only this single experience with the Luther model, they suggest that PC-based models may hold future promise as a part of the new-product–evaluation process.

Based upon this brief analysis, it would appear that PC models such as the Luther model provide limited managerial diagnostics compared to larger-scale PTM models. However, the simpler PC-based models may prove to be a valuable decision aid as a first-cut to the more extensive PTM-type models such as BASES or NEWS. For instance, given the firm's previous experience in certain product categories, inputs based on this experience (i.e., awareness levels, size of market, units per trial and repeat) might be used in a model to screen potential concepts or to initially evaluate the potential of a full PTM test.

In summary, the chapters presented in this part may certainly impress the reader of the value of pre–test-market testing. This is not to downplay the disadvantages as pointed out by Shocker and Hall, but the evolution of new-product–introduction models do provide marketing management with a competitive tool that should not be overlooked. As the models and methodologies are refined and more experience with their use is revealed, managers will become more comfortable with selecting a model or method that best meets the requirements of their firms in terms of new-product development.

References

Urban, Glen L., and Hauser, John R. (1980). *Design and Marketing of New Products*. Englewood Cliffs, N.J.: Prentice Hall.

Urban, Glen L., and Katz, Gerald M. (1983). "Pre–Test-Market Models: Validation and Managerial Implications," *Journal of Marketing Research* 20 (August): 211–234.

8

Pre–Test-Market Models: A Critical Evaluation

Allan D. Shocker
William G. Hall

T he job of a marketing manager has been described as one of creating monopolies—developing products that are new and different from those of the competition, thereby giving certain consumers reasons to select and, perhaps, pay a premium for them. A company that continues to market the same products will soon find its markets and profit margins eroded as competitors counter the differences that have been erected. If only to maintain its position in the marketplace, a company must periodically introduce new products and improve old ones.

But developing new products is a complex and risky business. Many ideas that are potentially promising lose their luster when subjected to early cost/benefit analysis. Others move far along the path to development. The ultimate test of a product's commercial value is, of course, the marketplace. But a great many dollars must be invested in any product before it is even ready to be tested in that arena. And if it fails there, many more dollars, sometimes well into the millions, can be lost. There may also be a certain public embarrassment for the firm (Crawford [1979]). An ideal system for product development would pass only eventual winners and kill losers early. But real systems are not ideal and sometimes kill winners or continue investment in losers (Assmus [1984], Elrod and Kelman [1984]). Despite the fact that a product-reaching test market can cost a firm in excess of a million dollars, the A.C. Neilsen Company reported that only about 40 percent of new grocery products taken to test market "succeed" (Blackburn and Clancy [1983], Crawford [1979]). As the costs of test marketing (both in terms of out-of-pocket expenses and opportunity) have increased, marketing managers have realized that better ways of weeding out the probable failures prior to test marketing are needed.

Enter pre–test-market (PTM) modeling, a relatively new concept made commercially useful only in the the past fifteen years or so. Thus far, devel-

Reprinted with minor alterations by permission of the publisher from *The Journal of Product Innovation Management* (June 1986): 89–104. Copyright 1986 by Elsevier Science Publishing Co., Inc.

opment of the methodology has been confined mainly to high–purchase-frequency, low-involvement consumer goods. The purpose of this chapter is to evaluate critically PTM models as a part of such a consumer-goods–development process. What are PTM models and how do they work? Why and when are they useful? What are their strengths and weaknesses? Within this framework, the chapter will describe and contrast four popular PTM models: BASES II, ASSESSOR (and its successor, ASSESSOR-FT), LITMUS II, and NEWS/PLANNER.[1]

PTM Models

 The aim of PTM models is to turn readily obtainable information into forecasts of market share or sales volume and recommendations for improving the product, its pricing, and, especially, the advertising and promotional plans for introduction. The data required typically come from simulated test markets, the proposed marketing plan, past product-category experiences, and the judgments of one or more experienced marketers and researchers.

Simulated Test Markets

Simulated test markets (STMs), sometimes referred to as LTMs or laboratory test markets, were developed in the late 1960s to help marketers predict whether new products would be successful. Pessemier (1963) had earlier demonstrated the usefulness of laboratory data in predicting price elasticities and demand. STMs were a natural outgrowth of this earlier work. Many firms now provide STM services, not simply those whose models will be discussed.[2] One better-known firm is Yankelovich, Skelly, and White, Inc., which created the acronym LTM.

The goal of an STM is to measure, in a controlled way, the trial and repurchase intentions of a target market toward a new product as a consequence of certain proposed marketing plans. STMs are conducted in both permanent and traveling laboratories, which are generally located in shopping centers, but are occasionally conducted in the home. The procedure is substantially as follows (Silk and Urban [1978], Yankelovich, Skelly, and White, Inc. [1981]):

1. Respondents are intercepted at shopping centers and are surveyed about attitudes and usage behavior toward the product category (assuming there is one that is well defined).

2. They are exposed to concept boards or commercials for the new product (and possibly for competitors).

3. They are given an opportunity to receive the new product if they are interested in it (through purchase in either a real or mock store).

4. Nonbuyers or those not interested may be given a sample of the new product as a gift.

5. After an in-home usage period (possibly several weeks), they are contacted by phone and surveyed for attitudes, use, and intention to repurchase.

6. Sometimes, a "sales wave" (repeated offers to sell and deliver more of the product to those who used it) is conducted.

The STM provides estimates of the percentage of aware consumers who will buy the product and the percentage of triers who will repurchase, for a given advertisement, product concept, and packaging. These percentages must be adjusted downward to correct for the obvious upward bias of the lab procedure. But those who conduct such research claim to have been able to find systematic relationships between STM results and product performance in subsequent test market and commercialization (Blackburn and Clancy [1982, 1984], Burke Marketing Services [1984], Lin et al. [1982], Silk and Urban [1978], Urban and Katz [1983]). The cost of an STM starts at approximately $40,000 (1984). (Actual costs vary with the sample size used, number of different cities in which the STM is run, and so on.)

The Development of PTM Models

The contention is that an STM, if interpreted correctly, can predict sales or market share with sufficient accuracy to decide whether or not further investment in the new product's development is warranted. PTM models have been developed to go further—to systematically translate STM data into accurate market-share predictions and to simulate the effects on share and profits of different advertising and sales promotional mixes, packaging designs, product positioning, pricing plans, and distribution plans. Like many models used by the marketing community, they are not based on a well-tested scientific theory. Rather, they incorporate a conceptual framework, historical data, and managerial judgment (Little [1970], Parfitt and Collins [1968]). Their goal is to replace "gut feel" with a more systematic approach, thereby (it is hoped) introducing a higher degree of consistency and accuracy in predicting the sales or market share of new products.

Figure 8–1 is a family tree showing the parentage of the BASES II (Burke Marketing Services [1984], Lin et al. [1982]), ASSESSOR (and ASSESSOR-FT) (Information Resources, Inc. [1985], Silk and Urban [1978]), LITMUS II (Better [1983], Blackburn and Clancy [1982]), and NEWS/PLANNER (Pringle et al. [1982]) models[3] that are discussed here (as well as several competing others). Though related, they have diverged significantly in their methodology, with BASES appearing different from LITMUS and NEWS, and all different still from ASSESSOR (as ASSESSOR is from ASSESSOR-

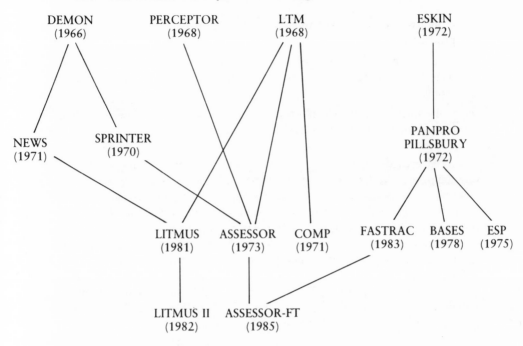

DEMON
(1966)

PERCEPTOR
(1968)

LTM
(1968)

ESKIN
(1972)

NEWS
(1971)

SPRINTER
(1970)

PANPRO
PILLSBURY
(1972)

LITMUS
(1981)

ASSESSOR
(1973)

COMP
(1971)

FASTRAC
(1983)

BASES
(1978)

ESP
(1975)

LITMUS II
(1982)

ASSESSOR-FT
(1985)

Figure 8–1. Family Tree of PTM and Test-Market Models

Source: Redrawn from Clancy, Shulman, and Associates (1983) and Information Resources, Inc. (1985).

FT). Other related models, most notably TRACKER and SPRINTER (Mahajan et al. [1984], Narasimhan and Sen [1983], Wind [1982]), are test-market models in that they make predictions on the basis of early test-market, not STM, data (i.e., data from a field test conducted over a time period sufficient to measure actual repeat purchase). Because BASES, ASSESSOR, LITMUS, and NEWS are representative of the family of such models (figure 8–1), because they are among the more widely used, and importantly, because the latter three have especially good documentation, we shall describe and compare only these. Other reviews (e.g., Mahajan et al. [1984], Narasimhan and Sen [1983], Robinson [1981], and Wind [1982]) consider some of the same models but are not necessarily critical reviews or fail explicitly to consider the models' appropriateness using STM data. We first examine why and when PTM models should be used.

Reasons for Pretest Marketing

Pretest marketing has become widespread in the past few years because it can reduce the cost of new-product development significantly. Assume that, on average, new consumer products have roughly a 40 percent chance of succeeding (i.e., meeting their market-share goals) in test market. This implies that 2.5 products must go into test market for each product that will go on to a national introduction.

Assuming that the pretest methodology is valid and of sufficiently low cost, the information gained from this research should help to screen out most of the failures before going to test market. As a result, the products that proceed to test market should have a much higher chance of going to a national introduction. Data published by Better (1983) and Urban and Katz (1983) indicate that products successful in PTM[4] have about an 80 percent chance of succeeding in test market. This relationship can be expressed by relations similar to those of figure 8–2. The left curve is proposed to describe the relationship between the market share attained[5] in PTM and the probability of succeeding in test market.[6] The curve indicates an 80 percent chance of succeeding in test market when the PTM achieves its goal (indicated by a 0 percent difference on the horizontal axis).

Figure 8–3 illustrates a typical case, in which a PTM could decrease the cost of introducing a successful new product by about $1.6 million. Most of the savings comes from simply avoiding test-market failures. (This still permits the test market to be used to confirm results for the marketing plan that emerges from the PTM and/or refine that marketing plan, and it may result in a shorter test market or preclude a need for several test markets.) The probability of success in the PTM is slightly higher than for the test market alone (0.45 versus 0.40), because there is more variance in the PTM share estimate. The additional screening realized through pretest marketing is assumed to lead to a slightly higher probability of a successful introduction (0.9 versus 0.85). The PTM also increases the likelihood that potentially successful products will be killed; hence, more product concepts are required for each successful introduction (3.09 versus 2.95). This cannot be avoided, for at every screening stage in the new-product–development process, some potential successes will be wrongly killed. (See Elrod and Kelman [1984].) Fortunately, given the overall validity of the PTM models, the successes that are more likely to be weeded out by a PTM are those likely to be marginal (those that the model may have trouble discriminating between because they are close to the cutoff levels for determining success).

The probability of a successful test market should decrease as the market share required to pass the PTM is reduced. Despite this, Urban and Katz (1983) indicate that products are often passed through pretest with a lower predicted-share estimate than would be necessary to succeed in test market. Although, as noted, a lower share might be accepted to decrease the possibility of weeding out successes; more likely this occurs because a product champion is seeking to keep its "baby" alive, explaining away any deviation from target as a problem with the forecasting model or providing reassur-

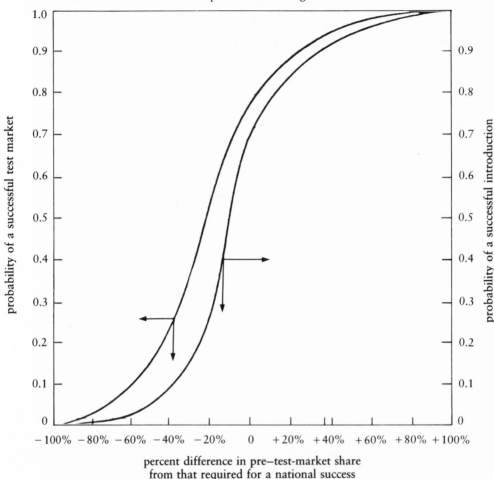

Figure 8–2. **Proposed Relationship between PTM Performance and Probabilities of Test-Market Success and Introduction Success without Test Market**

ances that a newly revised marketing strategy (often one that will not be tested itself) will improve the product's performance in test market.

The right curve in figure 8–2 relates pretest results to the probability of succeeding nationally without a subsequent test market. In those cases where the PTM forecast exceeds the required share by, say, 30 percent or more, skipping test market might be called for, particularly if the company has a lot of experience with the new brand's category. (The PTM does not, of course, provide a firm with experience in implementing its plan or in dealing with competitive reaction, so that such risks must be assumed if a test market is skipped.)

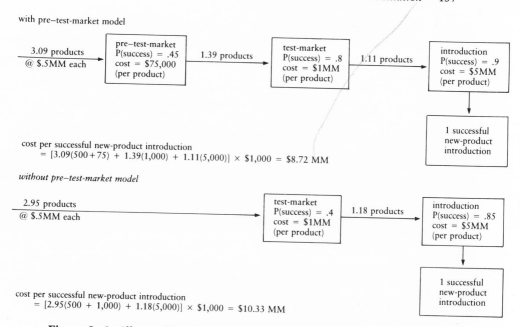

Figure 8–3. **Illustration of How a PTM Model Can Lower the Total Cost of Introducing New Products**

Even though it is far from a perfect substitute, pretest marketing might be substituted for test marketing to avoid "tipping one's hand" to the competition, to avoid test-market sabotage, or because there is simply not enough time to test market. In the race to bring new products to market, it is often advantageous to be first. (See Robinson [1985], Urban et al. [1985].) Test markets can often take a year or more to complete, increasing the likelihood that a competitor will monitor your test, copy the product, and possibly beat you to national introduction. If pretest marketing is substituted, the share forecast required for a "go" should normally be set well above that required for national success. A wider margin for error is advisable because failing nationally can cost many millions of dollars. Strong results in PTM, when not quite good enough to go national, might still be good enough to suggest skipping test market and rolling the product out regionally, because the costs of failing in a rollout are likely to be lower (although a rollout certainly tips one's hand).

Good PTM models can forecast the effects of different levels of advertising and sales promotion (e.g., sampling, couponing) on the market share attainable using product-category norms (when that is all that is available) or actual experience from the STM. This can be a particularly valuable exercise for companies with little or no experience in the product category.

Through such exercises, the models can accelerate learning how different advertising, promotion, and planned distribution intensity interact to affect the profitability of the new product. An inexperienced company can avoid, to some degree, the slow and costly process of learning by trial and error in test markets. However, again such models reveal little of a firm's ability to execute its marketing plan, and thus it is always possible that results predicted by the model may not be attainable.

Pretest marketing can pinpoint problems early so that they can be corrected and the corrections can be retested away from the public eye. Low market share for a new product may be the result of low trial rates, low repurchase (repeat) rates, or both. Low trial can result from poor advertising copy, unattractive packaging, a weak product concept, or inferior distribution (e.g., penetration, shelf positioning, facings). Low repeat, on the other hand, often means that the product itself has some major problems (at least relative to what advertising and promotion claimed). (Competent product testing can do a great deal to insure that the product is well received, so that obtaining trial is often the more difficult problem.) If the problem is low repeat, however, it may take months for the product to fail (because trial may overshadow repeat as a cause for sales in the early stages of introduction), making the failure all the more noticeable when it finally occurs. Whatever the cause, a company is less likely to reformulate a product and retest if it has failed in the eyes of many consumers. The uphill battle to regain consumer confidence may simply make such an attempt too costly.

Strengths and Weaknesses of Pretest Marketing

Strengths

The strengths of pretest marketing discussed previously can be summarized as follows:

1. PTM can reduce the cost of developing and introducing new products (i.e., less "finished" advertising, limited media expense, only small quantities of product needed).

2. PTM provides more timely data (weeks rather than months) and diagnostics to help improve the concept product and/or its marketing plan (e.g., packaging, positioning, advertising, pricing).

3. Such research is easier to keep secret from competitors and/or minimizes their influence.

4. The existence of models potentially allows "optimization" of certain aspects of the marketing mix.

5. By providing a framework for analysis, such models increase managerial understanding of (and involvement in) the new-product–introduction process. They provide a way, for example, of making use of particular historical data (e.g., product-category norms) and, later, more new-product–specific data in a meaningful way.

Weaknesses

The weaknesses of pretest marketing and the models for forecasting sales or shares for a new product are also numerous:

1. PTM models do not address potential *problems in implementing* marketing decisions (e.g., trade acceptance or support, sales-force acceptance, delays in manufacturing or delivery).

2. Competitive reactions are essentially not considered; changes in economic conditions are ignored.

3. Some model parameterization is based on judgments that may not prove valid because, with new products, they may extend beyond the manager's direct experiences (Chakravarti et al. [1981]).

4. STMs are unrealistic and unrepresentative and thus may lack validity.

5. PTM models are less applicable to minor-line extensions and more difficult for "new-to-the-world" products or products that may be faddish or have irregular usage patterns. It may be difficult to provide "go/no-go" advice for products that can succeed with very low volumes or market shares. PTM models are also less applicable when the new product is to be sold in outlets other than supermarkets or drug stores.

Perhaps the greatest weakness of PTM models is that implementation issues, particularly those concerned with bringing about desired trade behaviors, are not addressed. Smaller, lesser known firms may have particularly difficult problems in execution. In using these models, the analyst will develop, based upon analogous experience, an estimate of the level of distribution intensity, say, that they believe could be achieved, and this along with other elements of the marketing plan are input into the model so that it may render its forecast. Data from the PTM may be able to shed light upon the actual effect of the product itself and its packaging, its pricing, its position and number of facings on store shelves, different advertising copy, sampling and, possibly, couponing or other sales promotion in the plan. Knowledge of reach and frequency can often be established with reasonable confidence (based on prior experience) from the media and budget plans, although these plans may not be optimal. Detailed scheduling may not be determinable in an optimal fashion either. However, whether distributors will actually carry the new product, shelve it next to desired competitors, give it the desired shelf facings and location, price it according to plan, promote it as desired, and so forth, remains an open question. A company should thus find that predicted results are acceptable, even with conservative estimates of distribution, if it intends to skip test marketing or use forced distribution in test markets.

PTM models also generally do not model competitive effects (e.g., the vigor with which existing competitors will seek to defend their franchises). Some models may consider *relative* pricing, but most do not even do this. (Advertising may sometimes be represented as "share of voice" [e.g., LIT-MUS] or specific ads for the new product evaluated in the presence of existing competitive ads [e.g., ASSESSOR].) Although this admittedly represents a weakness, it must be acknowledged that there is simply no way to incorporate the unpredictable behavior of competitors into any model. By better understanding which competitors may be more affected by the firm's new product and marketing plan, one is more able to anticipate from whom major retaliation will come. Then, one may approximate competitor effects upon repeat purchase by an informed guess based on competitor behavior in the past or by an assumption of an action—"optimal" reaction "game" (Hauser and Shugan [1983]) or some other heuristic. But such approximations (which may be misleading) may not prove superior to procedures that feign ignorance of competitive action. In fairness, we would note that a test market may also be unable to reveal the extent of competitor response if competitors decide not to show their hand in the test market because it is limited in scope or may use that time to develop and refine their counter-strategy (possibly themselves using a PTM simulation for this purpose).

The predictions of PTM models or the data on which they are calibrated usually must be adjusted by judgmental parameters or "fudge factors" (which one author has termed "clout" or "salience/novelty" factors), applied by personnel experienced with prior application of the models (e.g., members of the model-developing firms) (Urban and Katz [1983], Yankelovich, Skelly, and White, Inc. [1981]). Judgment may be required, for example, to incorporate product-class effects or to estimate the degree of retention of brand awareness in the absence of additional exposures. One reason that many research firms can maintain comparatively high margins on their PTM services (BBDO positions NEWS as a service to clients and seeks only to recover costs) is that they have accumulated data and experience in applying these corrections or adjustments. Several firms have chosen to disclose selected details of otherwise proprietary models through publication in the academic press, which, arguably, adds legitimacy to the firm and its model. (In some cases, however [e.g., BASES, ESP, SPEEDMARK, and COMP], the proprietary model itself is not published but represents an elaboration on prior academic research.) By analyzing the performance of products that have experienced PTMs, test markets, and commercialization, it becomes possible to obtain estimates of such correction factors analytically.

A pertinent question is whether past product-category experience is sufficient to generate valid bases for modifying PTM model results (Yankelovich, Skelly, and White, Inc. [1981]). First of all, there is a sampling bias, because products that do not perform well in a PTM market may never be test-marketed or commercialized; therefore, analytically determined correction factors can only be estimated based on a truncated population consisting only of PTM successes. Second, all products are somewhat different, and there is no theory to indicate why average historical relations should have predictive validity in any given case. Judgment of experienced managers may be no substitute either, particularly if their experience does not encompass the nature of the new product and its marketing plan (e.g., levels of expenditure not previously undertaken). Third, the passage of time between the PTM and the test market or commercial rollout and difference in the populations from which data are obtained for these activities make generalizations dangerous. Consequently, there will always be a *need* for a market test of the entire marketing program prior to commercialization. Finally, we would note that each new product in a category enters into a different competitive environment than did the one before (e.g., a second entry must contend with the fact that the first entry is already there; a third entry with the reality of the presence of a first and second entry, etc.), so that historical generalization may, for this reason, also prove inadequate. All of these reasons argue the necessity for judgment in adjusting any model results, but such adjustments create their own problems.

STMs (without adjustment) lack external validity and may lack internal validity in some instances as well, because subjects know they are participating in research. The artificiality of the laboratory task setting is an obvious problem limiting external validity. Many customers may recognize the brand being tested simply because it is the "unfamiliar one" or its advertising is in storyboard or animated form. Awareness resulting from customer word of mouth, or retail sales effects resulting from factors such as retail promotion, packaging, or in-store displays, is rarely modeled explicitly because too many variations would need to be captured (an exception being the LITMUS model). Instead, all awareness is presumed to be generated by producer advertising and promotion. Depth of repeat purchasing (Urban and Hauser [1980, pp. 390–395], Wind [1982, pp. 456–459]) often cannot be obtained empirically because the short duration of a PTM can permit no more than one "repeat-purchase" measure. This need not be a particularly serious limitation, both because it may be possible to extend the duration of the PTM and offer sales waves, and also because second and higher repeat frequencies may often be reliably forecast from first repeat (Eskin [1973], Kalwani and Silk [1980]). (If use of the product requires habit changes or if the product is a fad, there may be no easy substitute for extended testing.) The effects of advertising may often be modeled as a function of dollars expended rather than the content of the ads. Media other than television and certain print (e.g., radio or billboard) may not be tested. Such limits on reality add to the burden of the adjustments just alluded to. Further, the population samples used for most STM studies are convenience samples (e.g., mall shoppers). Sometimes subjects are screened to be users of the product category or for particular demographics. The distribution of the sample tends to be limited to a comparatively few locations. Finally, most models are generally unable to capture market expansion that could result from the introduction of a product that is truly new (i.e., has appeals that broaden the market) and that may trigger unpredictable amounts of favorable or unfavorable publicity and word-of-mouth and social acceptance. Rather, their concern is often with predicting sales or market share for the new brand under an assumption of zero or "normal" growth in the product category.

There are several new-product situations that are not good candidates for PTM analysis. If a new product can succeed with a very low market share or sales volume, the forecasts may not be sufficiently precise to provide unambiguous go/no-go advice. Minor line extensions or slight product modifications may represent very little expense or risk (e.g., adding a new flavor to a food-product line or a packaging redesign) and, thus, neither a PTM nor a test market may be worth its cost.[7] The cheapest "research" may actually be marketing the product, because manufacturing is similar, distribution is available, prices are unchanged, and the product category and brand name are known to customers. The considerable brand awareness that subjects bring to the STM task may also contaminate results if a PTM were to be attempted. At the other extreme, products that are totally new to respondents present a different problem in that responses may be unstable because respondents lack a suitable frame of reference. Virtually all pre–test-marketing models rely on the ability to estimate category demand outside the model. When a unique product class does not exist to which the tested product can be related, a "share-of-market" forecast may be arbitrary. Placement in a supermarket may be essential to cuing competitive associations, and this may not be controlled. The relatively short duration of the PTM may not permit respondents to develop a full appreciation for a new-to-the-world product or for those other products that will ultimately come to define a category. Finally products with long purchase cycles (e.g., luggage), irregular usage patterns (e.g., frozen pies and barbecue sauces), or highly seasonal patterns (e.g., eggnog, Easter-egg dye) have also been difficult to model accurately, possibly due to difficulties in getting representative repeat-intentions data because interest in the category will vary with the immediacy of need and timeliness of the research (e.g., LITMUS makes use of seasonality indices in order to improve its ability to deal with such instances).

It is desirable that most pretest marketing be conducted after the product concept has been brought to a state of readiness for test marketing.[8] The product and its packaging, price, advertising and promotional copy, and budgets should have been developed, tested, and planned prior to pretest marketing. (Simulations may be possible, with resulting diagnostics, to help this planning process.) Refining the promotional mix is impossible without this initial marketing plan. Further, each time a major change is made to the product or advertising copy, it is desirable to run another STM (but, unfortunately, it usually is not done). Pretest marketing prematurely or not conducting pretest marketing after significant marketing-plan changes are made can destroy much of the value of the earlier information gained.

A Discussion of Four PTM Models

We now turn to a discussion of the four models we have chosen that use PTM data to forecast demand for the new product: BASES, ASSESSOR and its successor ASSESSOR-FT, LITMUS and its successor LITMUS II, and NEWS. BASES, ASSESSOR, and LITMUS were originally developed as PTM models; NEWS began as a test-market model, but a version was developed for the PTM situation before either BASES or ASSESSOR existed.

Table 8–1 compares major features of the models. ASSESSOR and LITMUS integrate an STM or require that one be performed prior to use, BASES uses some, but not all, of the elements of an STM, and NEWS typically uses consumer-survey data (but can use STM data when available from its clients). Some require that an estimate of product-category demand be available. The cost per PTM ranges between $50,000 and $75,000 for ASSESSOR and LITMUS, compared with only $26,000 to $36,000 for NEWS (i.e., approximately $15,000 for NEWS itself plus $15,000 to $25,000 for the cost of the survey on which runs will be based.)[9] ASSESSOR-FT is probably more expensive, depending on the number of modules chosen. A BASES II test (one cell, 600 respondents) was estimated by Burke personnel to cost between $40,000 and $55,000. Of course, such costs will change over time and can vary considerably with specifics of the research design. They are presented here for guidance only. The cost of running each model is generally small compared to the cost of an STM, survey, or other fieldwork.

Published Validation Results

Each company has published the results of case histories comparing forecast and actual product performance. The models appear to be quite accurate, though there is probably some bias in the reporting. Such a bias can be a consequence of the conflict of interest that results when authors are reporting on a procedure from which they expect to derive income. It is quite common for both the commercialized product and its marketing plan to be changed from that used in a test market or PTM. After all, it is a purpose of such product-development stages to provide guidance to improve marketing plans.

Table 8–1
Comparison of BASES II, ASSESSOR (ASSESSOR-FT), LITMUS II, and NEWS/PLANNER

		Model		
Characteristic	*BASES II*	*ASSESSOR (ASSESSOR-FT)*	*LITMUS II*	*NEWS/PLANNER*
Type of model	Trial-repeat	Trial-repeat and preference	Trial-repeat	Trial-repeat
Data sources	Survey and marketing plan	Simulated test market and survey, marketing plan (IRI Fact Book [FT])	Simulated test market and survey, marketing plan	Survey, marketing plan, and copy test (if available)
Categories represented (1982 data)	Packaged goods (90%), food products (35%)	Packaged goods (99%), food products (22%) (not available [FT])	Packaged goods (95%), food products (50%)	Packaged goods (97%), food products (46%) [23]
Forecasts by time period?	Yes	No, steady-state (yes [FT])	Yes	Yes
Marketing-plan inputs	Advertising, price, promotion, distribution build (by period)	Advertising, price promotion, distribution (aggregate) (by period [FT])	Advertising, promotion, distribution build (by period)	Advertising, price, promotion, distribution build (by period)
Cannibalization effects considered?	Yes, through source-of-volume model	Yes, through STM and preference model	Some, through STM	When appropriate data available
Competitive reactions considered?	No, relative price in STM	No, competitive ads shown, relative price in STM (source of competition identified [FT])	No, competitive ads shown, relative price in STM	No

Respondent screening	Security, basic demographics (category usage possible)	Security, category usage, desired demographics (BehaviorScan panelists [FT])	Security, category usage, desired demographics	Security category, usage, desired demographics
Output	Sales-volume trial rate, repeat rate, average time between purchases, average number of units trial/rep	Market-share aggregate trial, aggregate repeat (sales volume [FT]) (trial, repeat development broken down by heavy user, deal buyer, etc. [FT])	Market share, sales volume, trial rate, average repeat rate, number of users, awareness by period, profitability	Market share, sales volume, trial rate, average repeat rate, number of users, awareness by period
Diagnostics	Trier profile, nontrier profile, positioning analysis, segmentation summary	Trier profile, nontrier profile, test-brand profile, draw/cannibalization, attribute trade-offs (product map [FT])	Trier profile, nontrier profile, test-brand profile, profitability	Trier profile, nontrier profile, test-brand profile
Sensitivity/optimization	Sensitivity	Sensitivity, what-if simulation (FT)	Sensitivity, limited optimization	Sensitivity, what-if simulation
Average sample				
Initial	500–700	300	500–600	200–300
Call back	190–200	200–240 users	100 (min.)	Depending on client data
Time to complete	12 weeks	8–10 weeks (faster with FT)	6–12 weeks	10–12 weeks
Approximate cost	$40–55,000[a]	$50,000 [27]	Approx. $75,000 $15–100,000[b]	$35,000[c]

[a] An estimate provided by William Moult.
[b] An estimate provided by Joseph D. Blackburn.
[c] Survey at $15–25,000 plus analysis at $15,000.

Consequently, to correct for this "noncomparability," the earlier PTM results may be "adjusted" to reflect that product and marketing plan actually utilized at the later stage.[10] Such adjustments are subjective and, however legitimate in intention, contain the possibility of bias in execution. Further, the fact that the test market and PTM occur at different and, possibly, widely separated time periods (a year or more) complicates inferencing because changes in the market environment over so long a time could render a PTM forecast less valid. Differing competitive action in the test market may bias results. There may be measurement error in computing shares in test market (Urban and Katz [1983]). A further problem arises due to "curtailment." Products that are revealed by the PTM to be unlikely to succeed pragmatically are also less likely to be taken further to test market or commercialization. Because, as noted earlier, only products that experience both stages can be compared, such comparisons cannot consider products that fail in PTM (or, more accurately, prior to commercialization). Some fraction of such products might have been successful if commercialized (see Elrod and Kelman [1984] for an estimate), but the published data do not normally consider the costs of these "mistakes." Neither can they show reliably the correspondence between predicted and actual shares for those products that had low shares in the PTM.

With the factors just mentioned as caveats (and with the further realization that reported validation results often combine forecasts based on test markets with those based on PTM data), we would note that Blackburn and Clancy (1982) report that of 20 LITMUS share forecasts, 8 were "bull's-eyes," 8 were "near misses," and only 4 were "disappointments" (the authors' subjective interpretations). Better (1983) reports that of 50 LITMUS forecasts, the average error was about 10 percent. Pringle, et al. (1982) report that of 28 NEWS share forecasts, the average error was 18.5 percent. Further, Pringle et al. state that NEWS predicts market share within 1 share point 68 percent of the time, and within 1.5 points 77 percent of the time. Similar results are reported for ASSESSOR, for example, 80 percent within 1 share point (Silk and Urban [1978]) and 68 percent (after adjustment) within 1 share point, with an average absolute deviation of error of 11.6 percent of actual (Urban and Katz [1983]). It is worthwhile noting that the ASSESSOR-FT is a sufficiently new and different service from the original ASSESSOR that validation results are not yet available. One should not assume that the results just cited for ASSESSOR will necessarily be applicable to this new service. Finally, BASES (Burke Marketing Services [1984] and Lin et al. [1982]) reports over 140 validated case histories, which indicate first-year sales-volume estimates within ±10 percent of actual marketplace performance in 66 percent of the cases (35 percent within ±5 percent of actual). They also report trial and repeat estimates within ±10 percent of actual marketplace performance in 75 percent of the cases (and within ±20 percent in over 90 percent of cases) and test-retest reliability of trial estimates about 0.99 (based on six concepts).

BASES

BASES is an organization offering a number of interrelated services designed to make sales forecasts for new products at virtually every stage in the new-product–development process (from business analysis through test marketing and commercialization) (Burke Marketing Services [1984] and Lin et al. [1982]). At the earliest stages, historical data representing product-class norms or averages are used, refined by managerial and research-firm judgment. At later stages, data pertinent to the specific product or brand and its marketing plan are substituted for these averages or approximations: The product concept is replaced by the actual product and packaging, advertising mock-ups or storyboards by actual advertising, and concept tests by actual product usage. BASES I is a concept test conducted during a shopping-mall intercept. BASES II involves data from an in-home test of the physical product, whereas BASES III is designed to measure the effect of in-store environmental factors, such as packaging and merchandising materials, shelf placement, and the presence of competitive brands. These latter stages most closely resemble pretest marketing conditions. Most of Burke's experience is with BASES I and II applications; BASES III is conducted infrequently. An important reason for this appears to be the claimed forecasting accuracy of BASES II, which is very similar to the more expensive BASES III.

BASES II uses a new-product prototype, as well as a finished concept board (or commercial), with a package photograph, product description, and key selling messages. Personal interviews are conducted at shopping malls to identify high-potential triers. These individuals are given the product to try at home. Participants are later surveyed, either via self-administered questionnaires or by telephone interviews for after-usage data, including buying intentions and intended frequency of purchase, as well as price/value assessment, hedonic score, and other key diagnostics. These, in addition to secondary assumptions on marketing variables, are used to forecast first-year trial rate, first-repeat rate, average time between purchases, average trial- and repeat-purchase units, and end-of-year consumer-sales volume. In BASES III, the test product in finished packaging is priced and shelved in its expected competitive environment in 6 to 12 retail stores in 3 to 6 geographically separated markets. Temporary interviewing facilities are set up at these stores, and 1,200 to 3,000 shoppers are intercepted individually. These shoppers are *not* usually screened for product-category usage or specific demographics. This is an important characteristic not only of BASES but also of LITMUS and NEWS because it makes estimation of sales possible without reference to a prior product-category definition. Basic demographics are collected, however, as well as information regarding category and brand usage where feasible. TV commercials or print ads for the test product are shown. Each participant receives a 20-percent–off coupon for the test product and a $1-off coupon for any product bought in the store during the shopping trip. They then go on about their shopping. Coupon redemptions become the basis for estimating trial volume, and coding permits identification of triers and nontriers. Several weeks later, a minimum of 240 triers are surveyed by phone regarding repurchase intent and other reactions to the test product.

The BASES forecasting model, shown in abstracted form in figure 8–4, takes into account media plans, advertising-impact assumption, trade and promotion plans, distribution build, seasonal indices (SI), and brand-and category-development indices (CDI) (which reflect prior experience with the category in the test cites) to build a first-year trial estimate.

$$\text{Trial Estimate} = \left(\begin{array}{c} \text{Calibrated} \\ \text{Buying} \\ \text{Incentive} \\ \text{Score} \end{array} \right) (\text{Distribution}) \times (\text{Awareness}) \frac{1}{\text{SI}} \frac{1}{\text{CDI}}.$$

The calibration of stated buying intentions is based on more than twelve years of historical data and is designed to "correct" stated buying intentions for overstatement. Calibration attempts to take account of the respondent's nationality or cultural background, the product category, and unit-price level.

Repeat-rate estimates are based on three after-use measures: stated buying intentions, an average hedonic (like/dislike) score, and a measure of average price/value. After-use buying intentions are calibrated in a manner similar to the trial measures and are combined with the other two measures in a function similar to that just given to obtain a refined first-repeat rate. The *average purchase cycle* is estimated based on after-use intended-purchase frequency adjusted for overstatement via historical panel experience and consideration of the build of the trial curve. Long-term repeat-rate decay is calibrated using the after-use hedonic scores and price/value measures for the test product, rather than some constant rate or a rate based on category norm. BASES claims that by so doing, it is better able to evaluate volume potential for innovative products. Finally, *average purchase units* at trial and repeat are estimated from potential buyers' statements of intended purchase quantities adjusted for overstatement based on historical relationships.

The preceding measures are combined to produce sales estimates using the following model:

$$S_t = T_t + R_t, \tag{1}$$

where

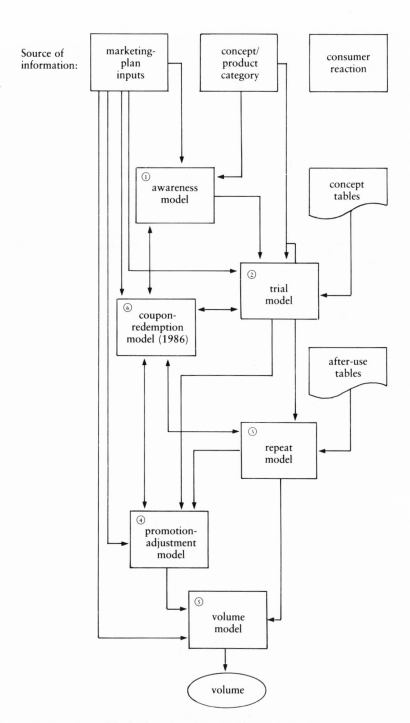

Figure 8–4. A Simplified Flowchart for BASES Volume Forecasts

Source: Courtesy Burke Marketing Services.

S_t = total sales volume up to time t,

T_t = trial volume up to time t,

R_t = repeat volume up to time t,

and

$$T_t = (TM)P_tU_o, \tag{2}$$

where

TM = target-market size (number of households in the target-market area)

P_t = cumulative trial (or penetration) rate up to week t

U_o = average units purchased at trial

and

$$R_t = \sum_{i=1}^{\infty} (N_{i-1,t}Y_{it}U_i) \tag{3}$$

where

$N_{i-1,t}$ = cumulative number of customers repeating at least $(i$-1$)$ times by week t, where $(N_{o,t} = (TM)P_t)$

Y_{it} = conditional cumulative ith repeat rate at week t given that $(i$-1$)$ repeat purchases were made up to week t

U_i = average units purchased at repeat level i

As figure 8–4 implies, there is much more to BASES than we are able to examine because Burke has not chosen to disclose much detail beyond that reported here. If assumptions on distribution level, awareness level, and/ or approximate marketing plans are available, a second-year sales-volume forecast is possible in addition to the first-year forecast. Forecasts of coupon redemption, independent of those assumed by the marketer, are to be incorporated in the latest changes to the model. The output of BASES includes sales-volume forecasts, trial rates, repeat rates, average time between purchases, and average number of units per trial/repeat. Diagnostics include postexposure measures of recall, key messages, and purchase intent; demographics and usage behavior profiles of triers and nontriers; and hedonic and price/value measures. Because BASES I and II do not make use of an

STM and do make greater of use of product-category norms than the other techniques discussed, their forecasting success makes the value of the specific product data provided by an STM at least open to question. We do not know enough regarding the mix of products in the applications of BASES and the other approaches to reach any conclusions regarding the relative desirability of the different types of data (STM vs. category norm) for different product applications. Such uses must assume a well-defined category already exists.

ASSESSOR

Figure 8–5 shows the basic structure of ASSESSOR. It actually involves two models: a trial-repeat model and a preference model. Data are collected for both models from a STM and a telephone follow-up. Each produces a long-run, steady-state market-share estimate. The two estimates should be similar, but if not, there is an attempt to reconcile data to produce convergence. A claimed advantage for ASSESSOR is this dual approach. One model (preference) is based on judgmental data, whereas the other (trial-repeat) is based on behavior (choice) in the STM. The judgment-based model is presumed to have greater diagnostic value in suggesting *why* the predicted share is achieved and from which existing alternatives the new brand would draw share. As long as the two models agree in their predictions, the fact that different premises lead to similar results increases confidence in the predictions. Should they disagree, the attempts at reconciliation could necessitate favoring one model over the other as an indicant of "truth" or some averaging of the two predictions. Both models involve the use of "analyst judgment" to arrive at their predictions, and thus a basis for such reconciliation can rest on a suitable recalibration of such judgmental parameters.

The preference model makes use of Luce's (1959) choice axiom and work done by Pessemier et al. (1971). Key in Luce's theory is that choice probabilities can be linked to measures of brand preference. Prior to being exposed to commercials in the STM, respondents are asked to list their consideration set ("evoked" set) of brands from among those being tested in the product category. They are then asked to allocate a fixed number of "chips," or points, among this evoked set. This exercise results in relative preference ratings for each product (averaged across respondents). During a follow-up telephone call, the respondents are again asked to allocate points among the brands, but this time the new product is included. A market-share estimate can be calculated from the relative preference for the new product, and its "draw" from competitors' products can be determined from the change in relative preferences (Silk and Urban [1978]).

The trial-repeat model is similar to that proposed by Parfitt and Collins (1968). The underlying premise is that the steady-state, long-run market

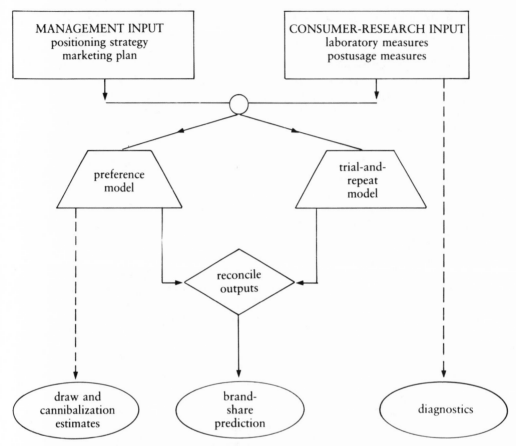

Figure 8–5. Structure of ASSESSOR

Source: Reprinted from Alvin J. Silk and Glen L. Urban, "Pretest Market Evaluation of New Packaged Goods: A Model and Measurement Methodology," *Journal of Marketing Research* (May 1978), published by the American Marketing Association.

share (*S*) achieved by a new brand will be the product of the long-run levels of trial and repeat purchasing it attains:

$$S = T R B$$

where *T* is the long-run cumulative trial rate (the proportion of all buyers in target group who ever try the product), *R* is the long-run repeat-purchase rate (new brand's share of subsequent purchases in the product category made by previous triers), and *B* is the index to adjust for the usage of buyers of the new brand relative to other buyers in the category.

ASSESSOR estimates T by assuming that trial comes about either from the receipt and use of free samples or through initial purchase; it does not distinguish between these sources (although the latter involves more initiative on the part of the consumer). First purchase is taken to be dependent on the level of awareness brought about through advertising and promotion and on the availability of the product in stores. Thus, T can be written as follows:

$$T = F * K * D + C * U - (F*K*D)(C*U)$$

where F is the long-run probability of trial of the new brand (for a consumer in the target market) given 100 percent awareness and availability, K is the long-run probability that a consumer in the target market will become aware of the new brand, D is the long-run level of distribution (probability that the new brand will be available), C is the probability that a consumer in the target market will receive a sample of the new brand, and U is the probability that a consumer who receives a sample will use it.

The laboratory test market provides an estimate of F: it is simply the corrected proportion of respondents who buy the new brand in the mock store. During follow-up, the respondents who received a sample of the new brand are asked if they used it, and U is calculated as the proportion that did. The advertising budget specified in the marketing gives rise to an estimate of K. The marketing plan also specifies plans for achieving some level of distribution (D) and sampling penetration (C).

ASSESSOR estimates R as the equilibrium share of a first-order, two-state Markov process. Two estimates must be obtained before this share can be calculated:

1. The probability that a consumer who last purchased any of the estimated brands will switch to the new brand on the next occasion.

2. The probability that a consumer who last purchased the new brand will repeat.

The first quantity is estimated based on preference ratings given by nonpurchasers during follow-up. The second quantity is estimated as the proportion of buyers in the STM who state (during follow-up) that they would like to repurchase the new brand (Silk and Urban [1978]). Obviously, such single measures of repeat purchase require subjective judgments based on experience to (hopefully) improve their validity.

ASSESSOR-FT

ASSESSOR-FT is an outgrowth of the acquisition of Management Decision Systems, Inc. (ASSESSOR) by Information Resources, Inc. (IRI) (FASTRAC). From its description (Information Resources, Inc. [1985]), however, it seems more to resemble FASTRAC, a forecasting and data-analysis system built to utilize IRI's vast UPC scanner data base. This data base contains household purchases of virtually every item sold through grocery stores and drugstores in over twenty communities nationwide. Several hundred thousand UPC codes are monitored. Purchases by members of a large panel of store customers are recorded by household over time. In addition, store pricing, display, sales promotion, and couponing are monitored, as are television viewing and other media habits (advertising exposure) of the customer panel. IRI has argued that this way of measuring panel purchases is more objective than the older diary method and that its extensive monitoring of virtually every purchase by the panel gives it the historical base to track sales, marketing, and competitive activity (e.g., price, sales, promotion, advertising, distribution intensity) for the thousands of new products introduced each year. It provides demographics and purchase histories for those households that do and do not purchase specific new products and permits separate analyses of purchases by heavy and light users of the product category. ASSESSOR-FT, by making use of the FASTRAC models, permits sales-volume forecasts for a new product, rather than the share of market that ASSESSOR alone provides, and it is claimed to have the capability of predicting new-product growth (and trial and repeat components) over time (which other models do as well).

ASSESSOR-FT consists of a *base module,* which uses data from an in-home concept test as input to a model that predicts consumer response to the new product. The past purchasing behavior of those households has been previously tracked. A study is typically conducted in eight geographically dispersed cities. The ASSESSOR-FT model takes account of competitive activity, purchase frequency, household assortment buying activity, and the like at the household level to construct its forecast. In the early stages of the new product's development, the model relies on historical norms, but as the product nears market introduction, the optional modules allow testing the new product's unique appeals and actual concept execution.

There is a *product-exposure module,* which involves concept testing and in-home usage followed by measurement of repurchase intent and hedonic scaling, as well as other diagnostic data. A *competitive set module* identifies competing product alternatives and provides a measure for the strength of preference for the new brand within this competitive context. Stronger and weaker competitors are identified, and cannibalization estimates are provided. These can be tracked, much as in the original ASSESSOR. The *advertising-exposure module* provides the capacity of adding the reality of full video exposure in the home to the base module's concept-board exposure for those products where IRI experience indicates that advertising exposure is disproportionately important to the final result (or where a unique selling approach is envisioned). The *simulated-store module* offers services similar to that phase in the original ASSESSOR. The *perceptual-map module* projects the new product's image (prior to use) on a map of the existing market to discover strengths and weaknesses. After use, its image is again projected to investigate change and verify market segmentation and segment expectations. This was also part of the original ASSESSOR (Urban and Hauser [1980]). Finally, a *profit-optimum module* (misnamed, because it does not globally optimize) provides a PC-based simulation that utilizes information from the other analyses (e.g., elasticities of price, promotion, and advertising repeat rates over time) to make projections for changes in the product and marketing plan.

ASSESSOR-FT is supposed to be a replacement for the older ASSESSOR. It is not clear from the description of the service, however, in what form the original survives. Indeed, both services are currently marketed. Thus, although ASSESSOR-FT bears the same name, the validation evidence reported for AS-SESSOR may no longer be applicable because of the changed format. ASSES-SOR-FT makes sales *volume* predictions, whereas ASSESSOR predicted share (which could easily be converted to volume if market size were known). It predicts buildup over time of trial and repeat components, which the older version did not. The FT version makes use of UPC scanner data collected from stores in a limited number of small to midsized cities across the United States, which may not prove completely representative of the distribution plans and customer base for each new product. The availability of substantial prior product-category data and analyses may encourage management to make greater use of historical norms and deemphasize research that explores the uniqueness of the new concept. One of ASSESSOR-FT's claimed advantages is a substantially shortened response time (time from inception of the research to report delivery), which may also encourage such compromise. Finally, by restricting its data collection to panel members in those cities where IRI has its BehaviorScan monitoring facilities, burnout or panel "fatigue" may occur, which diminishes the usefulness of projections made from panel purchase behavior. These criticisms are, to some extent, speculative, and IRI may be able to take steps to overcome them. Nonetheless ASSESSOR-FT is itself a new product, and its track record needs to be better established.

LITMUS II and NEWS

Although NEWS is the older procedure, LITMUS II and NEWS are structurally similar, so they will be described together (Blackburn and Clancy [1983], Mahajan et al. [1984], Pringle et al. [1982]). Figure 8–6 shows their basic structure. Both can be characterized as "decision-process" or "hierarchy-of-effects" models. Unaware consumers become aware through exposure to advertising and/or promotion for the new product. "Awareness to trial" is affected by promotion, ad persuasion, product concept, packaging, price, and distribution. Price and product quality are the main factors affecting "trial to repeat." Unlike ASSESSOR, both model at the aggregate level. They afford the advantage of period-by-period forecasts of awareness, trial, share, sales, and even profitability—very useful for fine-tuning a marketing plan.

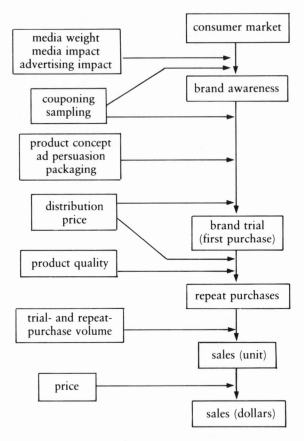

Figure 8–6. The New-Product–Introduction Process as Modeled by LITMUS

Source: Reprinted from Blackburn and Clancy (1982).

There are several differences between LITMUS II and NEWS. First, we have noted that NEWS uses consumer-survey data, rather than the STM data used by LITMUS II, to estimate trial and repeat probabilities.

The awareness coefficient is estimated from the brand name recall component of one of many commercially available copy evaluation methods. These copy evaluation methods provide a percentile score for the tested advertisement, which is then transformed into the comparable awareness coefficient based upon prior experience with the model. The awareness-trial rate is estimated from the "definitely intend-to-buy" score of a standard concept test. The trial-repeat rate can be estimated from the "definitely will repurchase" score in an in-home product-use test (Pringle et al. [1982, p. 20]).

This can make the cost of NEWS run much lower than that of LITMUS. A second difference is that LITMUS allows consumers three time periods to move from awareness to trial and from trial to repeat, whereas NEWS allows only two. This may provide a more flexible or realistic model, but the real value of this difference is unknown. In addition to such structural differences, LITMUS II also calculates an estimate of "profitability" and offers an "optimization" routine that is not available with NEWS to help a manager improve the product's marketing plan.

Table 8–2 shows the data inputs required for both NEWS and LITMUS II runs. Notice that the trial and repeat probabilities (items 15, 16, 21, and 22) are estimated from an STM, whereas, as noted, NEWS uses consumer-survey data. Figure 8–7 shows how LITMUS II models the awareness-to-trial process. (The process is identical in NEWS, except that the third period is not

Table 8–2
Model Inputs Required by LITMUS

	Model Inputs	
Type	*Input*	*Source*
Market characteristics	1. Size of potential market (millions of buyers)	
	2. Number of units per case	
	3. Size of market (millions of cases)	
	4. Estimated number of purchase cycles per year	Marketing plan
Marketing-plan characteristics	5. Average cost per 1,000 GRPs	
	6. Average cost per sample dropped	
	7. Average cost per coupon	
	8. Maximum likely brand awareness	Normative data
	9. Advertising dollars or GRPs per period	
	10. Percentage of market couponed per period	Marketing plan
	11. Percentage of market sampled per period	
	12. Attention-getting power of advertising (1.0 = average)	Copy and media research
	13. Attention-getting power of media (1.0 = average)	Normative data or
	14. Probability of remembering brand one period in the absence of additional exposures (1.0 = maximum)	management judgment
		Management judgment
	15. Probability of brand trial intention given awareness of advertising	Laboratory-test-market estimates
	16. Probability of brand trial given intention and distribution	
	17. Probability of brand trial given coupon	Normative data or
	18. Probability of brand trial given sample	customer research
	19. Distribution per period	marketing plan
	20. Trial purchase size (1.0 = average)	
	21. Probability of first repeat purchase in period following trial	Laboratory-test-market estimates
	22. Probability of second repeat purchase in period following first repeat	
	23. Repeat purchase size (1.0 = average)	
	24. Price per standard unit (1.0 = average)	Marketing plan

Source: Reprinted from Better (1983).

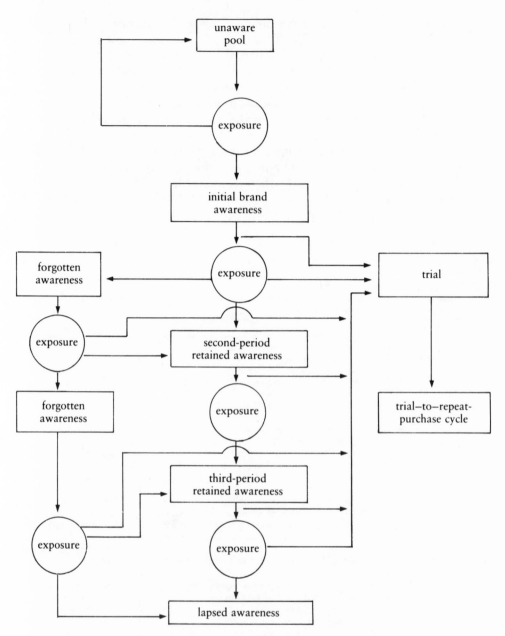

Figure 8–7. The Process of Awareness as Modeled by LITMUS

Source: Reprinted from Blackburn and Clancy (1982).

considered.) Both models consider seven sources of awareness: (1) advertising, (2) sales promotion (sampling), (3) couponing, and (4–7) all possible pairwise and three-way combinations of the first three. In both models, the probabilities of a customer becoming aware through advertising, promotion, and couponing are assumed to be independent. Though this may be questionable, the assumption is necessary for tractable modeling of the process. The mathematical structures of both LITMUS II and NEWS are beyond the scope of this chapter.

NEWS is somewhat simpler and, depending on field costs, can be less expensive to use than LITMUS. But whether the differences between them are consequential is, of course, an empirical question. The reliance of NEWS on consumer-survey data may imply lower validity (i.e., what people say they would do versus what they actually do in a simulated purchase environment). There are, however, well-known methods for adjusting measures of purchase intent (Urban and Hauser [1980]). But for the additional cost of a simulated test market, one gets more control over the product and situation being tested. For example, factors such as facings, shelf placement, presence of competitive brands, and relative pricing can be tested more realistically and, hopefully, more validly than would be possible with concept or usage tests (although such factors are far from constant across different stores even within the same chain). Competitive brands can be displayed and serve as purchase cues. Second, the three states of awareness modeled by LITMUS would appear to capture the complexity of the new-product–introduction process better than the two states modeled by NEWS by permitting some fraction of subjects to become aware in a third period, although the value of this difference cannot be determined by us from available information. Lew Pringle of BBDO has claimed that in personal communication that the difference is not material. Third, although LITMUS calculates profitability for a new product under the assumed marketing plan, such calculations have a great deal of arbitrariness. Cost must be estimated for different sales levels; sales are not forecast for more than one or two years so that only early-year profitability is emphasized. Fourth, the optimization routine provided by LITMUS II may make it easier for a marketer to fine-tune the marketing plan for the new product. NEWS uses sensitivity analyses alone to suggest improvements to the plan that would increase the sales predictions made by the model. Because the optimization provided by LITMUS II is conducted at extra cost, the benefit/cost value of this feature remains to be established. It also remains for the manager to determine feasibility of implementation for such "optimal" plans.

Conclusion

The pre–test-marketing idea seems clearly to have been worthwhile. In terms of managerial acceptance, these forecasting models and systems have become among the more widely used of all marketing models. They fulfill goals of all research to provide benefits, through reduction of risk, which substantially exceed their costs. New-product development and introduction remains a costly enterprise. Research that aids the process of putting a greater percentage of resources behind new-product winners and that helps winners to become even more profitable is worthwhile research indeed. NEWS and, more recently, the LITMUS, BASES, and ASSESSOR-FT systems offer an intriguing approach— taking a basic forecasting model or approach and systematically refining estimates for its parameters as new or better product- and/or market-specific data become available through subsequent research.

We would repeat again that these models do not constitute theories of market behavior. Consequently, we do not fully understand the limits of their applicability and usefulness. It is unfortunate that BASES and ASSESSOR-FT have not yet chosen to reveal their complete logic and structure so that these models could be examined in the same detail as have ASSESSOR, NEWS, and LITMUS. Further, this lack of disclosure precludes academic research to compare the several models. The validation evidence published in working-paper form by NEWS (Pringle et al. [1982]) and in articles by ASSESSOR (Silk and Urban [1978], Urban and Katz [1983]) encouraged competing models to report their own validation results. Such results have, of course, implied that all these competing frameworks are valid, but such reports are self-serving. Subjectivity in the validation process makes for possible conflicts of interest in reporting. Thus, full disclosure of the models themselves and their parameterization methods—as NEWS and, to a lesser extent, LITMUS and the original ASSESSOR have done—could encourage more impartial studies and comparisons.

Table 8–1 summarizes our discussion of the four approaches (and includes, perhaps, a few new facts). Although the table emphasizes differences, one should not conclude that the approaches are enormously different. Their common heritage has already been stressed and, insofar as we can judge, the validation evidence (not reported in the tables) appears equivalent. Rather, it is useful to think of these as complementary, each with distinctions that may prove more useful than others in certain product applications. ASSESSOR and ASSESSOR-FT each have their bases in two conceptually different models, and this can give rise to greater confidence in estimates when their predictions converge. Having two independent estimates precludes making possible large forecasting mistakes because disagreement implies a "red flag" and subsequent search for possible sources of bias and error. (Management Decisions Systems, Inc., has not reported how often such disagreement occurs in practice or provided examples of strategies for dealing with such occurrences.)

ASSESSOR-FT, BASES, LITMUS, and NEWS estimate sales (as well as trial and repeat) on a period-by-period basis, permitting better forecasts of profitability and encouraging financial planning in a manner that could prove superior to that provided by the singular forecast of ASSESSOR. (Such forecasts, however, are made under steady-state assumptions regarding pricing, couponing and other promotion, advertising spending, distribution build, and so forth, which ignore word-of-mouth, competitive reaction, and implementation issues that could prove consequential at launch for some products.) Also, the fact that ASSESSOR considers only total spending levels while the other approaches permit inputs on a period-by-period basis means that the effects of different expenditure schedules can also be tested. LITMUS and NEWS explicitly model interactions between advertising, promotional spending, and distribution build; thus, trade-offs between these factors can be considered.

ASSESSOR-FT provides a module that identifies competitors to a new product. For certain new-to-the-world or company products, the entire set (product category) may not be known with confidence or assumptions regarding it may prove too naive. (As noted previously, a poorly specified category can be *fatal* to the forecasting ability of virtually all of these models.) The new product may, for example, have alternative positioning against different types of competitors, which could be equally plausible but carry different profit implications. Consequently, the choice of competitive products for an STM shelf display may be an important decision variable that users may wish to test. Where it is not, all approaches that assume prior specification of category and competitors should prove acceptable. The STM provides data concerning the new product's cannibalization and draw. ASSESSOR and ASSESSOR-FT also provide diagnostic data helpful in analyzing the reasons behind such substitutions, using the preference-modeling and perceptual-product-mapping exercises. Similar research is not, but could readily be, incorporated in conjunction with the other frameworks, however.

When the test product is truly new in the sense that it is expected to create its own category, bring new users into a category, or enter a category that is thought to be ill defined, BASES, LITMUS, or NEWS would appear to have some advantage. by not using prior screening for category usage or using (as in BASES III) the more realistic setting of the supermarket, the precise a priori category definition that other approaches require is less critical. When the target market is largely unknown, this methodology will provide the information that may help in discriminating between people who could be induced to buy and nonusers. The use of real stores, as in the BASES III approach, may also help to ascertain the effect that specific in-store location may have on trial and provide some (albeit limited) guidance to potential problems that may arise in obtaining distribution.

When the test product is part of a well-established category and is likely to appeal to consumers already using brands in that category, approaches such as those of ASSESSOR (both versions) and BASES I and II are able to provide diagnostics that help explain the test brands' strengths and weaknesses relative to competitive brands. Concept tests and in-home usage are prior data to LITMUS and NEWS. These models are able to examine weaknesses of the marketing and promotion program. As we have noted, LITMUS offers an optimization capability that makes it easier to ask "what-if" questions and converge more rapidly to marketing programs that look superior to the model. The other approaches provide analysis of sensitivity to changes in specific marketing inputs and provide guidance in more of a trial-and-error manner. Although LITMUS promises more, its optimization has not been validated in real-world terms (i.e., will the "feasible" marketing plan that the model likes best produce the results predicted for it?). Joseph Blackburn, one of the developers of LITMUS, has stated that his experience with optimization indicates that it almost always leads to better plans than the original in the client's judgment.

If sampling is part of the marketing program for the new brand, ASSESSOR (both versions) or LITMUS might be preferable because all participants in the study can be given the new product to use after their laboratory experience. ASSESSOR probably has the greater experience in using their "sampling" procedure to forecast sales. Receiving a sample at the conclusion of a simulated shopping trip is probably not identical in its impact to receiving a sample through more conventional means. ASSESSOR, as well as several of the other approaches, has developed empirical estimates of the relation between sampling and trial. ASSESSOR does not explicitly consider the effects of couponing, whereas BASES, LITMUS, and NEWS do. The ASSESSOR-FT data base provides historical data regarding purchases on "deal" in the product category and which customers are likely to be more deal-prone. Thus, these latter approaches might be preferred for product categories where extensive couponing is common or contemplated.

ASSESSOR-FT provides access to the enormous IRI data base. A major advantage of such a data base is that ASSESSOR-FT can provide *some* "experience" even in product categories where it may not have conducted prior pre–test-marketing studies and it knows a great deal about the prior purchase histories and behaviors in response to advertising, promotion, and pricing for customers in its test cities. BASES, by virtue of having the largest collective market share among PTM models, may also provide a substantial experience advantage. Because this share represents three services combined, it may not be directly comparable to that of other models. Such experience can be a two-edged sword, however. Historical results do not necessarily generalize to each and every new alternative in a category. A new product may have idiosyncratic characteristics that may make fitting into an established category more arbitrary than is presumed, so that historical analyses or category norms may prove misleading. As we have noted previously, market conditions tend to change over time so that a second entry into a category is affected by the fact that the first entrant is already there, a third by the presence of the first two, and so forth. Some competitors may have responded more effectively or dramatically to such entrances in the past, as well. Similarly, added model complexity may also prove deceptive because of the increased knowledge and insight required to model effectively and the added parameterization necessary. In discussing LITMUS, for example, Pringle et al. acknowledged its greater complexity in relation to their NEWS approach but concluded that "the added complexity of LITMUS does not seem to yield materially more accurate results" (1982, p. 5).

Finally, an issue that goes beyond the scope of this chapter, but can be important in deciding which framework to use, is the question of how easy it is to work with a supplier's staff. Some supplier personnel may be more technically trained and more able to answer questions regarding their model or its assumptions. Others may prove more insightful managerially in helping the client address the unique problems posed by its new product and its marketing program. This kind of experience and skill at developing an appropriate research design and model inputs and in interpreting model outputs may prove extremely valuable. Although there are also differences in cost and some in timeliness between approaches (e.g., ASSESSOR-FT claims faster results because it is able to make extensive use of its computerized data bases), these more qualitative factors may prove more important in choosing a supplier. A client may be well advised to solicit proposals from several suppliers or to experience several suppliers over time with different new products to acquire a basis for future choice. Because the models have different strengths and weaknesses, a firm might consider using different suppliers for different types of product and marketing programs.

All four models appear to represent worthwhile applications of marketing science and are worthy additions to the product planner's set of research alternatives. The success that such models and approaches have enjoyed has already encouraged further research to improve these models and to provide more relevant data. The fact that all such models are not identical also means that each may find a different client-product market niche and keep alive the competitive incentive necessary to improve research and service in this area. There does not currently appear to be one single, dominant approach for all new products and situations, and that may well be good.

Notes

1. ASSESSOR, NEWS and LITMUS are the best documented in the literature. BASES and ASSESSOR are the market leaders as of 1985 (William Moult, personal communication). ASSESSOR-FT is supposedly the successor to ASSESSOR, although both continue to be marketed. It is quite different and not well documented, but its discussion is included for completeness.

2. We are aware of at least twelve PTM forecasting services (although not all use STM data): ADOPTER (Data Development Corp., New York), ASSESSOR and ASSESSOR-FT (Management Decision Systems, Waltham, Mass., which was acquired by Information Resources, Inc., Chicago), BASES (Burke Marketing Services, Cincin-

nati, Ohio, acquired by SAMI, New York), COMP (Elrick and Lavidge, Chicago), CRITIQUE (Custom Research, Inc., Minneapolis Minn.), ESP or SIMULATOR ESP (NPD Research Inc. Port Washington, N.Y.), LITMUS (Clancy, Shulman, and Associates, Westport, Conn., which was acquired by Saatchi and Saatchi of London, England), LTM (Yankelovich, Skelly, and White, Inc., New York), which was also acquired by Saatchi and Saatchi), MICROMARKET (TeleResearch, River Edge, N.J.), NEWS (BBDO, New York), PURCHASE ACTION (Audience Studies, Inc., New York), and SPEEDMARK (Robinson Associates, Bryn Mawr, Pa.).

3. BASES services address four distinct stages in the product-planning process: BASES I (at the concept-test stage), BASES II (at the home-use–test stage), BASES III (at the in-store–test stage), and Early Market Cast (at the test-market and commercialization stages). Each stage makes use of better, more brand-specific data as they become available. BASES I and II are the most "popular" levels. ASSESSOR-FT combines the large-scale data base that is part of FASTRAC volume estimates with the preference-structure models that were part of ASSESSOR. ASSESSOR-FT is a modular system consisting of six modules plus a base module and can also be used at various stages of the product-planning process. LITMUS II is the successor to the original LITMUS model. NEWS was developed to analyze both test-market (NEWS/MARKET) and PTM (NEWS/PLANNER) data. Both versions employ the same model structure but make use of different data available in the two situations. NEWS/PLANNER will be referred to as both NEWS and NEWS/PLANNER in the ensuing discussion.

4. Successful simply means achieving the same sales or market share that management requires for success in test market.

5. Actually, forecast to be attained, based on STM data.

6. If the model were a perfect predictor, the curve would follow the x-axis from -100 percent to 0, would go straight up to $y = 1.0$, and would then go straight across from $x = 0$ to $+100$ percent. Deviation from this pattern indicates the amount of variance between predicted and actual values, i.e., the accuracy of the model.

7. Product modifications, such as a new sauce recipe or a new package, may or may not prove to be minor. Thus, judgment must enter in deciding whether or not to test rather than assuming hard and fast rules based on an arbitrary categorization.

8. However, new products can easily acquire a momentum that keeps them alive. If one tests too late, such momentum can carry even a losing proposition in to the marketplace. Thus, some testing is necessary at the earliest possible times even if the product, package, promotion, and so forth are not completely finished. The methods used, however, will be different.

9. Lew Pringle of BBDO states that NEWS is priced only to recover its costs and includes no profit or overhead. Moreover, he indicates that the survey data required are almost always provided by clients and would be gathered even if the model were not run.

10. Lew Pringle states that BBDO does not adjust the data reported in NEWS validation evidence.

References

Assmus, Gert (1984). "New Product Forecasting," *Journal of Forecasting* 3 (April–June): 121–38.

Better, Rona (1983). "Analysis of the Predictive Accuracy of the LITMUS Pre-Test Market Model." Paper written for K.J. Clancy, Boston University.

Blackburn, Joseph D., and Kevin J. Clancy (1982). "LITMUS: A New Product Planning Model," in *Studies in the Management Sciences—Marketing Planning Models,* Andris Zoltners, ed. North-Holland, pp. 43–61.

———— (1983). "LITMUS II: An Evolutionary Step in New Product Planning Models from Marketing Plan Evaluation to Marketing Plan Generation," in *Advances and Practices of Marketing Science 1983,* Fred Zufryden, ed. Providence, R.I.: Institute of Management Sciences, pp. 48–55.

———— (1984). "Awareness Forecasting Models: Comment," *Marketing Science* 3, no. 3 (Summer): 198–201.

Burke Marketing Services (1984) "BASES. Introduction. Services. Validation History." Descriptive brochure. Cincinnati, Ohio: Burke Marketing Services.

Chakravarti, Dipankar, Andrew A. Mitchell, and Richard Staelin (1981). "Judgment Based Marketing Decision Models: Problems and Possible Solutions," *Journal of Marketing* 4(45). (fall): 13–23.

Clancy, Shulman, and Associates (1983). "How to Reduce the Risk in New Product Marketing." Internal client publication.

Crawford, C. Merle (1979). "New Product Failure Rates—Facts and Fallacies," *Research Management* 22 (September): 9–13.

Elrod, Terry, and Alan P. Kelman (1984). "Reliability of New Product Evaluation as of 1968 and as of 1981." Working paper. Graduate School of Business, University of Chicago (December).

Eskin, Gerald J. (1973). "Dynamic Forecasts of New Product Demand Using a Depth of Repeat Model," *Journal of Marketing Research* 2, no. 10 (May): 115–29.

Hauser, John R., and Steven M. Shugan (1983). "Defensive Marketing Strategies," *Marketing Science* 2, no. 4 (fall): 319–60.

Information Resources, Inc. (1985). "ASSESSOR-FT: The Next Generation." Descriptive brochure. Chicago: IRI.

Kalwani, Manohar, and Alvin J. Silk (1980). "Structure of Report Buying for New Packaged Goods," *Journal of Marketing Research* 3, no. 17 (August): 316–22.

Lin, Lynn Y.S., Alain Pioche and Patrick Standen. (1982). "New Product Sales Forecasting: Recent BASES Model Experience in Europe and in the United States." Paper presented to the ESOMAR Conference, Vienna, Austria (September 2).

Little, John D.C. (1970). "Models and Managers: The Concept of a Decision Calculus," *Management Science* 16 (April): 466–85.

Luce, R. Duncan (1959). *Individual Choice Behavior.* New York: Wiley.

Mahajan, Vijay, Eitan Muller, and Subhash Sharma. (1984). "An Empirical Comparison of Awareness Forecasting Models of New Product Introduction," *Marketing Science* 3, no. 3 (summer): 179–206.

Narasimhan, Chakravarthi, and Subrata K. Sen. (1983). "New Product Models for Test Market Data," *Journal of Marketing* 1(47) (winter): 11–24.

Parfitt, J.H., and B.J.K. Collins (1968). "Use of Consumer Panels for Brand Share Prediction," *Journal of Marketing Research* 2, no. 5 (May): 131–45.

Pessemier, Edgar A. (1963). *Experimental Methods for Analyzing the Demand for Branded Consumer Goods with Applications to Problems in Marketing Strategy.* Pullman, Wash.: Washington University Press.

Pessemier, Edgar A., Philip Burger, Richard Teach, and Douglas Tigert (1971). "Using

Laboratory Brand Preference Scales to Predict Consumer Brand Purchases," *Management Science* 6, no. 17 (February): 371–85.

Pringle, Lewis G., R. Dale Wilson, and Edward I. Brody (1982). "NEWS: A Decision-oriented Model for New Product Analysis and Forecasting," *Marketing Science* 1, no. 1 (winter): 1–29.

Robinson, Patrick J. (1981). "Comparison of Pretest Market New Product Forecasting Models," in *New Product Forecasting*. Wind Yoram et al., eds. Lexington, Mass.: Lexington Books, pp. 181–204.

Robinson, William T. (1985). "Market Pioneering and Sustainable Market Share Advantages in Industrial Goods Manufacturing Industries." Paper presented at the Marketing Science Conference, Vanderbilt University, Nashville, Tenn. (March).

Silk, Alvin J., and Glen L. Urban (1978). "Pretest Market Evaluation of New Packaged Goods: A Model and Measurement Methodology," *Journal of Marketing Research* 2, no. 15 (May): 171–91.

Urban, Glen L., and John R. Hauser (1980). *Design and Marketing of New Products*. Englewood Cliffs, N.J.: Prentice-Hall.

Urban, Glen L., and Gerald M. Katz (1983). Pretest Market Models: Validation and Managerial Implications," *Journal of Marketing Research* 3, no. 20 (August): 221–34.

Urban, Glen L., Theresa Carter, Steven Gaskin and Zofia Mucha (1985). "Market Share Rewards to Pioneering Brands: An Empirical Analysis and Strategic Implications." Paper presented at the Marketing Science Conference, Vanderbilt University, Nashville, Tenn. (March). (Urban is at MIT.) A previous version appears in *Strategic Marketing and Management*, Howard Thomas and David Gardner, eds. New York: Wiley, pp. 239–52.

Wind, Yoram J. (1982). *Product Policy: Concepts, Methods, and Strategy*. Reading, Mass: Addison-Wesley, pp. 436–61.

Yankelovich, Skelly, and White, Inc. (1981). "LTM Estimating Procedures," in *New Product Forecasting*, Wind Yoram et al. eds. Lexington, Mass.: Lexington Books, pp. 249–67.

9
Advances and Issues in New-Product–Introduction Models

R. Dale Wilson
David K. Smith, Jr.

The decade of the 1980s has seen tremendous advances in the area of new-product forecasting and analysis models as they are applied to individual brand decisions. During the six-year period encompassing 1980–85, advances have included publications that review and evaluate various models, provide new information on established models, and delve into new areas and applications. The various new-product models made available through companys' in-house market research groups, consulting firms, research suppliers, and advertising agencies have been quite successful in providing forecasts and diagnostic information and are now firmly established as an important part of the modern marketing manager's repertoire of decision tools. As a result, these models comprise one of the most dynamic and important areas of marketing and thus are of interest to both the academic and practitioner communities. With the costs of new-product introductions continuing to increase rapidly (cf. *Fortune* [1985]), the importance of these models is unlikely to diminish.

In this chapter, we focus upon new-product models for individual brand introductions that rely on data stemming from early test-market results (i.e., test-market models) and from consumer research prior to the introduction of the brand into test market (pre–test-market models). Examples of such new-brand–introduction models include well-known tools such as ASSESSOR, BASES, COMP, LITMUS, LTM, NEWS, SPRINTER, and TRACKER. We make no attempt at dealing with innovation/diffusion models of new-product introductions (e.g., Mahajan and Muller [1979]) since they are considerably more difficult to apply to individual brand-level decisions (Narasimhan and Sen [1983], Wilson and Machleit [1985]).

The purpose of this chapter is threefold. First, we examine recent developments in new-brand–introduction modeling by reviewing the literature published between 1980 and 1985. Second, we identify and discuss a large number of areas for future research that would continue to expand our knowledge about new-product models, the role these models play in organizations, and the characteristics of new-brand successes and failures. Third, we use a new-product–introduction model developed by Luther (1985) as a mechanism to illustrate the trend toward the use of models that can be run on personal computers by individual managers. We briefly describe this model, present a sample run using previously published input data, and evaluate the model's characteristics.

Advances in the Literature of the 1980s

The literature on new-brand–introduction models published in the 1980s has contained numerous contributions. For the purpose of discussing these advances in the literature, we have classified these publications into four categories: (1) reviews and anthologies, (2) model evaluations, (3) new models and new information on established models, and (4) new areas and applications. To summarize this literature in each of the four categories, appendix 9A identifies the model(s) discussed, the publication's primary content, and its major contributions.

One of the most significant contributions of the 1980s was the publication of *New-Product Forecasting*, edited by Wind et al. (1981). This book contains several important chapters, with insight into using and evaluating new-brand–introduction models (e.g., Levine [1981], Robinson [1981]), updates on previously published models (e.g., Dodson [1981]), and new information on models that are available commercially but previously unpublished, such as COMP (Burger et al. [1981]), LTM (Yankelovich, Skelly, and White, Inc. [1981]), and the Hendry model (Rao [1981]). Another important contribution in the reviews and anthologies category is Wind's (1982, pp. 436–47; also in Wind et al. [1981]) presentation of a taxonomy for classifying new-product–forecasting models and a set of criteria for evaluating these models. Wind's evaluation criteria, which are highly relevant for academics and practitioners alike, deal with several aspects of predictive accuracy; the ability to develop, implement, and maintain a model; and diagnostic power. Because of the importance of Wind's criteria for evaluating new-product–forecasting models, they are presented in table 9–1. Other sets of criteria have been proposed and used by Robinson (1981) and Narasimhan and Sen (1983) and have been discussed by Wind and Mahajan (1981).

The article coauthored by Wind and Mahajan (1981) is quite interesting. Seven previously published review papers are summarized along with the criteria used to evaluate various types of new-product models. In addition, Wind and Mahajan call for a program of research designed to empirically evaluate competing models (which was partially executed two years later by Mahajan et al. [1984]). In a slightly different vein, Assmus (1975) describes the characteristics of several different pre–test-market and test-market models and nicely illustrates how various managerial-decision variables are incor-

Table 9–1
Criteria for Evaluating New-Product–Forecasting Models

Criteria	*Specific Elements*
1. Predictive accuracy	A. Short- and long-run forecasting accuracy in terms of various stages in the sales history of the product
	B. Ability to accurately forecast product triers, repeat purchasing, sales volume, and market penetration
	C. Ability to identify future turning points
	D. The economic consequences of forecasting error
2. Ability to develop, implement, and maintain the model	A. The technical skills (i.e., mathematical, statistical, and programming) required for the development and implementation of the model
	B. Management acceptance of the model and willingness to take action based upon the model's results
	C. The data required and the ability to generate it within acceptable time and cost constraints
	D. The time and cost required for model development, implementation, and maintenance
3. Diagnostic power	A. Forecasting for individual market segments
	B. Forecasting under various marketing strategies
	C. Forecasting under various competitive and environmental conditions
	D. Assessing the uncertainty involved in the forecasts

Source: Wind (1982, pp. 444–47).

porated into them. An important lesson to be taken from Assmus's work is his demonstration of (1) the identification of relevant decision variables and (2) the various ways they can be specified in new-product models.

In the area of model evaluations, three important contributions have been made since 1980. Both Robinson (1981) and Narasimhan and Sen (1983) provide *nonempirical* comparisons, while Mahajan et al. (1984) provide the first *empirical* test of competing models. Robinson's review of pre–test-market models is especially insightful since he evaluates several models that had not previously been published in the academic literature. He also discusses the similarities and positioning of six models and compares the output of the models with the information obtained from limited rollouts and conventional test markets. Narasimhan and Sen focus their attention on test-market models and critically evaluate six popular models according to several theoretical and managerial criteria. Of the models considered, Narasimhan and Sen found that the model proposed by Parfitt and Collins (1968) was superior for sales predictions alone and that TRACKER (Blattberg and Golanty [1978]) and NEWS (Pringle et al. [1982]) were superior when sales predictions and diagnostic information were required.

The work by Mahajan et al. (1984) is in the rather unique position of being a clearly important piece of research that makes a significant contribution, but yet it is exceptionally easy to criticize. Its contribution lies in the fact that it provides the first attempt at empirically comparing new-brand–introduction models. Also, several interesting philosophical and mechanical issues are addressed such as model specification, parameter estimation, and input-data requirements. However, only the *awareness* components of the models were tested without considering sales or market-share predictions. Also numerous other difficulties were identified by the authors of the five models that were compared. The most serious of these difficulties seem to include: (1) the alteration of the models to highly simplified forms that could be estimated by ordinary least squares, (2) the exclusion of several variables that clearly affect awareness (e.g., sampling and couponing activity), (3) problems with the data used in the test (or a misinterpretation of these data), and (4) problems in handling various aspects of awareness building such as *initial* awareness and forgetting. (See, for example, Blackburn and Clancy [1984], Dodson [1984], and Pringle et al. [1984].) Because of these and other problems, it is not surprising that Mahajan et al. results indicated few important differences in the performance of the models. At the same time, however, the Mahajan et al. paper raises many thought-provoking issues and lays the foundation for additional research comparing model performance.

Another important set of contributions has been the publication of new models as well as the publication of new information on well-established models. In this category, articles have appeared on models such as PLANNER (Roy and Nicolich [1980]), COMP (Burger et al. [1981]), the Ayer model (Dodson [1981]), the Hendry model (Rao [1981]), LTM (Yankelovich, Skelly, and White, Inc. [1981]), LITMUS (Blackburn and Clancy [1980, 1983]), NEWS (Pringle et al. [1982]), Wilson and Pringle [1982]), ASSESSOR (Urban and Hauser [1980, pp. 394–417], Urban and Katz [1983], Urban et al. [1983]), and PROD II (Zufryden [1985]). The specific nature of these articles as well as their contributions are summarized in appendix 9A.

Especially interesting are the publications on ASSESSOR by Urban and Katz (1983) and Urban et al. (1983). Taken together, these articles provide irrefutable evidence of the value of pre–test-market models in general and ASSESSOR in particular. Urban et al. (1983) even provide statements by users of the model attesting to its value. Without question, these articles are "must reading" for any serious student of new-product modeling.

Two new areas in new-product forecasting and analysis models have been tackled by John Hauser and his colleagues. Specifically, Hauser and Urban (1982) and Hauser et al. (1983) deal with new consumer-*durable*–brand introductions, while Hauser and Shugan (1983) and Hauser and Gaskin (1984) propose and test the Defender model. Defender is appropriate for use by a company wishing to defend its market position against *competitive* new-product introductions. While the work on consumer-durables introductions and Defender are still at an early stage of development, Hauser and his colleagues have already made ample progress in these areas.

Our review of approximately twenty-five publications on models of new-brand introductions indicates that a significant amount of progress has been made in the 1980s. These publications seem to have pushed the state of the art in new-product modeling forward by a substantial margin. Despite these advances, however, new frontiers remain to be conquered. Additional research is needed to provide new insights and to resolve numerous issues.

Open Issues and Needed Research

In reviewing the literature discussed thus far in this chapter, it quickly becomes apparent that a comprehensive program of research needs to be conducted that will fill rather large holes in the literature. In this section of the chapter, we present a research agenda designed to continue the recent momentum associated with new-product–introduction model work. The various aspects of this research agenda contain twenty-four specific issues or questions to be addressed and can be conveniently categorized into five groupings: (1) model validations and comparisons, (2) model extensions, (3) modeling philosophies, (4) organizational and operational considerations, and (5) marketing generalizations. Appendix 9B is designed to summarize the needs for future research.

Numerous research opportunities exist in the area of model validation and comparison. Despite recent works to validate models such as ASSESSOR, COMP, Defender, LITMUS, and NEWS, much more work needs to be done. Of particular interest would be documentation of the validation of widely used models such as the Ayer model, BASES, the Hendry model, LTM, SPEEDMARK, TRACKER, and other procedures that would benefit from such exposure. Additional emphasis should be placed on empirical model comparisons such as the pioneering work of Mahajan et al. (1984) as well on larger-scale simulations run under varying conditions. Also, since many models can be broken down into awareness, trial, and repeat-purchasing components, "replacement testing" (e.g., replacing one model's trial function with another model's trial function) may prove insightful. Other topics of interest include the determination of the relative importance of the awareness, trial, and repeat-purchase functions in determining forecasting accuracy; assessing the quality of the diagnostic information stemming from the models; assessing the uncertainty associated with model forecasts; and comparing individual model forecasts with subjective managerial judgment and with combined forecasts from several models.

In addition to validating and comparing existing models, there is considerable room for extending the models into new areas. Examples include the analysis of model predictions under varying competitive conditions; determining the value of optimizing the levels of marketing inputs (such as the advertising budget) for new-brand introductions; the inclusion of additional decision-process variables such as concept tests, product tests, communication tests, advertising strategy, and creative decisions; and the investigation of cannibalization caused by new-brand introductions. Also of interest would be research studies that focus on forecasts and diagnostics for line extensions rather than on "newer" products; the analysis of awareness, trial, and repeat forecasts by market segments; and the further development and validation of models for products other than consumer packaged goods.

In terms of modeling philosophies, there are three issues that have been identified as deserving attention. One important issue is the appropriateness of using "norms" from previous new-brand introductions in models such as TRACKER, and this leads to the larger issue of the overall similarity of new-product introductions across product categories and over time. Also, it would be interesting to attempt to determine the importance of price and other marketing controllable variables as model parameters. Another interesting issue is the appropriateness of low-involvement constructs as they relate to new-product modeling. Should low involvement be integrated into the models? If so, how should such models be specified?

Appendix 9B also identifies several organizational and operational considerations to be studied. These include the influence of management "enthusiasm" for the brand, the role of the "product champion," the cost and reward functions operating on managers, and the effect of microcomputers on new-brand–introduction modeling. The last category, marketing generalizations, is also quite important. It refers to the determination of the relative importance of the controllable and uncontrollable variables in new-product success, and it includes examples such as the importance of distribution increases and the nature of the advertising-media plan. Finally, we need to determine what if any generalizations about the new-product–introduction process can be made that are based on our experiences with new-brand–introduction models.

Illustration of a Current Trend: PC-based Models

Thus far, our literature review has examined recent developments and emergent issues related to new-product–forecasting models. A recent trend not yet examined, however, is the development within both new-product forecasting specifically and marketing in general of relatively simple models designed to run on personal computers. In its November 1985 issue, *Marketing News* lists approximately two dozen vendors of personal-computer–based models relating to radio media planning, sales analysis, product planning, advertising and promotional analysis, and forecasting. We turn now to a description and evaluation of one such personal computer-based model designed to address the question of new-product forecasting.

Description of the New Product Buyer Model

The New Product Buyer Model developed and marketed by Luther (1985) is one specific example of the generic microcomputer sort of model just described. Unlike the new-product–forecasting models alluded to earlier, the Luther model is positioned not as a decision tool but rather as a frame model designed to teach managers what key variables are likely to significantly impact sales of their new products. The objective of this model, however, like those positioned as decision tools, is to forecast market share. The dependent measures are the monthly share for the new product in units and dollars over a twelve-month period. Independent variables include levels of awareness over time, an awareness to trial percentage, depth of repeat data, and distribution percentages. Because the model is structured in four schedules and because the variables utilized vary from schedule to schedule, we turn now to a discussion of the structure of these schedules and the data they require.

Schedule 1: Penetration. The first schedule of the New Product Buyer Model deals with market penetration. Inputs made by the user include the number of potential buyers (1), the percentage of aware buyers who try the product (2), a schedule showing the percentage of potential buyers aware by month (3), and a schedule showing the product-distribution percentage by month (4).

Given these inputs, the model calculates the number of newly aware buyers each month by multiplying total potential buyers (1) by the percentage of potential buyers aware this month less the percentage for the previous month (from schedule 3). Cumulative monthly aware is a running total of the number of buyers aware of the product. New trial is computed by multiplying the newly aware each month by the awareness/trial percentage (2) and by the product-distribution percentage for that month (4). Cumulative trial is a running total of the number of buyers who have made the initial trial purchase. Potential buyers trying is the cumulative trial for each month divided by the total number of potential buyers (1).

Schedule 2: Repeat Purchasing. Inputs made by the user at this point include the average repeat-purchase cycle in months (5), the percentage of triers repeating once (6), the percentage of triers repeating twice (7), and the percentage of triers who repeat three times (8).

Given these inputs, the model calculates the number of first-, second-, and third-repeat purchases made each month. The number of first repeats is calculated by multiplying new triers (schedule 1) by input (6); the number of second repeats is the number of first repeaters multiplied by input (7), and the number of third repeats is the number of second repeaters multiplied by input (8). The timing of these repeat purchases is based on the repeat-purchase cycle (5); the underlying behavioral assumption is that no repeat purchase occurs until the previous purchase is used up. Given a four-month repeat-purchase cycle, therefore, no first repeats will occur until month 5, no second repeats until month 9, and no third repeats until month 13. The total-repeat column is a running total by month of all incidences of repeat behavior, while the total-transactions column is a running total of all incidences of either trial or repeat. The repeat/total-transaction percentage is simply the total number of repeat transactions over the twelve-month period divided by the total number of trial and repeat transactions over the same period.

Schedule 3: Unit and Dollar Volumes. Inputs made by the model user at this point include the average number of units per trial transaction (9), the average number of units per repeat transaction (10), and the manufacturer's price per unit (11).

Given these inputs, the model calculates the number of units consumed by triers each month by multiplying the number of new triers (schedule 1) by the average units per trial (9) figure. The number of units consumed each month by repeaters is calculated by multiplying the total number of repeat transactions by month (schedule 3) by the average number of units per repeat (10) input; the total-units column is a running total that sums the trial and repeat units. The dollar trial, repeat, and total figures are calculated by multiplying the unit figures from the first part of this schedule by the manufacturer's price per unit.

Schedule 4: Share of Market. Inputs made by the user at this point include the average retail-selling price (12), the size of the total market in units (13), and the size of the total market in dollars (14).

Given these inputs, the model calculates the incremental unit and dollar shares of market for the new product on a monthly basis. Monthly unit shares are calculated by dividing monthly unit volumes by the total market in units (13). Monthly dollar shares are calculated by multiplying monthly unit sales by the average retail-selling price (12) and then dividing each monthly total by the total unit market (13) times that same average retail-selling price (12). Note that the model produces incremental monthly unit-

and dollar-share forecasts, rather than cumulative estimates of unit and dollar shares.

Trial Run of the Model

While the Luther model is positioned as a teaching tool rather than as a decision aid, the issue of whether it could be used as a managerial-decision tool is an interesting question. As a first step in the effort to evaluate the usefulness of the Luther model, the authors made a trial run using data from a case history of the NEWS new-product–forecasting model reported by Pringle et al. (1982). Table 4 from that article provided values for most of the thirteen inputs required to run the Luther model.

Because the data used to run NEWS do not correspond exactly with the data necessary to run the Luther model, certain assumptions and adjustments were made, including the following:

1. NEWS inputs not required by the Luther model (initial trial, initial repeat, the media budget, and the attention coefficient) were ignored.
2. The NEWS "Loyalty" figure was used as a surrogate for the percentage of first-repeat purchasers who will make a second-repeat purchase; the "Maximum Loyalty" figure was used as a surrogate for the percentage of second-repeat purchasers who will make a third-repeat purchase.
3. The NEWS model includes purchases by "initially aware" buyers, that is, those aware of the product before advertising begins. Because the Luther model does not include purchases by this group, the 8 percent initially aware figure from the case history was changed to 0. This adjustment insures that both initially aware buyers and buyers who become aware through advertising are included in both analyses.
4. Because NEWS does not require users to input an awareness schedule, it was necessary to create one. Levels of awareness were generated by dividing cumulative gross rating points (GRPs) in each period by the total number of GRPs in all three periods and then multiplying these percentages by the NEWS "maximum-awareness" figure, which was redefined to be the level of awareness achieved by the third purchase period, when all GRPs have been purchased.
5. The NEWS forecast based on the case data covered a period of one year. Given the four-month purchase cycle and the fact that levels of awareness change between (rather than within) purchase cycles, all forecast data generated by the Luther model over a twelve-month period is available by looking only at the results for months 0, 1, 5, and 9. In the interests of space, our trial-run printouts in table 9–2 show only those results.

Table 9–2
Sample Run of the New-Product–Buyer Model

Schedule 1   Penetration

				Assumptions
Total number potential buyers (000)				52,200
Conversion awareness to trial				23.00%
Distribution reduces trial 100%				

		Awareness				Trial	
Month	Potential Buyers Aware	Newly Aware (000)	Cumulative Aware (000)	Product Distribution	New Trial (000)	Cumulative Trial (000)	Potential Buyers Trying
0	0.00%	0	0	0.00%	0	0	0
1	41.00	21,402	21,402	62.00	3,052	3,052	5.85%
5	68.00	14,094	35,496	77.00	2,496	5,548	10.63
9	92.00	12,528	48,024	89.00	2,564	8,112	15.54

Schedule 2   Repeat purchasing

				Assumptions
Average repeat-purchase cycle (months):				4
Percent triers repeat once:				47.00%
Percent triers repeat twice:				76.00%
Percent repeat twice repeat $3\times$:				95.00%

Month	New Triers (000)	First Repeat (000)	Second Repeat (000)	Third Repeat (000)	Total Repeat (000)	Total Trans (000)	Repeat % Total Trans
0	0				0	0	
1	3,052				0	3,052	
5	2,496	1,434	0	0	1,434	3,930	
9	2,564	1,173	1,090	0	2,263	4,829	
Total	8,112	2,608	1,090	0	3,698	11,810	31.31%

Given these adjustments and assumptions, it was possible to run the Luther model and to make unit- and dollar-share forecasts for the new product at the end of the first year of sales. As indicated in table 9–2, the Luther model forecast for this product was 19,266,000 units out of a total market of 305,000,000 units, which is a 6.32 share. This is lower than the 7.1 share that was actually achieved and slightly further from the actual figure than the NEWS forecast of a 7.6 share.

Evaluation of the Model

As mentioned earlier, Wind (1982) suggests that the following three categories of variables should be used for the evaluation of new-product–forecasting models: predictive accuracy, ability to develop and implement the model, and diagnostic power. Using these general criteria, it is possible to

Schedule 3   Unit and dollar volumes

				Assumptions
Average number units trial per transaction:				1.60
Average number units repeat per transaction:				1.70
Manufacturer's price per unit:				0.50

| | Units | | | Dollars | | | Repeat |
Month	Trial (000)	Repeat (000)	Total (000)	Trial (000)	Repeat (000)	Total (000)	% Total Dollars
0	0	0	0	$0	$0	$0	
1	4,883	0	4,883	$2,442	$0	$2,442	
5	3,994	2,438	6,432	$1,997	$1,219	$3,216	
9	4,103	3,848	7,951	$2,052	$1,924	$3,975	
Total	12,980	6,286	19,266	$6,490	$3,143	$9,633	32.63%

Schedule 4   Share of market

Average retail selling price:	1.00
Total market in units (000):	305,000
Total market in dollars (000):	$179,411

Month	Unit Share Market	Dollar Share Market
0	0.00%	0.00%
1	1.60	2.72
5	2.11	3.59
9	2.61	4.43

make several evaluative comments on the Luther New Product Buyer Model. First, given the assumptions and adjustments previously set forth, its prediction was about 11 percent lower than the actual share achieved by the product and somewhat less accurate than the NEWS prediction. In other words, the predictive accuracy of the Luther model in this one instance was fair. Because we have only this one experience with the model, however, no validation history is yet established; and no claims about the predictive accuracy of the model can be made.

Second, the ability of most users to develop and implement the model should be excellent. This New Product Buyer Model, as well as the other models presented by Luther, run within Lotus 1-2-3. Since Luther provides copies of his models to all seminar members, any participant possessing a personal computer and Lotus 1-2-3 can run the New Product Buyer Model. In other words, access to the model is very easy and the incremental cost of using it is very small. In addition, the fact that the model operates within Lotus means that reprogramming the model to take account of unique product situations and/or characteristics is simple and that much more complicated programming is possible if necessary. Furthermore, since Lotus is a widely used business spreadsheet program, time and dollar costs of learning how to work with the Luther model are small, while the probability that management will be able to understand the process being utilized should be high.

Regarding diagnostic power (the third general criterion mentioned by Wind), the Luther model has little to offer managers. While changes in marketing efforts could be factored into the model indirectly (for example, a manager might generate alternative awareness schedules depending on the magnitude and/or timing of promotional efforts), the model does not directly consider promotional activities. Similarly, while managers might modify the size of the potential market depending on the price established for the product, the model does not directly consider the effect of price on demand. Furthermore, the model gives no estimation of the accuracy of the forecast nor of a range within which actual results are likely to lie.

Conclusion

In this chapter, we have reviewed the literature on new-product forecasting and analysis modeling that has been published during 1980–85. In the process, we have identified and discussed numerous contributions to this important area and have outlined a program of research that would alleviate many of the open issues in new-product–forecasting research. In addition, we have illustrated an important trend in new-product modeling (as well as in marketing modeling in general)—the development and use of personal-computer–based models that are designed to aid managerial decision making. The features of a simple new-product model were discussed, and it was evaluated according to several criteria that included a limited empirical test of the model. While the future holds a great deal of promise for the use of PC-based models, it will be interesting to track the *quality* of the decisions that are made on the basis of these models. Further research is necessary to determine whether the increased access of PC-based models will promote or hinder our progress in new-brand introductions.

Appendix 9A: Advances in the Literature

Classification and Author(s)	Model(s) Discussed	Primary Content of the Work	Major Contribution(s)
Reviews and anthologies			
Wind, Mahajan, and Cardozo (1981)	Many	Gives a variety of readings on pre–test-market and test-market forecasting models as well as other new-product–forecasting topics.	Pulls together a large amount of information on new-product models; provides previously unpublished information on several models.
Wind (1982)	Several different models	Develops a taxonomy for classifying new-product–forecasting models and a set of criteria for evaluating these models.	Both the classification framework and the evaluation criteria were new contributions. Both have stimulated thinking on the attributes associated with new-product–forecasting models.
Levine (1981)	Pillsbury's Supertest model and the Hendry model	Describes the appropriate uses and limitations of pre–test-market research.	Provides insight from a practitioner's point of view; briefly describes some of the elements of Supertest.
Assmus (1981)	ASSESSOR, TRACKER, Ayer model, DEMON, NEWPROD, SPRINTER, Hendry model	Describes the characteristics of several models.	Illustrates how various managerial-decision variables are incorporated into the models; suggests relevant variables and discusses how the models are specified to incorporate them.

Classification and Author(s)	Model(s) Discussed	Primary Content of the Work	Major Contribution(s)
Wind and Mahajan (1981)	None	Synthesizes previous review papers from several areas of new-product forecasting.	Uses previous reviews to evaluate the current status of the models; identifies six different sets of criteria used to describe and evaluate the models; calls for a program of research designed to empirically evaluate competing models.
Model evaluations Robinson (1981)	ASSESSOR, SPEEDMARK, COMP, LTM, Tele-Research, ASI Research models	Evaluates each model according to 37 criteria; discusses the similarities and positioning of the various models.	Gives a well-thought-out set of criteria for evaluating the models; provides a great deal of information previously unpublished in the academic literature; compares the models with the information stemming from limited rollouts and conventional test markets.
Narasimhan and Sen (1983)	Fourt/Woodlock, Parfitt/Collins, STEAM, SPRINTER, Eskin, Nakanishi, NEWPROD, TRACKER, NEWS	Critically evaluates test-market models according to theoretical and managerial criteria.	Provides a succinct review of the models; assesses the advantages and disadvantages of each model; discusses how the models stack up against each criterion; selects the best models for sales prediction alone (the Parfitt/Collins) or

			sales prediction and diagnostic information (TRACKER and NEWS).
Mahajan, Muller, and Sharma (1984)	TRACKER, NEWS, LITMUS, Dodson/Muller, Ayer model	Uses the awareness components of new-product models to generate awareness forecasts in a limited empirical model comparison.	Provides the first published evidence on the quality of awareness forecasts stemming from new-product models; raises many interesting philosophical and mechanical issues regarding model specification, parameter estimation, input data requirements, etc. Authors of the five models compared respond with their comments.

New models and new information on established models

Roy and Nicolich (1980)	PLANNER	Describes the model and its performance.	Provides the first published information on this unique model; includes validation data.
Burger, Gundee, and Lavidge (1981)	COMP	Describes the model, its uses, and its performance.	Provides a great deal of insight into the model; describes the use of a simulated shopping experiment to serve as input. Several submodels are described in detail; a few validation results are presented.

Classification and Author(s)	Model(s) Discussed	Primary Content of the Work	Major Contribution(s)
Dodson (1981)	Ayer model	Essentially updates the N.W. Ayer model originally published by Claycamp and Liddy (1969); also relates practical experience with test-market models.	Provides important insights into the evolution and current application of the model and the managerial value of test-market models in general.
Rao (1981)	Hendry model	Describes the Hendry procedure for new-product–sales forecasting.	Summarizes the PARSHARE component of the model rather nicely; includes some of the technical aspects of the model as well as an actual application of the procedure.
Yankelovich, Skelly, and White, Inc. (1981)	LTM	Describes the LTM model, how data are collected, and how estimates are made.	Does a good job of describing the model for the first time in the literature; discusses the use of simulated test-market experiments and the data stemming from them. The artificiality of the data is nicely assessed.
Blackburn and Clancy (1980)	LITMUS	Describes the model in a great deal of detail by emphasizing model structure and validation.	Provides insight into how the model was developed; does a good job specifying the mathematical details of the model. Empirical results are categorized according to the accuracy of the forecasts.

Blackburn and Clancy (1983)	LITMUS II	Describes the updated version of LITMSU.	Nicely describes the evolution of the model as well as why and how the modifications came about; provides a good lesson in evolutionary model building.
Pringle, Wilson, and Brody (1982)	NEWS	Thoroughly describes the model and its mathematical specification; provides validation data as well as information on parameter estimation and a detailed case study of the model's usage.	Describes how the model evolved; provides a great amount of technical information; clarifies the specification, input-data requirements, and other details of this popular but previously unpublished model.
Wilson and Pringle (1982)	NEWS, SPRINTER, TRACKER	Compares the three models on a variety of (nonempirical) dimensions.	Clarifies the similarities and differences among the models; corrects some misperceptions about the models; updates previously published information; suggests several avenues of future research.
Urban and Hauser (1980, pp. 394–417)	ASSESSOR	Describes the model, how it is used, its validation, and how input data are collected.	Provides considerable information above and beyond that available in the original description of the model (Silk and Urban [1978]). Emphasis is placed on the application of the model to actual new-product introductions.

Classification and Author(s)	Model(s) Discussed	Primary Content of the Work	Major Contribution(s)
Urban and Katz (1983)	ASSESSOR	Analyzes the predictive accuracy of the model; emphasizes the value of the information stemming from an application of ASSESSOR.	Nicely looks at the managerial aspects of pre-test-market modeling with ASSESSOR; documents the value of the model; discusses the risks of not having information coming from pre–test-market and test-market procedures.
Urban, Katz, Hatch, and Silk (1983)	ASSESSOR	Documents the model further with emphasis on its usage by managers; deals with the impact of the model in the marketplace.	Firmly establishes the substantial value of pre–test-market models in general and ASSESSOR in particular; provides comments made by users of the model.
Zufryden (1985)	PROD II	Describes the features of a new microcomputer-based model.	Lays out major elements of the model in nontechnical, easily understood terms. The model is integrated into an a microcomputer software system.
New areas and applications Hauser and Urban (1982)	Consumer-durables model	Discusses several different theoretical phenomena from economics and marketing that likely affect consumers' purchase behavior for durable products; also discusses measurement and estimation procedures.	Provides the first published attempt at modeling *durable-*product introductions; proposes a framework for developing a model and provides new food for thought.

Hauser, Roberts, and Urban (1983)	Consumer-durables model	Presents a modeling and measurement methodology for forecasting sales of a new durable product prior to market introduction; uses a series of laboratory measures; reports top-line results on a minitest in the automobile market.	Provides the first empirical results for a forecasting model for new durable products; lays of a great deal of detail for a model still being developed; discusses a series of challenges that must be faced in building a durable-forecasting system.
Hauser and Shugan (1983)	Defender	Develops a model that can be used by a firm wishing to defend its share of the market against competitive new-product introductions; describes a consumer-market model and several theorems that indicate the activities to be undertaken by managers.	Provides the first attempt at looking at a defensive–marketing-strategy model; provides a great deal of insight into the problem and suggests many areas for future research.
Hauser and Gaskin (1984)	Defender	Provides two applications of the model in order to test it in a realistic environment.	Provides considerable insights into how the Defender model is operationalized; provides model tests in order to assess the model's predictive validity.

Appendix 9B: A Research Agenda

Area of Interest	Specific Issue or Question to be Addressed
Model validations and comparisons	Continued validation of existing models. Recent examples have been provided by Burger et al. (1981), Blackburn and Clancy (1980), Pringle et al. (1982), Urban and Katz (1983), and Hauser and Gaskin (1984), but a great deal more work needs to be conducted in this area.
	Comparison of new-product–model forecasts with subjective managerial forecasts based upon judgment and experience. Does the use of a model lead to better forecasts and diagnostic information as opposed to no formal model?
	Does the use of forecasts generated by combining forecasts from individual models yield better results than the use of an individual model in isolation? How can model triangulation improve forecasting results?
	Additional emphasis should be placed on empirical model comparisons. The work of Mahajan et al. (1984) needs to be extended to other dependent variables, models, and competitive situations. One question to be addressed is whether the more sophisticated models (e.g., Hendry, SPRINTER MOD III) outperform simpler models.
	The assessment of the uncertainty involved in new-product modeling needs additional work.
	How do we assess the quality of the diagnostic information provided by new-product models? Do the various models differ substantially in the quality of their diagnostics? Are new-product decisions any better due to this diagnostic information?
	Numerous opportunities exist for model testing and comparison research. Examples include the use of simulation, "replacement testing," and alternative "goodness-of-fit" measures.
	What are the most important "ingredients" in new-product models? One hypothesis supported by the authors suggests that the key factor in modeling new-brand introductions is trial. The awareness and repeat-purchasing components would seem to be less crucial than the trial component.

Area of Interest	*Specific Issue or Question to be Addressed*
Model extensions	The effect of varying competitive and economic conditions on the accuracy of model forecasts.

Most new-product models forecast sales only up to one year past the brand's introduction. Can these models be used to forecast sales after the first year, but prior to the brand's maturity?

What is the value of providing *optimal* levels of advertising, promotional spending, price, and so on for the introduction of a new brand? How accurate are the sales forecasts stemming from these optimal levels, and how accurate are these optimal levels themselves?

Models need to be expanded to incorporate a more complete decision process in order to determine the results of concept tests, product tests, communication tests, advertising-strategy and creative decisions, and so on.

How important is the distinctiveness of the product being introduced in new-product–forecasting situations? More attention needs to be paid to "line extensions" rather than products that are clearly "new." This need is due to the trend toward more line extensions that are currently being introduced (*Marketing News* [1986]). As a result, the entire range of the degree-of-innovation scale needs to be investigated.

The issue of cannibalization needs to be addressed in detail. Although several models provide cannibalization estimates, we have no knowledge as to their accuracy.

Model forecasts need to be generated and assessed by market segments. There is virtually no information on this important aspect of new-product–model performance and analysis.

More work needs to be conducted on the development and validation of models for non–consumer-packaged goods such as consumer durables (à la Hauser and Urban [1982], Hauser et al. [1983]), consumer services, industrial products, health-care products, and business-to-business products and services.

Area of Interest	*Specific Issue or Question to be Addressed*
Modeling philosophies	How does the use of "norms" from previous new-brand introductions in models such as TRACKER and the Ayer model affect model validity? Related to this is the larger issue of how "similar" new-product introductions are across product categories and over time. See Wilson and Pringle (1982) and Pringle et al. (1982) for more details.
	What is the importance of the explicit inclusion of the *price* of the new brand in new-product models (see, for example, Narasimhan and Sen's 1983 criticism of NEWS on this attribute) as well as other controllable marketing variables? What is the impact of not including such variables?
	How can recent developments in the area of low-involvement research (e.g., Antil [1984], Robertson [1976]) be incorporated into new-product models? Low-involvement constructs are highly touted by their supporters, but they have had virtually no impact on the decision-modeling literature (e.g., Wilson and Machleit [1985]). Incorporation of these developments should lead to considerable insight into the viability of the low-involvement area.
Organizational and operational considerations	How do management "enthusiasm" for a new brand and other organizational factors (such as the role of the "product champion") interact with new-product modeling? For example, how do organizations use model forecasts to justify decisions that have already been made?
	More research needs to be focused on various cost functions and reward functions operating on managers in new-product–modeling situations. Urban and Katz (1983) have laid the foundation in this area, but additional work would provide considerable insight.
	What is the effect of the increased usage of microcomputers on new-product–forecasting models? Since these models are currently in evidence (e.g., Luther [1985], Zufryden [1985], we need to evaluate their characteristics, their accuracy, and their impact on organizational decision making.
Marketing generalizations	How important are the various controllable variables and uncontrollable factors in new-product success? For example, how important is distribution build

Area of Interest	Specific Issue or Question to be Addressed
	(both the quantity and speed of distribution increases) and the nature of the advertising-media plan in influencing the sales of a new brand?
	What empirical generalizations can be made about new-product–marketing response stemming from validated case studies of new-brand introductions?

References

Antil, J.H. (1984). "Conceptualization and Operationalization of Involvement," in *Advances in Consumer Research*, 11, Thomas C. Kinnear, ed. Provo, Utah: Association for Consumer Research, pp. 203–9.

Assmus, G. (1975). "NEWPROD: The Design and Implementation of a New Product Model," *Journal of Marketing* 39 (January): 16–23.

Blackburn, J.D., and K.J. Clancy (1980). "LITMUS: A New Product Planning Model," in *Proceedings of the ORSA/TIMS Special Interest Conference on Market Measurement and Analysis*, R.P. Leone, ed. Providence, R.I.: Institute of Management Science, pp. 182–93.

——— (1983). "LITMUS II: An Evolutionary Step in New Product Planning Models from Marketing Plan Evaluation to Marketing Plan Generation," in *ORSA/TIMS Marketing Science Conference Proceedings*, F.S. Zufryden, ed. Providence, R.I.: Institute of Management Science, pp. 48–54.

——— (1984). "Comment," *Marketing Science* 3 (summer): 198–201.

Blattberg, R., and J. Golanty (1978). "Tracker: An Early Test Market Forecasting and Diagnostic Model for New Product Planning," *Journal of Marketing Research* 15 (May): 192–202.

Burger, P.C., H. Gundee, and R. Lavidge (1981). "COMP: A Comprehensive System for the Evaluation of New Products," in *New-Product Forecasting*, Y. Wind, V. Mahajan, and R.N. Cardozo, eds. Lexington, Mass.: Lexington Books, pp. 269–83.

Claycamp, H.J., and L.E. Liddy (1969). "Prediction of New Product Performance: An Analytical Approach," *Journal of Marketing Research* 6 (November): 414–20.

Dodson, J.A. (1981). "Application and Utilization of Test-Market-Based New-Product Forecasting Models," in *New-Product Forecasting*, Y. Wind, V. Mahajan, and R.N. Cardozo, eds. Lexington, Mass.: Lexington Books, pp. 411–21.

——— (1984). "Comment," *Marketing Science* 3 (summer): 202–3.

Fortune (1985). "Products of the Year," 112 (December 9): 106–12.

Hauser, J.R., and S.P. Gaskin (1984). "Application of the Defender Consumer Model," *Marketing Science* 3 (fall): 327–51.

Hauser, J.R., and S.M. Shugan (1983). "Defensive Marketing Strategies," *Marketing Science* 2 (fall): 319–54.

Hauser, J.R., and G.L. Urban (1982). "Prelaunch Forecasting of New Consumer

Durables: Ideas on a Consumer Value-Priority Model," in *Analytic Approaches to Product and Marketing Planning: The Second Conference,* R.K. Srivastava and A.D. Shocker, eds. Cambridge, Mass.: Marketing Science Institute, pp. 276–96.

Hauser, J.R., J.H. Roberts, and G.L. Urban (1983). "Forecasting Sales of a New Consumer Durable," in *Advances and Practices of Marketing Science 1983,* F.S. Zufryden, ed. Providence, R.I.: Institute of Management Science, pp. 115–28.

Levine, J. (1981). "Pre–Test-Market Research of New Packaged-Goods Products—A User Orientation," in *New-Product Forecasting,* Y. Wind, V. Mahajan, and R.N. Cardozo, eds. Lexington, Mass.: Lexington Books, pp. 285–90.

Luther W.M. (1985). "How to Use Personal Computers in Marketing and Sales Management," American Management Association Seminar, New York, July 8–10.

Mahajan, V., and E. Muller (1979). "Innovation Diffusion and New Product Growth Models in Marketing," *Journal of Marketing* 43 (fall): 55–68.

Mahajan, V., E. Muller, and S. Sharma (1984). "An Empirical Comparison of Awareness Forecasting Models of New Product Introduction," *Marketing Science* 3 (summer): 179–206.

Marketing News (1986). "Firm: Consumers Cool to New Products," 20 (January 3): 1, 45.

Narasimhan, C., and S.K. Sen (1983). "New Product Models for Test Market Data," *Journal of Marketing* 47 (winter): 11–24.

Parfitt, J.H., and B.J.K. Collins (1968). "Use of Consumer Panels for Brand-Share Prediction," *Journal of Marketing Research* 5 (May): 131–45.

Pringle, L.G., R.D. Wilson, and E.I. Brody (1982). "NEWS: A Decision-Oriented Model for New Product Analysis and Forecasting," *Marketing Science* 1 (winter): 1–29.

———— (1984). "Issues in Comparing the Awareness Component of New Product Models," *Marketing Science* 3 (summer); 203–5.

Rao, V.R. (1981). "New Product Sales Forecasting Using the Hendry System," in *New-Product Forecasting,* Y. Wind, V. Mahajan, and R.N. Cardozo, eds. Lexington Mass.: Lexington Books, pp. 499–527.

Robertson, T.S. (1976). "Low Commitment Consumer Behavior," *Journal of Advertising Research* 16 (April): 19–24.

Robinson, P.J. (1981). "Comparison of Pre–Test-Market New-Product Forecasting Models," in *New-Product Forecasting,* Y. Wind, V. Mahajan, and R.N. Cardozo, eds. Lexington, Mass.: Lexington Books, pp. 181–204.

Roy, R.A., and M.J. Nicolich (1980). "PLANNER: A Market-Positioning Model," *Journal of Advertising Research* 20 (April): 61–66.

Silk, A.J., and G.L. Urban (1978). "Pre-Test Market Evaluation of New Packaged Goods: A Model and Measurement Methodology," *Journal of Marketing Research* 15 (May): 171–91.

Urban, G.L., and J.R. Hauser (1980). *Design and Marketing of New Products.* Englewood Cliffs, N.J.: Prentice-Hall.

Urban, G.L., and G.M. Katz (1983). "Pre-Test Market Models: Validation and Managerial Implications," *Journal of Marketing Research* 20 (August): 221–34.

Urban, G.L., G.M. Katz, T.E. Hatch, and A.J. Silk (1983). "The ASSESSOR Pre-Test Market Evaluation System," *Interfaces* 13 (December): 38–59.

Wilson, R.D., and K.A. Machleit (1985). "Advertising Decision Models: A Managerial Review," *Current Issues and Research in Advertising 1985*, 2. Ann Arbor: University of Michigan, pp. 99–187.

Wilson, R.D., and Pringle, L.G. (1982). "Modeling New Product Introductions: A Comparison of NEWS, SPRINTER, and TRACKER," in *Analytic Approaches to Product and Marketing Planning: The Second Conference*, R.K. Srivastava and A.D. Shocker, eds. Cambridge, Mass.: Marketing Science Institute, pp. 297–311.

Wind, Y.J. (1982). *Product Policy: Concepts, Methods, and Strategy*. Reading, Mass.: Addison-Wesley.

Wind, Y.J., and V. Mahajan (1981). "A Reexamination of New Product Theories and Applications," in *1981 Marketing Educators' Conference Proceedings*, Kenneth Bernhardt et al., eds. Chicago: American Marketing Association, pp. 358–63.

Wind, Y.J., Mahajan, V. and R.N. Cardozo, eds. (1981). *New-Product Forecasting*. Lexington, Mass.: Lexington Books.

Yankelovich, Skelly, and White, Inc. (1981). "LTM Estimating Procedures," in *New-Product Forecasting*, Y. Wind, V. Mahajan, and R.N. Cardozo, eds. Lexington, Mass.: Lexington Books, pp. 249–67.

Zufryden, F.S. (1985). "PROD II: A Model for Predicting from Tracking Studies," *Journal of Advertising Research* 25 (April/May): 45–51.

Part V
New-Product–Diffusion Modeling and Its Development

D iffusion is the process by which an innovation is communicated through certain channels over time among the members of a social system (Rogers [1983]). Understanding the diffusion process of new products is an indispensable step for their success once the products are introduced in the market. The objective of this part is to review the major developments in the modeling of new-product diffusion and innovation over the past decades. In chapter 10, Norton and Bass present a new model encompassing the two concepts: diffusion and substitution processes of new technologies. This chapter has previously been published by *Management Science*. In chapter 11, Takada investigates the diffusion process of durable goods in international markets.

The Basic Diffusion Models

Diffusion models prior to 1969 are classified as pure innovative or pure imitative (Lilien and Kotler [1983]). A pure innovative model, such as a market-penetration model by Fourt and Woodlock (1960), assumes that innovative or external influences are operative in the diffusion process, while a pure imitative model assumes that the only effects on the process are driven by imitation or word of mouth. A model of the imitative-diffusion process developed by Fisher and Pry (1971) was widely applied to industrial products. Their technological-substitution model has less predictive power, however, when little data are available and when it is unclear that one technology completely substitutes for another. Blackman et al. (1973) and Blackman (1974), building on the work of Mansfield (1961, 1968), provide a means of making projections for substitution in the absence of an adequate historical data base. Among the most well known and widely applied diffusion models is the one by Bass (1969). His model has integrated innovative and imitative models. The premise of the Bass model is that initial purchases of a product are made by both "innovators" and "imitators." Innovators are not influenced in the timing of their initial purchase by the number of previous buyers. The model states that the likelihood of purchase at time T given that no purchase has yet been made is given by a linear function of the number of previous adopters. Thus, $f(T)/[1-F(T)] = p + qF(T)$, where $f(T)$ is the likelihood of purchase at time T and $F(T)$ is the fraction of the ultimate potential that has adopted by time T. Constants p and q are referred to as the coefficients of innovation and imitation, respectively.

Extension of the Bass Model

The Bass model has been adopted, extended, and employed by marketing researchers (Nevers [1972], Dodds [1973]) and used by many companies for forecasting purposes (Bass [1980]). Mahajan and Muller (1979) provided an extensive review of the developments of alternative model specifications. One of the general and comprehensive extensions is provided by Dodson and Muller (1978) proposing a three-stage, consumer-adoption process. Horsky and Simon (1983) included advertising among a variety of extended models incorporating the marketing-decision variables. Bass (1980), Bass and Bultez (1982), Dolan and Jeuland (1981), and Robinson and Lakhani (1975) developed the models with a price variable. Bass (1980) incorporated price in a dynamic demand model in which the diffusion process is exogenous and does not interact with price, as opposed to the models by Robinson and Lakhani and by Dolan and Jeuland in which price interacts with the diffusion process. The model indicates that the myopically optimal price will decline monotonically, in contrast with the optimal multiperiod price in the Robinson and Lakhani formulation that the price rises at first and later declines. Furthermore, Bass and Bultez showed that the multiperiod optimal price is always less than the myopically optimal price and therefore also is monotonically declining.

Norton and Bass developed a new model presented at the workshop that provided the impetus for this book. Encompassing both diffusion and substitution, the model is believed to be the first to combine the two concepts. In chapter 10, they illustrate the development of their model based upon the Bass model and show that the model works extremely well on the data from the semiconductor industry involving successive generations of dynamic and static random-access memory devices through estimation of parameters by nonlinear simultaneous equation regression. An empirical comparison of the models shows that their model outperforms a technological-substitution model by Fisher and Pry (1971). Consequently, the model demonstrates impressive forecasting performance.

New Estimation Procedures

Another development of the new-product–diffusion models is new estimation procedures. The parameters of the original Bass model have been estimated through conducting regression analysis to the discrete analog model in many studies. Bass (1969) provided corrections for possible biases of the estimated parameter values. This procedure has been widely used since it is easy to implement. However, this procedure suffers from certain shortcomings. Parameter estimates are sometimes unstable or produce wrong signs. The standard errors for the estimates p, q, and m are not available since they are nonlinear functions of parameters of the discrete analog model. There is a time-interval bias since discrete time-series data are used for estimating a continuous-time model. To solve these problems, alternative estimation procedures have been suggested in the marketing literature. Mahajan et al. (1986) provide comprehensive review of these procedures with empirical evaluation, including a maximum-likelihood estimation (MLE) procedure by Schmittlein and Mahajan (1982) and nonlinear least squares estimation procedures by Srinivasan and Mason (1986) and Jain and Rao (1985).

The Bass model is widely applied to a variety of durable goods, and it is empirically proven that the model performs very well in predicting future peak time and demand as indicated in the marketing literature. Most of the applications are confined to the U.S. markets, however, and the number of studies in other markets is limited. One major study investigating the U.S. and overseas markets was conducted by Heeler and Hustad (1980). They examined forecasting validity of the Bass model for fifteen products in a variety of countries by estimating parameters of the discrete analog model using the OLS method to the comprehensive data set. Empirical findings indicate some problems with the forecasting capability of the model. For instance, frequently the time of peak is estimated too early, perhaps reflecting different communication patterns and economic restraints than in the United States. In chapter 11 Takada applies the nonlinear estimation procedures to the data of a wide variety of products in international markets. Contrary to the previous studies, his empirical results indicate that the Bass model has a very good fit to the data with reasonable accuracy of predicting the peak period of sales and peak magnitude. In particular, the nonlinear estimation outperforms the OLS estimation for predicting the time of peak sales.

References

Bass, Frank M. (1969). "A New Product Growth Model for Consumer Durables," *Management Science* 15 (January): 215–227.

———— (1980). "The Relationship between Diffusion Rates, Experience Curve, and Demand Elasticities for Consumer Durable Technological Innovations," *Journal of Business* 53: S51–67.

Bass, Frank M., and A.V. Bultez (1982). "A Note on Optimal Strategic Pricing of Technological Innovations," *Marketing Science* 1 (fall): 371–78.

Blackman, A.W., Jr. (1974). "The Market Dynamics of Technological Substitutions," *Technological Forecasting and Social Change* 6 (February): 41–63.

Blackman, A.W., Jr., E.J. Seligman, and G.C. Solgliero (1973). "An Innovation Index Based upon Factor Analysis," *Technological Forecasting and Social Change* 4: 301–16.

Dodds, W. (1973). "An Application of the Bass Model in Long-Term New Product Forecasting," *Journal of Marketing Research* 10 (August): 308–11.

Dodson, J.A., and E. Muller (1978). "Models of New Product Diffusion through Advertising and Word-of-Mouth," *Management Science* 24 (November): 1568–78.

Dolan, R.J., and A.P. Jeuland (1981). "Experience Curves and Dynamic Demand Models: Implications for Optimal Pricing Strategies," *Journal of Marketing* 45 (winter),: 52–62.

Fisher J.C., and R.H. Pry (1971). "A Simple Substitution Model for Technological Change," *Technological Forecasting and Social Change* 2 (May): 75–88.

Fourt, L.A., and J.W. Woodlock (1960). "Early Prediction of Market Success for Grocery Products," *Journal of Marketing* 25 (October: 31–38.

Heeler, R.M., and T.P. Hustad (1980). "Problems in Predicting New Product Growth for Consumer Durables," *Management Science* 26 (October): 1007–20.

Horsky, D., and L.S. Simon (1983). "Advertising and the Diffusion of New Products," *Marketing Science* 2 (winter): 1–17.

Jain, D., and R.C. Rao (1985). "Effects of Price on the Demand for Durables." Working paper. School of Management and Administration, University of Texas at Dallas.

Lilien, G.L., and P. Kotler (1983). *Marketing Decision Making: A Model Building Approach.* New York: Harper & Row.

Mahajan, V., and E. Muller (1979). "Innovation Diffusion and New Product Growth Models in Marketing," *Journal of Marketing* 43 (fall): 55–68.

Mahajan, V., Charlotte H. Mason, and V. Srinivasan (1986). "An Evaluation of Estimation Procedures for New Product Diffusion Models," in *Innovation Diffusion Models of New Product Acceptance,* Vijay Mahajan and Yoram Wind, eds. Cambridge, Mass.: Ballinger.

Mansfield, E. (1961). "Technical Change and the Rate of Imitation," *Econometrica* 29 (October): 741–66.

—— (1968). *Industrial Research and Technological Innovation*. New York: W.W. Norton.

Nevers, J.V. (1972). "Extensions of a New Product Growth Model," *Sloan Management Review* 13 (winter): 78–89.

Norton, John A., and Frank M. Bass (1986). "A Diffusion Theory Model of Adoption and Substitution for Successive Generations of High-Technology Products." Working paper no. 31-2-86. School of Management, University of Texas at Dallas.

Robinson, B., and C. Lakhani (1975). "Dynamic Price Models for New-Product Planning," *Management Science* 21 (June): 1113–22.

Rogers, E.M. (1983). *Diffusion of Innovations*, 3rd ed. New York: Free Press.

Schmittlein, D., and V. Mahajan (1982). "Maximum Likelihood Estimation for an Innovation Diffusion Model of New Product Acceptance," *Marketing Science* 1 (winter): 57–78.

Srinivasan, V., and C.H. Mason (1986). "Nonlinear Least Squares Estimation of New Product Diffusion Models," *Marketing Science* 5; Spring 169–78.

Takada, Hirokazu (1987). "Does the Bass Model Perform Well for International Marketing Data?" Working paper. Graduate School of Management, University of California, Riverside.

10

A Diffusion-Theory Model of Adoption and Substitution for Successive Generations of High Technology Products

John A. Norton
Frank M. Bass

Newer technologies are continually replacing older ones. In marine power, steam replaced sail and, in turn, was replaced by the internal combustion engine. As a source of industrial fuel, oil substituted for coal, and natural gas and nuclear energy have substituted for oil. In recent years, the time interval between successive generations of high tech electronic products has been demonstrated to be relatively brief in comparison with the time interval between replacing technologies using historical norms. As the time interval between technologies decreases, the importance of understanding the impact of recent technologies on earlier ones increases. No matter what their advantages, newer technologies are not adopted by all potential buyers immediately. Rather, a diffusion process is set into motion. The newer technology may widen the market by allowing applications that were not feasible before. It will also provide an opportunity for buyers of earlier technologies to substitute the more recent technology for earlier ones. These substitution effects will ultimately diminish the potential, if not the actual sales, of earlier technologies, in the following ways. First, customers who would otherwise have adopted the earlier device will, instead, adopt the later one. Second, customers who have already adopted the first device

We are grateful for a grant from United Technologies Mostek to the Morris Hite Center for Product Development and Marketing Science at the University of Texas at Dallas, which supported this research. Our thanks to R.L. Schultz, Director of the Hite Center, for arranging this support; to Chris Hann and Bert Kehren of United Technologies Mostek for information, advice, and counsel; and to Dataquest for supplying the data used in this study.

We gratefully acknowledge the thoughtful critical review by three anonymous referees. Any remaining errors and omissions are, of course, our responsibility.

This chapter originally appeared in *Management Science* (September 1987) and is reprinted courtesy of the Institute of Management Sciences.

may switch from (disadopt) the earlier device in favor of the later one. When the time interval between technologies is short, the earlier technology may continue to diffuse through a population of potential buyers even as the substitution process is underway. Therefore, the demand for an earlier technology may continue to grow even as the substitution process occurs, as illustrated in figure 10–1. We develop a model that explains the conjunction of diffusion and substitution. In this way we provide a basis for assessing and forecasting the influence of recent technologies on earlier ones. We study here certain electronic devices, but other work underway indicates that the model and concepts apply more widely.

There is a substantial literature on the diffusion of innovations (that is,

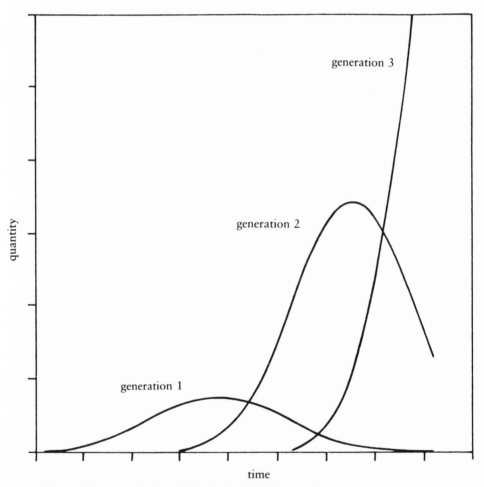

Figure 10–1. A Series of Technological Generations

literature dealing with the growth in level of demand, acceptance, or use of something as a function of time and other variables). There is also a considerable literature dealing with technological substitution. Most substitution models are market-share models; indeed, a principal distinction between substitution and diffusion models is that models of technological substitution assume there is a market there to be substituted, and, many times, the size of that market is known, whereas diffusion models make no such assumptions, in general. In fact, it is often the case that one of the principal reasons a diffusion model might be of interest in the first place is its ability to estimate or forecast a market potential.

The Literature

Diffusion Models

In the model to be developed for demand growth and decline of successive generations of technological innovations, we shall make use of diffusion effects as well as substitution effects. In this section, we review briefly some of the more popular diffusion models.

The Bass (1969) model is one of the more well known and widely used models of first-purchase demand. It is a model of the timing of adoption of an innovation and will be central to subsequent developments.

The Bass model has a behavioral rationale that is consistent with studies in the social science literature on the adoption and diffusion of innovations (e.g., Rogers [1983]) and is based on a simple premise about the hazard function (the conditional probability that an adoption will occur at time t given that an adoption has not yet occurred). Thus if $f(t)$ is defined as the probability of adoption at time t, or the fraction of the ultimate potential that adopts the innovation at time t, and $F(t)$ is the fraction of the ultimate potential that has adopted by time t, the fundamental premise is that the likelihood of adoption at time t given that one has not yet occurred is

$$f(t) / [1 - F(t)] = p + qF(t). \tag{1}$$

The parameter p is called the coefficient of innovation and q the coefficient of imitation. Adoptions of the product are made by "innovators" and "imitators." The importance of innovators will be greater at first but will diminish monotonically with time, while the imitation effect will increase with time. Equation (1) leads to the differential equation

$$f(t) = p + (q - p)F(t) - q[F(t)]^2. \tag{2}$$

If $F(0) = 0$, the solution to equation (2) is

$$F(t) = [1 - \exp(-bt)]/[1 + a \exp(-bt)], \tag{3}$$

and the density function of time to adoption will be

$$f(t) = (b^2/p) \exp(-bt)/[1 + a \exp(-bt)]^2, \tag{4}$$

where $a = q/p$ and $b = p + q$. It is easy to differentiate f to find the time of the peak in f or the inflection point of F to be $t^* = (1/b) \ln(a)$.

If the innovation is a consumer durable (such as television sets, power lawn mowers, room air conditioning units, or cellular mobile telephones), then sales during the period in which demand consists of initial purchases of the product will be proportional to f. On the other hand, in other circumstances when sales consist of repeat purchases or when adopters make multiple purchases of the innovation, it will be necessary to measure the adoption rate separately from the sales measure.

Other distributions used in connection with time to first purchase include the negative exponential, the logistic, and the Weibull. (For applications of these, see Fourt and Woodlock [1960], Mansfield [1961], and deKluyver [1982].)[1] Bass's original extended logistic formulation initiated a number of modifications and extensions. (For examples, see Bass [1980], Dodson and Muller [1978], Horsky and Simon [1983], Kalish [1985], Lekvall and Wahlbin [1973], Mahajan and Peterson [1978, 1979], and Mahajan et al. [1979]. For reviews of a number of diffusion models, see Kotler [1971], Lilien and Kotler [1983], and Mahajan and Muller [1979].) While most of these refinements add something to the paradigm, none overrides the essential character of the model as originally formulated. Further, as Jeuland (1981) points out, given the nature of the data available for most new-product–forecasting tasks (approximate) and the quantity of information available (scant), there is considerable difficulty in reliably extrapolating the early-sales path of a new product. He argues that "if improved forecasting models are to be built, it must be within the constraint of highly parsimonious models" (p. 3). From the point of view of developing a first model incorporating the effects of diffusion and substitution, the original formulation is conceptually sound and captures the essence of the process.

Substitution Models

An important and often-used model of technological substitution was proposed by Fisher and Pry (1971). Their model is based upon three assumptions. The first of these is that "many technological advances can be considered as competitive substitutions of one method of satisfying a need for another" (p. 75). Second, they observed that new technologies often completely supplant older ones. Third, they expressed their market-share model in terms of Pearl's Law: "The fractional rate of fractional substitution of new for old is proportional to the remaining amount of the old left to be substituted." They assert that the rate constant of a substitution, once begun, does not change. Rather, it is the number and magnitude of such substitutions that measure more properly the pace of technological change in society. Their model is

$$d/dt[s(t)] = ks(t)[1 - s(t)], \tag{5}$$

where $s(t)$ is the fractional market share of the innovation of time t, and k is a constant of proportionality. The time scale t may be chosen such that $s(0) = 1/2$. When this is done, it is possible to solve equation (5) to yield the following expression for the fractional market share of the newest innovation:

$$s(t) = 1/[1 + \exp(-kt)]. \tag{6}$$

Equation (6) is a form of logistic function. Using the assumption that there are only two competing technologies, Fisher and Pry derive a more convenient form for purposes of estimation. The result is that the log of the ratio of the market share of the succeeding technology to that of the first is a linear function of time:

$$\ln [s/(1 - s)] = kt. \tag{7}$$

(In their notation, $k = 2a$ and $t = t - t_0$.)

The Fisher-Pry model has been shown to fit the data well for a number of successive innovations. Peterka (1977) extended their model to apply to several generations. His formulation was

$$\ln (s_j/s_i) = kt, \tag{8}$$

where i and j are technologies, j newer than i.

There have been very few studies in the technological-substitution literature of a series of technological substitutions. The most intense and interesting competition may indeed be taking place between the two newest technologies, but there are a number of examples of simultaneous competition of more than two generations. (But see, for example, Peterka [1977] and Sharif and Kabir [1976a].) As each innovation is studied in finer detail, it is often clear that the process is evolutionary, not revolutionary. The process of multilevel substitution is central to the development of the model we propose.

Blackman (1974) modified the Mansfield (1961) model and suggested the model

$$\ln [s/(S - s)] = a + bt \tag{9}$$

where S is the upper limit on market share obtainable by the new technology, s = the market share of the new technology at time t, a is a constant, and b is a linear function of investment and profitability. A number of other variations of the Fisher-Pry share-substitution models exist, such as those by Floyd (1968) and Sharif and Kabir (1976b). The existing substitution models deal either in share or in number of adopting firms as opposed to sales. Each of them has a dynamic time component, thus implying delayed learning about the advantage of the innovations.

The Fisher-Pry model is particularly nice in that it describes in very simple terms a very powerful generalization. However, it does not address the level of sales for each generation. And, as we shall observe later, market shares exhibit a much nicer regularity than do absolute sales levels. In certain environments, managers require insight into the development of a market in absolute as well as relative terms. Clearly, if we can successfully forecast in absolute terms, we can use that knowledge to derive the relative- or market-share information.

The model we develop deals with sales and it explicitly incorporates diffusion effects and substitution effects. Time-varying factors are subsumed in the model and not explicitly taken into account.

The Model

The model development will be facilitated by introducing some simple definitions. We shall use the word *device* to refer to a component part of a larger product. We will use the word *application* to refer to a use of the device in a particular product, and *adoption* to refer to the incorporation of the device into the design of the product. Applications are things, not people, but it may be useful to think of applications as an adopting population. More properly, design engineers decide to incorporate a certain level of integrated-circuit (IC) content (say) into a particular product. That IC content presumably makes the product better in some way and becomes a standard part of the product's design. The product has "adopted" the use of ICs.

Let us make a few assumptions. We assume that once an application incorporates some level of the new technology, it does not revert to earlier technologies during the relevant period of time.

In the case where adopters buy multiple units of a new innovation, sales will consist of the number of units purchased per user times the number of users. Let us assume that the average rate of consumption per time period approaches a constant. More specifically, let the usage rates associated with applications be independently and identically distributed with a constant overall mean rate. (The argument for the constancy of this rate is based on the fact that, as the number of consuming units gets large, the change in the average amount consumed will be little affected by the inclusion of an incremental user.)

Based on several phenomena, we can assume that the number of uses of a given device changes over time. The device may have been invented to go into a particular product or solve a particular problem. It may also have uses that are not imagined until it exists. Finally, a device may perform better than something currently available. It is readily observable that the uses of some generations of innovations are growing in number, some explosively. Nonetheless, however rapid its growth appears, each device must have some upper limit on its applicability, and we assume that limit to be constant. We assume also that the rate of growth in applications incorporating a given device is related to the number of applications already existing and the number of potential applications yet to be made.

We recognize the simplification introduced by the second of the preceding assumptions. The assumption of the constancy of average per-period consumption implies that the growth of applications constitutes all of the variability in the process over time. Since in many situations we can observe neither the average rate of consumption of devices nor the number of applications but only their product, this may be a reasonable and workable simplification.

Model Development

Denote by M the upper limit of the number of applications for which the innovation is appropriate. Denote by r the rate at which an average application consumes the output of interest. These two variables, assumed constant, multiply together to yield the upper limit on sales per time period, notationally designated by m. The only thing changing, as discussed earlier, is the number of applications that adopt.

The process of incorporating a new technology into a given product is a process that involves the diffusion of knowledge about the characteristics of the technology. The specific functional form chosen to represent this process is that proposed by Bass and previously written as equation (3). Thus, in the case of a single generation with no successor, sales would be written

$$S(t) = mF(t). \tag{10}$$

Sales would be proportional to the (S-shaped) cumulative distribution function of the adoption rate. First differences in sales would be proportional to the adoption rate (approximately the [unimodal] density function of time to adoption).

We deal in this model with a series of generations of innovations. Each generation is introduced to the market before its predecessor has been fully diffused to its potential population. Each successive generation will obtain sales by (a) expanding applications, thus obtaining sales that would not have otherwise gone to earlier generations, and (b) capturing sales that would otherwise have gone to earlier generations. Some part of the sales that would have otherwise gone to earlier generations will consist of customers switching from the earlier to the later generation. Another part will consist of customers who would have adopted the earlier device but instead adopt the later one. The two may or may not be distinguishable in practice; in the empirical section that follows, they are not.

Let us introduce some additional notation. Let i index generations of a particular device type. Then we can denote by S_i the shipments of the ith generation, and, in the case of two generations, we may write, for the first generation's sales,

$$S_1(t) = F_1(t)m_1 - F_2(t - \tau_2)F_1(t)m_1$$
$$= F_1(t)m_1[1 - F_2(t - \tau_2)] \text{ for } t > 0 \quad (11)$$

and, for the second,

$$S_2(t) = F_2(t - \tau_2)[m_2 + F_1(t)m_1] \text{ for } t > \tau_2 \quad (12)$$

where $S_i(t)$ refers to sales of the ith generation in time period t, m_1 refers to the potential for the first generation, m_2 refers to the potential uniquely served by the second generation, and $F_i = [1 - \exp(- b_i t)]/[1 + a_i \exp(- b_i t)]$. Indexing the generations with i, of course, means that $a_i = q_i/p_i$ and $b_i = p_i + q_i$. Note that τ_2 is the time at which the second generation is introduced, and $F_2(t - \tau_2) = 0$ for $t < \tau_2$.

The simultaneous model indicated in equations (11) and (12) captures both adoption and substitution. $S_2(t - \tau_2)$ will increase monotonically after τ_2. The peak in $S_1(t)$ will occur at or after τ_2 depending on the relationship of F_2 to F_1. The ultimate level of sales of the second generation will be the sum of the potentials for both generations.[2]

The model may be applied to a number of generations simultaneously even though as the number of generations expands, the sales of earlier generations will approach zero because of substitution. For three generations, generation 1 loses to generation 2. Generation 2 gains from 1, but loses to generation 3, including the loss of actual and potential gained from 1.

The model assumes (a) the existence of a series of advancing generations, each of which can do everything the previous generation could do and possibly more, (b) a density function of time to adoption for each generation applying against a time-varying potential, and (c) the substitution of actual and potential sales from earlier to later generations.

If we relax the assumption that the adoption process differs by generations, we can write $p_i = p$ and $q_i = q$ for all i. This assumption has a certain plausibility in that for a given technology class, the behavioral processes for the adoption of advancing generations could be expected to be similar. If the assumption is approximately correct, the number of parameters to be estimated will be drastically reduced. For example, if F has k parameters and there are n generations, there will be $kn + n$ parameters to estimate, but if the k parameters of F are the same for each generation, the number of parameters to estimate will be $k + n$. The very strong assumption that p and q are constant across equations should be easily falsifiable on the basis of model fit: if the p_i and q_i are really different for different i, it should be difficult to obtain reasonable fits to the empirical data and reasonable forecasts using the simpler model.

The Data

The data employed in this chapter are from the semiconductor industry and were collected and supplied to us by Dataquest. We shall model the demand growth and decline for successive generations of two basic types of integrated circuits (ICs): memory and logic circuits. These devices are similar in that they are products of the highest technology, they are sold to industrial as opposed to consumer markets, and their markets are dynamic in the sense that technological advances influence their environment. They are also similar in that they are very important to the nations that manufacture and use them for geopolitical, economic, and military reasons. They are different in their applications, in their served markets, and in that the technology leading to improvement in one may not be applicable to the other. Descriptions of the devices are included in an appendix available from the first author, in case the terms *dynamic random access memory* (DRAM), *static random access memory* (SRAM), *microprocessor* (MPU), and *microcontroller* (MCU) are unfamiliar. The point is that they are sequential innovations. The successive generations studied are the 4k, 16k, 64k, and 256k DRAM, the 4k, 16k, and 64k SRAM, and 8-bit logic devices (MPU and MCU). The data comprise 44 quarterly observations of DRAM shipments from 1974 through 1984, 36 quarterly observations of SRAM shipments ending in mid-1984, and 32 quarterly observations of 8-bit logic devices, ending with the fourth quarter of 1983.

Estimation and Fitting

DRAM Shipments

Operating under the assumption of constant diffusion parameters p and q for all generations of DRAMs, we can write the following system of joint nonlinear equations to describe their growth and interplay:[3]

$$S_1(t) = F(t)m_1[1 - F(t - \tau_2)], \tag{13}$$

$$S_2(t) = F(t - \tau_2)[m_2 + F(t)m_1][1 - F(t - \tau_3)], \tag{14}$$

$$S_3(t) = F(t - \tau_3)\{m_3 + F(t - \tau_2)[m_2 \\ + F(t)m_1]\}[1 - F(t - F(t - \tau_4)], \tag{15}$$

$$S_4(t) = F(t - \tau_4)\bigg(m_4 + F(t - \tau_3)\{m_3 \\ + F(t - \tau_2)[m_2 + F(t)m_1]\}\bigg) \text{ where} \tag{16}$$

$S_i(t)$ = shipments of generation i,

$F(\cdot) = [1 - \exp(-b\cdot)]/[1 + a \exp(-b\cdot)]$ (where a is q/p and b is $p + q$, as before), and

m_i = the incremental potential served by the ith generation, that is, that not capable of being served by any generation $j < i$.

This set of equations requires the estimation of six parameters: the coefficient of innovation p, the coefficient of imitation q, and the incremental potentials m_1 through m_4. These equations have been estimated jointly using the nonlinear three-stage least squares procedure SYSNLIN, available as part of the Statistical Analysis System (SAS).[4] For details of the program, please refer to the documentation in SAS (1984, pp. 505–50). Table 10–1 shows the parameter estimates using DRAM data to estimate equations (13)–(16). All of the parameter estimates are positive as expected and highly statistically significant with small standard errors relative to the estimates. Moreover, the parameter estimates are plausible. The m_is increase monotonically with i as might be expected for DRAMs and the values of p and q are within the range of experience of parameter estimates for other innovations.

Table 10–1
Parameter Estimates for Equations (13) through (16)

Parameter	Estimate	Approx. Std. Error	t Ratio	Approx. Prob. >|t|
m_1	22523.24	654.24	34.43	0.0001
m_2	59789.50	1778.39	33.62	0.0001
m_3	338834	9796.27	34.59	0.0001
m_4	762917	33995.63	22.44	0.0001
p	0.00370603	0.00013041	28.42	0.0001
q	0.33692	0.00710933	47.39	0.0001

Table 10–2 shows the fit of the model to the data for DRAMs. The R^2 values are remarkably high, the lowest value exceeding 0.96. Any test of the hypothesis that the parameters p and q are equal across generations would reject the hypothesis only if the fit of the model to the data without the constraints that $p_i = p$ and $q_i = q$ were markedly superior to the fit with the constraint. Clearly, the data and the model are in such a high degree of correspondence that we may assert that the data do not reject the notion that the assumption of constant p and q for all generations is reasonable.[5]

Figure 10–2 shows the fit of the model to the data. Clearly, there is close correspondence between the model and data. A plot of fitted versus actual aggregate demand derived from these data (not reproduced here) similarly shows very close correspondence.

As previously indicated, when there is only one device and no substitution, the first differences in sales will be proportional to the adoption rate. Figure 10–3 shows the theoretical graph of first differences when substitution comes into play. At some point, first differences will turn negative and will remain so, but at a later point the rate of substitution will diminish as the higher technology begins to saturate its potential from substitution. Eventually the sales of the first generation will approach zero and there will be little potential left for the second to capture. Figure 10–4 shows, for the 4k DRAM, the fit of the estimated derivative of shipments for the devices to the actual first differences. Although the data are noisy, the trend supports the model predictions. The prediction of the upper peak of differences corresponds chronologically to the time of the inflection point of sales.[6] We note also that as soon as the next generation is introduced, the derivative of sales of the older generation starts to slow, clearly indicating the link between the two generations. Graphic representations of the first differences of later devices (again, not reproduced in the interest of brevity) showed similar correspondence.

SRAM Shipments

Applying the model to the market for three generations of SRAMs, we write

Table 10–2
Model Fit to Data

Endogenous Variable	R^2
$S_1(t)$	0.9672
$S_2(t)$	0.9646
$S_3(t)$	0.9993
$S_4(t)$	0.9676

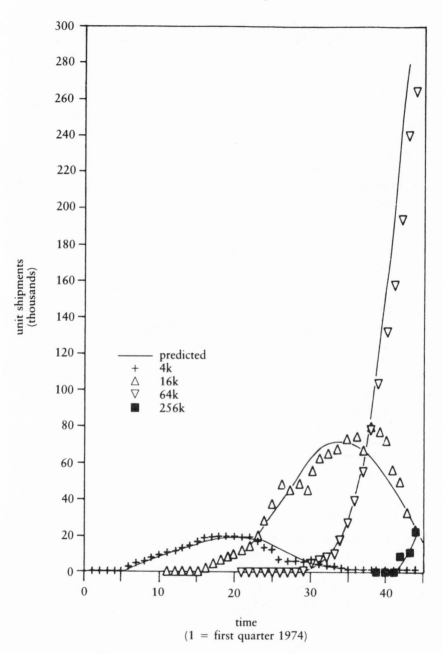

Figure 10–2. Model Fit to DRAM Data

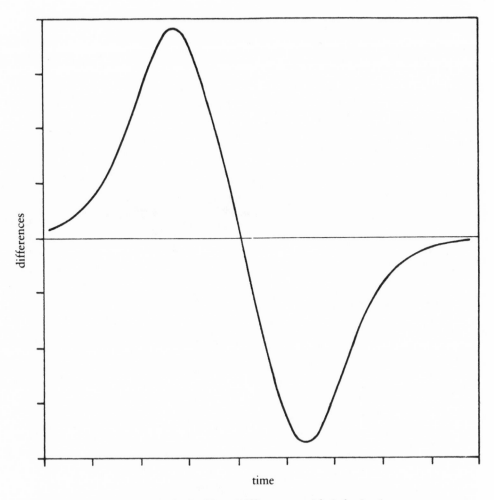

Figure 10–3. First Differences with Substitution

$$S_1(t) = F(t)m_1[1 - F(t - \tau_2)], \tag{18}$$

$$S_2(t) = F(t - \tau_2)[m_2 + F(t)m_1][1 - F(t - \tau_3)], \text{ and} \tag{19}$$

$$S_3(t) = F(t - \tau_3)\{m_3 + F(t - \tau_2)[m_2 + F(t)m_1]\}, \text{ where} \tag{20}$$

$S_i(t) =$ shipments of generation i,

$F(\cdot) = [1 - \exp(-b\cdot)]/[1 + a \exp(-b\cdot)]$ (where a is q/p and b is $p + q$, as before), and

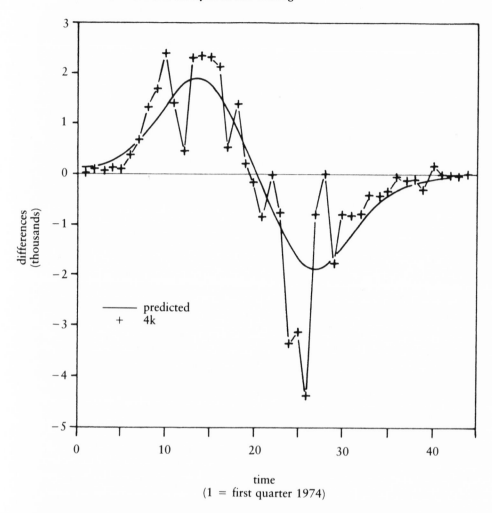

time
(1 = first quarter 1974)

Figure 10–4. 1st Differences, 4k DRAM

m_i = the incremental potential served by the *i*th generation, that is, that not capable of being served by any generation $j < i$.

The estimates of equations (18)–(20) are shown in table 10–3. As is the case for DRAMs, the estimates have the expected sign and reasonable values, and are all statistically significant.

Table 10–4 shows the fit of the model to the data for SRAMs. Again, we find a failure of the data to reject the model, in particular the constrained model.

Table 10–3
Parameter Estimates for Equations (18) through (20)

Parameter	Estimate	Approx. Std. Error	t Ratio	Approx. Prob. >|t|
m_1	32537.61	424.86	76.58	0.0001
m_2	180055	6135.39	29.35	0.0001
m_3	280094	19820.41	14.13	0.0001
p	0.002459	0.00015964	15.40	0.0001
q	0.23165	0.00548958	42.20	0.0001

Table 10–4
Model Fit to SRAM Data

Endogenous Variable	R^2
$S_1(t)$	0.9911
$S_2(t)$	0.9962
$S_3(t)$	0.9811

Logic-Device Shipments

Logic and memory differ in that an advanced-generation logic device will not necessarily easily substitute for an earlier-generation device. Our data indicated that the eight-bit microprocessor did not take over from the four-bit device, nor did the sixteen-bit from the eight-bit device. There are applications for which accessing a larger word or operating at very high speed is irrelevant. Furthermore, the peripherals used to control an MPU cost much more, in general, than the MPU itself. As a generation of MPUs matures, it will be integrated into more and more designs. With maturity it becomes expedient to put all the controlling devices, together with some instruction and a little memory, on a single chip. That chip is called a microcontroller. Therefore, one should expect that an MCU of a given word length would take over from an MPU of the same word length. We estimate the model of the relationship between both types of eight-bit logic, a set of equations similar to those presented earlier, with quarterly data during the eight-year period ending in 1983. Tables 10–5 and 10–6 show the parameter estimates and fit statistics. As was the case for both types of memory, the model fits the data extremely well. Eight-bit MPU sales are beginning to peak as MCUs take over.

Market Shares

Because of many successful applications, the Fisher-Pry model qualifies as a powerful generalization. Its limitations are that it is a share model only and

Table 10–5
Parameter Estimates: Logic

Parameter	Estimate	Approx. Std. Error	t Ratio	Approx. Prob. >|t|
m_1	79287.59	12687.67	6.25	0.0001
m_2	54756.73	17962.66	3.05	0.0049
p	0.00095211	0.00015277	6.23	0.0001
q	0.13370	0.01094	12.22	0.0001

Table 10–6
Model Fit to Logic Data

Endogenous Variable	R^2
$S_1(t)$	0.9916
$S_2(t)$	0.9858

does not account for sales levels of successive generations and that it considers only a single technological substitute at a time. The generalization of the model by Peterka (1977) permits the estimation of share relationships for a series of generations of a technology. A generalized form of the Fisher-Pry model is

$$\ln\,[s_i(t)/s_{i-1}(t)] = a + bt. \tag{21}$$

We note that while sales or shipments may exhibit highly irregular patterns, the process of substitution in relative or market-share terms shows remarkably regular patterns. With that in mind, we examined the performance of the Fisher-Pry model, comparing the results with market-share projections based on our model, to see whether the regularity captured by the Fisher-Pry formulation resulted in better market-share forecasts. Given the fits of our model to the shipment data, it may not be surprising that ours produced somewhat better results, measured in terms of mean absolute-percentage deviation. Again, we omit the results because of constraints on chapter length, but the results are available from the first author upon request.

Forecasting

In order to examine the forecasting properties of the model, we have estimated the parameters using different data intervals and then projected shipments of the devices using these parameter estimates. In general, we estimate using data for i devices ($i = 1, 2, 3, 4$) up until the time when the ith-plus-one is introduced; we then project shipments for all $i + 1$ devices.

Several studies of the sensitivity of the parameters of the Bass model indicate that estimates using data for first-purchase–adoption rates of single products are not very stable unless the period over which the estimates are formed extends past the peak of the curve. We expect something similar here. Fortunately, because there are a series of innovations, there will be a series of peaks. Thus we expect the estimates to improve with the data interval, making it possible to predict with some accuracy more recent and future innovation sales and to assess the impact of these upon the sales of earlier-generation innovations. In estimating in the way that we have, we develop estimates of p, q, and m_1, m_2, . . . , m_i. Thus, in order to project sales of the ith-plus-one, it will be necessary to guess m_{i+1}.

DRAMs

The 16k DRAM first captured 2 percent of the market in period 14. We have estimated p, q, and m_1 with these 14 observations. In order to forecast sales, we must guess m_2. We have taken m_2 to be equal to 4 times m_1, an arbitrary guess, but taken for the reason that the 16k device is 4 times as powerful (as dense) as the 4k. The resulting forecast values of shipments for 4k and 16k DRAMs captured the general shape of the shipment curves for the 2 devices, but the actual sales of the 4k device exceeded the forecast values, while the actual sales of the 16k device were below the forecast values. It should be emphasized that these forecasts were (a) developed from estimates made from data that do not extend to the peak in 4k shipments and (b) projected without the benefit of updating for 8 periods (2 years). We expect the relaxation of either (a) or (b) would improve the quality of the forecasts.

The 64k DRAM first captured 2 percent of the market in period 29. Estimates of p, q, m_1, and m_2, made on the basis of 29 observations, and m_3 (again taking as an estimated value for the new device's potential 4 times the previous potential), yield the results shown in figure 10–5. As expected, the quality of the fit using data that include a turning point is superior to that without one. From a strategic viewpoint, the projections in figure 10–5 might be considered to be adequate inasmuch as they capture the rapid growth of the 64k device and the decline in the 16k device.

The 256k DRAM first captured 2 percent of the market in period 38. The fitted values and projections through period 43 for the 4 devices are only slightly different from those shown using figure 10–5. Table 10–7 shows the parameter estimates for DRAMs for different data intervals. The estimates of p diminish and estimates of q increase with the number of observations used to obtain estimates. Systematic and monotonic changes in

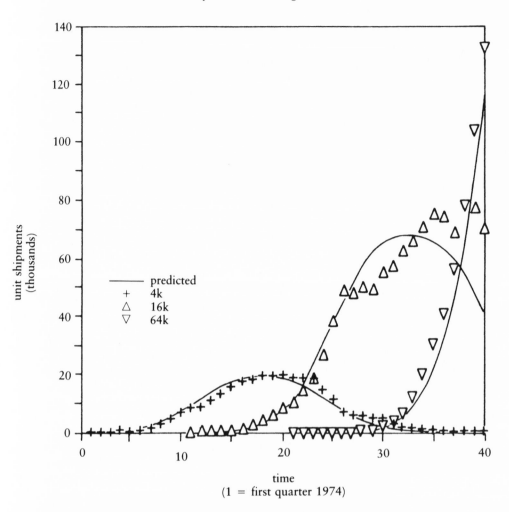

Figure 10–5. Forecast 4k–64k, Using 4k and 16k

Table 10–7
Parameter Estimates for DRAM Subsets

Observations	m_1	m_2	m_3	m_4	p	q
14	15171				0.0020	0.5065
29	22037	50499			0.0028	0.3938
40	22398	61230	390948		0.0030	0.2521
44	22523	59790	338834	762917	0.0037	0.3369

the m_i are also observed. Insofar as changes of this type occur over different innovations, there is the suggestion that one could estimate parameters based on observations from the first one or two generations and modify these to accord with the expectation for estimates based on a larger number of observations. Table 10–8 shows that the changes in the estimates for SRAMs for different data intervals are of the same character as those for DRAMs. Although we do not include the graphs, the forecast quality for SRAMs was similar to that of DRAMs for data over similar intervals.

Forecasts

Since the principal use of our model is in forecasting and planning, it seems reasonable to supply some forecasts based on the data on hand thus far. The following forecasts were made in early 1985, using data available at the time. The data series for memory devices ended at the fourth quarter of 1984. Therefore, we forecast quarterly shipments of 16k, 64k, and 256k, DRAMs for three years starting with the first quarter of 1985. The data series for logic devices ended with the fourth quarter of 1983, and therefore the logic forecasts are for three years starting with the first quarter of 1984.

Please note that all the following forecasts were developed in April 1985, and are three-year (twelve-step-ahead) forecasts, not one-step-ahead forecasts. None of the models is updated with information obtained since that time, with one exception: in June of 1985, we obtained from a planner in one of the semiconductor firms an estimate of the time when the 1M (one megabit) DRAM would capture 2 percent of the memory market. We used that guess to start the process of substitution for the earlier devices. (Only that introduction time matters, since m_5 would not enter the equation for the fourth generation's sales.)

Table 10–9 indicates the model forecasts of 16k, 64k, and 256k DRAMs beginning in the first quarter of 1985 and ending the fourth quarter of 1987. The model forecasts that, regardless of the price of the devices, the 64k DRAM will decline in shipment volume permanently following the fourth quarter of 1985. Table 10–10 summarizes three-year forecasts for 4k, 16k, and 64k SRAMs.

Table 10–8
Parameter Estimates for SRAM Subsets

Observations	m_1	m_2	m_3	p	q
21	21875			0.0013	0.3474
32	29659	206159		0.0016	0.2764
36	32537	180055	280094	0.0025	0.2317

Table 10–9
Three-Year DRAM Forecast

Period	16k	64k	256k
45	19823	309257	34515
46	14946	327619	54283
47	11056	338055	81710
48	8058	340318	118931
49	5806	334375	168157
50	4149	320364	231237
51	2947	298716	308997
52	2084	270381	400467
53	1469	237012	502364
54	1033	200924	609238
55	725	164752	714489
56	509	130917	811907

Table 10–10
Three-Year SRAM Forecast

Period	4k	16k	64k
37	22319	62739	7858
38	20701	73064	11120
39	18947	83737	15345
40	17102	94359	20774
41	15221	104463	27678
42	13359	113560	36355
43	11568	121176	47107
44	9890	126901	60222
45	8358	130421	75945
46	6988	131543	94438
47	5789	130210	115741
48	4758	126503	139732

Table 10–11 lists the estimates of shipments of eight-bit logic devices for the period from the first quarter of 1984 through the fourth quarter of 1986. We forecast a peak in eight-bit MPU shipments in the second quarter of 1985. When we compare the prediction with 1984 data that have since become available from Dataquest, sales appear to be flattening in accordance with the model predictions. This finding is interesting for a number of reasons, not the least of which is that a flattening of eight-bit MPU shipments was completely unexpected by a number of industry planners.

Conclusion

The model put forth in this chapter derives from prior work in the areas of diffusion and substitution, building upon knowledge gained in those studies.

Table 10–11
Three-Year Logic Forecast

Period	MPU	MCU
33	18540	31437
34	19109	35203
35	19520	39235
36	19760	43507
37	19819	47990
38	19697	52642
39	19399	57419
40	18934	62271
41	18321	67146
42	17578	71992
43	16731	76759
44	15802	81403

The unique contribution of the model is the casting of the process in such a way as to marry the two concepts to explain the process in a relatively accurate and yet parsimonious form. The model also has value in its ability to forecast overall industry demand as well as market shares of the various devices. Clearly, there are omitted variables, but from a practical forecasting viewpoint, the model serves in describing a generalization. To illustrate, consider the results of forecasting the 64k device using data from the 4k and 16k. A strategic planner using the model parameterized with data for 1974 through 1980 would not have been seriously wrong in forecasting global demand for each of the several generations for at least three years, even without updating.

Validation. By building upon the contributions of Mansfield, Fisher and Pry, and Bass, we can claim convergent validity. From the evidence supplied by the fit of the model to various data sets, we can assert event validity. We demonstrated predictive validity by using subsets of the data for parameterizing the model, then forecasting over remaining data points. We can assert hypothesis validity only to the extent that (a) the model does not reject the assumption of a constant substitution rate for a product class and (b) these data, at least, do not reject the assumption of the decline of sales to virtually zero for the earlier generations.

Future Research. The model is applied to data from the semiconductor industry. How would the model work in other applications? That is for future research to discover, but we offer some suggestions. First, the model needs to be applied to data wherein the distinction between the two types of succession can be discerned. That is, we need to be able to track separately those applications that choose the second generation (say) instead of the first and those that, having already adopted the first, switch to the second. Further, the model needs to be modified to allow switching by only a fraction of the market. For example, consider the substitution of acetaminophen for aspirin, and ibuprofin for both of those. The patient might need the antiinflammatory qualities of aspirin and not take acetaminophen at any price.

The incorporation of price seems necessary, in some cases, particularly where the device cost is a large fraction of the total value of the product. This matter has been addressed in the case of diffusion models, but much remains to be done.

Applications. The finding that the parameters stabilize considerably once a single generation has reached a turning point is a potentially powerful generalization, one that suggests that the model is particularly well suited to deal with industries undergoing rapid change.

We suggest also that the model could be incorporated as a component of larger models in the investigation of such research issues as optimal phasing out of "old" technological generations and/or optimal timing of the entry of new ones.

We have developed what we believe to be a unique and original model of demand growth and decline for a series of technological innovations. Our model is consistent with and builds upon well-known work on the diffusion of innovations. It incorporates both diffusion and substitution. The model works well for the technologies we have studied. In summary, it is simple, plausible, and historically accurate.

We believe that the model holds great promise for forecasting conditional on the timing of the introduction of successive generations of technology.

Notes

1. Because we anticipated the question of whether one density function is just as good as another in the model formulation, we did investigate the model formulated with these alternative distributions. We found that the negative exponential distribution was clearly inappropriate, which makes sense when one considers that it implies a memoryless process. We further found that the logistic and Weibull formulations did almost as well as that of Bass in terms of fit to the data over many observations. There were, however, considerable differences in the forecasts resulting from these distributions when few data points were used to parameterize the model. The resulting conclusion is that the function characterized as equation (3) was uniformly superior for forecasting, especially when few observations are available. The results are not published here in the interest of brevity, but are available from the first author upon request.

2. In theory, m_i may be any nonnegative number; it is an incremental market for all $i > 1$. For example, in the case of near-perfect substitutes, m_2 might be very nearly zero. For purposes of estimation, there is no constraint on any of the m_i. The use of an appropriate functional measure (e.g., tons of freight moved instead of number of steam or diesel locomotives) should avoid the consequence of a negative number for any of the m_i.

3. Here we let $G_k = m_k \prod_{i=k}^{M} F_i$, $i, k = 1, 2, \ldots, n$, and $F_i = F(t - \tau_i) \equiv 0$ for $t < \tau_i$. Then, in general,

$$S_n(t) = \sum_{k=1}^{M} G_k(1 - F_{n+1}). \tag{17}$$

4. Jain and Rao (1985) and Srinivasan and Mason (1986) demonstrate NLS estimation of the Bass diffusion model in its intrinsically nonlinear form. Our thanks to R. Rao for his helpful suggestions.

5. In this case, systems of equations are estimated with intercepts constrained to be zero. Therefore, R^2 cannot be unambiguously interpreted as a percentage of explained variance. Moreover, because of the large number of zero values that are perfectly "predicted" by the estimation, the significance estimates are very likely to be overstated. Nevertheless, visual inspection of the fits indicates that they are very good.

6. Given two competing devices, one the successor to the other, when will sales peak, and how high will that peak be? Rather than graph the equations, we can get an analytical answer by taking the time derivative of equation (14) to derive an expression for t^*, the peak time, and $S_1(t^*)$, the peak magnitude, in terms of the estimates of p, q, and m_1. An appendix available from the TIMS office provides details.

References

Bass, F.M. (1969). "A New-Product Growth Model for Consumer Durables," *Management Science* 15 (January): 215–27.

——— (1980). "The Relationship between Diffusion Rates, Experience Curves, and Demand Elasticities for Consumer Durable Technological Innovations," *J. Business* 53 (July): S51–67.

Blackman, A.W. (1974). "The Market Dynamics of Technological Substitutions," *Technological Forecasting and Social Change* 6 (February): 41–63.

DeKluyver, C.A. (1982). "A Comparative Analysis of the Bass and Weibull New Product Growth Models for Consumer Durables," *New Zealand Operations Research* 3, no. 2: 99–130.

Dodson, J.A., and E. Muller (1978). "Models of New-Product Diffusion through Advertising and Word-of-Mouth," *Management Science* 24 (November): 1568–78.

Fisher, J.C., and R.H. Pry (1971). "A Simple Substitution Model of Technological Change," *Technological Forecasting and Social Change* 3 (March): 75–88.

Floyd, A. (1968). "A Methodology for Trend Forecasting of Figures of Merit," in *Technological Forecasting for Industry and Government: Methods and Applications*, J. Bright, ed. Englewood Cliffs, N.J.: Prentice-Hall, pp. 95–109.

Fourt, L.A., and J.W. Woodlock (1960). "Early Prediction of Market Success for New Grocery Products," *Journal of Marketing* 25 (October): 31–38.

Horsky, D., and L.S. Simon (1983). "Advertising and the Diffusion of New Products," *Marketing Science* 2: 1–17.

Jain, D., and R. Rao "The Effect of Price on the Demand for Durables: Modeling, Estimation, and Findings." Paper presented at the Third Marketing Science Meeting. Nashville, Tenn. 1985.

Jeuland, A.P. (1981). "Parsimonious Models of Diffusion of Innovation Part A: Derivations and Comparisons," Working paper. Graduate School of Business, University of Chicago.

Kalish, S. (1985). "A New Product Adoption Model with Price, Advertising and Uncertainty," *Management Science* 31 (December): 1569–85.

Kotler, P. (1971). *Marketing Decision Making: A Model Building Approach*. New York: Holt, Rinehart and Winston.

Lekvall, P., and C. Wahlbin (1973). "A Study of Some Assumptions Underlying Innovation Diffusion Functions," *Swedish Journal of Economics* 75: 362–77.

Lilien, G., and P. Kotler (1971). *Marketing Decision Making: A Model-Building Approach*. Harper & Row. 1983.

Mahajan, V., and E. Muller (1979). "Innovation Diffusion and New Product Growth Models in Marketing," *Journal of Marketing* 43 (October): 55–68.

Mahajan, V., and R.A. Peterson (1978). "Innovation Diffusion in a Dynamic Potential Adopter Population," *Management Science* 24 (November): 1589–97.

——— (1979). "Integrating Time and Space in Technological Substitution Models," *Technological Forecasting and Social Change* 14: 231–41.

Mahajan, V., R.A. Peterson, A.K. Jain, and N. Malhotra (1979). "A New Product Growth Model with a Dynamic Market Potential," *Long Range Planning* 12 (August): 51–58.

Mansfield, E. (1961). "Technical Change and the Rate of Inflation," *Econometrica* 29 (October): 741–65.

Peterka, V. (1977). *Macrodynamics of Technological Change: Market Penetration by New Technologies*. Laxenburg, Austria: International Institute for Applied Systems Analysis.

Rogers, E.M. (1983). *The Diffusion of Innovation*, 3rd ed. New York: Free Press.

SAS Institute (1984). *SAS/ETS User's Guide, Version 5 Edition*. Cary, N.C.: SAS Institute.

Sharif, M.N., and C. Kabir (1976A). "A Generalized Model for Forecasting Technological Substitution," *Technological Forecasting and Social Change* 8: 353–64.

——— (1976B). "System Dynamics Modeling for Forecasting Multilevel Technological Substitution," *Technological Forecasting and Social Change* 9: 89–112.

Srinivasan, V., and C.H. Mason (1986). "Nonlinear Least Squares Estimation of New Product Diffusion Models," *Marketing Science* 5: 169–78.

11
Does the Bass Model Perform Well for International-Marketing Data?

Hirokazu Takada

Researchers and practitioners have shown much interest in the analysis of the diffusion process of products, and a number of models have been developed to capture this process in the marketplace. Among the major studies, the pioneering work of mathematical modeling by Bass (1969) demonstrated the successful application of his model to major durable goods in the U.S. market. The model has since been adopted, extended, and employed by many marketing researchers (Nevers [1972], Dodds [1973], Robinson and Lakhani [1975], Dodson and Muller [1978], Heeler and Hustad [1980], Tigert and Farivar [1981]). Mahajan and Muller (1979) provide a comprehensive review of the developments of the Bass model. Another development of the new-product–diffusion models is new estimation procedures. The parameters of the original Bass model have been estimated through conducting regression analysis to the discrete analog model in many studies. Bass provided corrections for possible biases of the estimated parameter values. This procedure has been widely used since it is easy to implement. However, it suffers from certain shortcomings. Parameter estimates are sometimes unstable or produce wrong signs. The standard errors for the estimates p, q, and m are not available since they are nonlinear functions of parameters of the discrete analog model. There is a time-interval bias since discrete time–series data are used for estimating a continuous-time model. To solve these problems, alternative estimation procedures have been suggested in the marketing literature. Mahajan et al. (1986) provide a comprehensive review of these procedures with empirical evaluation. First, Schmittlein and Mahajan (1982) have proposed a maximum-likelihood–estimation (MLE) procedure to estimate the parameters of the Bass model. An advantage of the MLE procedure is that the time-interval bias is eliminated since they use appropriate aggregation of the continuous-time model over the time intervals represented by the data. One of the disadvantages of this approach is that maximum-likelihood formulation considers only sampling

The author is grateful to Dipak Jain for providing valuable comments and suggestions for the entire manuscript.

error and ignores all other sources of error; thus, computed standard-error estimates may be too optimistic. The maximum-likelihood approach may be more appropriate in the case of survey data. Srinivasan and Mason (1986) suggested nonlinear least squares estimation procedure. This procedure overcomes the time-interval bias present in the OLS procedure. Also the derived standard errors for the parameter estimates incorporate the effect of sampling errors, missing variables, and misspecification of the density function. Jain and Rao (1987) presented an alternative nonlinear formulation where they utilized the information on the prior adopter population in the estimation equation.

Various product classes in the U.S. market have been modeled in the past decades, and the model performs very well. The results with international data, however, are not successful. One of the most comprehensive empirical studies of the diffusion of innovation in international marketing was done by Heeler and Hustad (1980). They examined forecasting validity of the Bass model for fifteen products in a variety of countries. They found that, first, the fit of the data to the model is sufficiently poor in about a third of the cases, which makes estimation impossible. Second, many of the time series have not yet peaked, perhaps indicating that first-purchase sales are still growing on an annual basis. Third, frequently the time of peak sales is estimated too early for international data, perhaps reflecting different communications patterns and economic restraints than in the United States. Fourth, the model is unstable as a forecasting tool with short periods of actual sales data. A dramatic improvement is obtained by providing an a priori estimate of potential market size. They suggested that the model will be most successful in predicting sales under two conditions: (1) A country is technologically advanced and is one of the first in the world to sell the product to its citizens. There will be no artificial constraints on sales (import restrictions, supply shortages). (2) A country is not technologically advanced nor is it one of the first in the world to sell the product; however, in this case, the country is isolated from markets where the product has been sold previously. The majority of studies focus on diffusion of durable goods in the U.S. market, and the studies of diffusion of durable goods in other markets are limited. Recently, the Pacific-rim countries have emerged as models of economic success and major competitors in the world market. Numerous books and articles have been written about the Japanese economic miracle or marketing strategies. Kotler et al. (1985), for example, shed their light on these countries to investigate the strategies and practices of, in particular, Japanese firms. Despite the growing interests in the Pacific-rim countries, studies on the diffusion processes in those nations are yet to be found in the marketing literature.

The objective of this chapter is to analyze diffusion process of consumer-durable products in the Pacific rim countries by identifying the diffusion models for each of the product categories in the respective market. For the purpose of modeling and parameterizing the diffusion process, recent developments of nonlinear estimation methods will be reviewed and applied to the data set available. The format of this chapter is to present the model formulation and the estimation methods, followed by the description of the data set available for this chapter and empirical results.

Estimation Methodology

In this section, I briefly describe the Bass model and discuss procedures of estimating parameters of this model. Let T denote the random variable representing the time of adoption of a new product and F(t) denote the cumulative distribution function of T. The probability that an adoption will take place in the time interval (t, $t+dt$) given that it has not yet taken place by time t, is h(t)dt where h(t) = f(t)/1 − F(t) and f(t) is the probability density function of T. Bass (1969) proposed the following linear relationship between h(t) and F(t).

$$h(t) \equiv f(t)/1 - F(t) = p + qF(t) \tag{1}$$

where p and q are the coefficients of innovation and imitation, respectively. The expression in (1) can be written as

$$f(t) = [p + qF(t)][1 - F(t)]. \tag{2}$$

Solving the differential equation in (2), we obtain

$$F(t) = \left[1 - e^{-(p+q)t} \right] \Big/ \left[1 + \frac{q}{p} e^{-(p+q)t} \right], \tag{3}$$

assuming

$$Y(t) = mF(t)$$

and

$$S(t) = mf(t) \tag{4}$$

where Y(t) denotes the cumulative sales prior to time t, and S(t) denotes the sales in period t, and m denotes the number of potential buyers of the product. Bass substituted equation (4) in equation (2) and used the following equation for estimation purpose:

$$S(t) = pm + (q-p) Y(t) - \frac{q}{m} [Y(t)]^2. \qquad (5)$$

The time at which the sales reaches its peak is given by

$$T^* = 1/(p+q)\ln(p/q) \qquad (6)$$

and the sales at its peak is

$$S(T^*) = m(p+q)^2/4q. \qquad (7)$$

To estimate the parameters p, q, and m in (5), Bass replaced the basic model in (5) with the following estimating equation for discrete time series data:

$$S_t = a + bY_{t-1} + cY^2_{t-1} + \mu_t \quad t = 2, 3, \ldots \qquad (8)$$

where

$$Y_{T-1} = \sum_{t=1}^{T-1} S_t = \text{cumulative sales through period } T-1$$

and

$$\mu_t = \text{error term.}$$

Bass used the ordinary least squares (OLS) to estimate a, b, and c. These values are then used to obtain estimates of p, q, and m using the following relationships:

$$p = a/m,$$
$$q = -mc, \qquad (9)$$
$$m = (-b - \sqrt{b^2 - 4ac})/2c.$$

Bass indicated that in substituting the cumulative sales in the discrete analogue for the cumulative sales in the continuous model, a certain bias was introduced. This bias can be crucial when there are only a few observations. To correct the bias, p, q, and m can be calculated from the following relationship where the original estimates are relabeled p', q', and m'.

$$p = 0.97p'/[1 + 0.4(1 + \vartheta)\, p'],$$

$$q = 0.97q'/[1 + 0.4(1 + \frac{1}{\vartheta})\, q'], \qquad (10)$$

$$m = m'/[0.97 - 0.4(p + q)],$$

and

$$\vartheta = q'/p'.$$

The estimates of p, q, and m were substituted in the following basic model to estimate the sales:

$$S(T) = [m(p + q)^2/p][e^{-(p + q)T}/(q/pe^{-(p + q)T} + 1)^2]. \qquad (11)$$

This procedure has been widely used since it is easy to implement. However, it suffers from certain shortcomings. Parameter estimates are sometimes unstable or produce wrong signs. The standard errors for the estimates p, q, and m are not available since they are nonlinear functions of parameters of the discrete analog model. There is a time-interval bias since discrete time series data are used for estimating a continuous-time model. To solve these problems, various researchers have proposed alternative methods of estimation for the parameters p, q, and m directly using the equation (3). For example, Schmittlein and Mahajan (1982) proposed a maximum-likelihood estimation procedure; Srinivasan and Mason (1986), and Jain and Rao (1987) proposed a nonlinear least squares (NLS) estimation. We discuss next the NLS procedure for estimating the parameters of the Bass diffusion model.

Consider an interval (t_{i-1}, t_i). The probability of an adoption in this interval is clearly $F(t_i) - F(t_{i-1})$. Therefore, the expected number of adopters in this interval will be

$$E(S_{t_i}) = m\,[F(t_i) - F(t_{i-1})] \qquad (12)$$

where S_{t_i} denotes the sales during the time interval (t_{i-1}, t_i). We can, therefore, write S_{t_i} as

$$S_{t_i} = m[F(t_i) - F(t_{i-1})] + u_i \qquad (13)$$

where u_i represents an additive error term with $E(u_i) = 0$. The model represented in (13) is formulated by Srinivasan and Mason (1986). They provide an explanation for the error term u_i and use the NLS estimation procedure to estimate the parameters p, q, and m of the model given in (13).

Jain and Rao (1987) have proposed an alternative model for S_{t_i}. They incorporate the information generated over time by continuous adoptions of the product. With every individual adopting a product, there is a decrease in the future market potential. Consequently, at any time epoch t_i, the future potential adopters are $m - X_{t_{i-1}}$ where $X_{t_{i-1}}$ represents the cumulative number of adopters prior to time t_{i-1}. The probability $p(t_i)$ of an individual adopting a product in the interval (t_{i-1}, t_i) given that he or she has not adopted it by time t_{i-1} is given by

$$[F(t_i) - F(t_{i-1})]/[1 - F(t_{i-1})]. \tag{14}$$

The number of potential adopters at time t_{i-1} is $(m - X_{t_{i-1}})$. Therefore, the expected number of individuals adopting the product in the interval (t_{i-1}, t_i) is

$$E(S_{t_i}) = (m - X_{t_{i-1}}) \, p(t_i) \tag{15}$$

or

$$S_{t_i} = (m - X_{t_{i-1}}) \, [F(t_i) - F(t_{i-1})]/[1 - F(t_{i-1})] + v(i) \tag{16}$$

where $v(i)$ is an additive error term. The model in (16) is the nonlinear formulation of the Bass model. Jain and Rao use the NLS estimation procedure to estimate p, q, and m.

Mahajan et al. (1986) characterize the NLS estimation of the parameters in (13) and (16) as ex ante estimation and ex post estimation procedures, respectively. They compare four different estimation procedures for the Bass model and conclude that the nonlinear least-squares appear to be generally the best among the four estimation procedures considered.

In this chapter, we confine ourselves to only the OLS and NLS estimation procedures.

Data and Results

The data include the eight product classes: electric refrigerators, black and white television sets, electric washing machines, room air conditioners, passenger cars, vacuum cleaners, calculators, and radios. The OLS estimation with bias corrections as previously suggested have been applied to the data set available in order to derive the starting values for the parameters p, q, and m necessary for the nonlinear estimation. The model has been applied to the early portion of the time–series data to help avoid repeat purchase.

Table 11–1 summarizes the estimation results of the Bass model for durable goods in the U.S. market using the OLS estimation. The F statistics

Table 11–1
OLS Estimation Results of the Bass Model for the U.S. Market

Product	F Statistic*	Adj. R²	Parameters		
			m	p	q
Electric refrigerators	86.13	0.88	80032	0.0019	0.2168
Black and white TVs	14.53	0.69	88202	0.0198	0.3240
Electric washing machines	26.05	0.79	48691	0.0060	0.3210
Room air conditioners	42.63	0.87	20594	0.0141	0.3360
Passenger cars	149.64	0.91	62034	0.0008	0.2499
Vacuum cleaners	46.87	0.84	59974	0.0098	0.1903
Calculators	32.21	0.85	154129	0.0159	0.3778
Radios	17.10	0.59	134126	0.0003	0.2635

*All F statistics are significant at the .01 level.

Sources: The Statistical Abstract of the United States, Bureau of the Census, Washington, D.C. *Abstract Statistics of the United States,* Bureau of Statistics, Washington, D.C. *Historical Statistics of the United States,* Bureau of the Census, Washington, D.C. *Electrical Merchandising,* McGraw-Hill, New York.

for all product classes are significant at .01 level, and the adjusted R^2 values lie in a range of .91 (passenger cars) to .59 (radios). For brevity, the OLS coefficients are not included in the table; instead, derived values for parameters m, p, and q are reported. Nonetheless, all of the parameters for the cumulative (Y_{t-1}) and squared cumulative (Y^2_{t-1}) terms in the model turned out to be significant at .01 level with proper signs. These results confirm the findings in other published diffusion studies of the U.S. market that the model fits the data fairly well, despite the fact that time series of four product classes (electric refrigerators, black and white television sets, radios, and vacuum cleaners) contain an interruption period during the war. Derived values for the parameters m, p, and q, after bias corrections, are within the plausible range.

Mahajan et al. (1986) have evaluated major estimation procedures for the Bass model including the OLS by Bass (1969), the maximum-likelihood estimation by Schmittlein and Mahajan (1982), and the nonlinear least squares estimation by Srinivasan and Mason (1986) and Jain and Rao (1987), among others. Their empirical results for consumer durables indicate that the nonlinear least squares estimation procedures outperform the OLS and MLE procedures on the basis of such criteria as goodness-of-fit of the models, one-step-ahead prediction performance, and values of parameter estimates of the models. Hereafter, I refer to the nonlinear estimation procedure by Srinivasan and Mason as model 1 and the latter by Jain and Rao as model 2 for the purpose of our discussion. Their comparisons of the results for the nonlinear estimation procedures indicate that for all the products studied, model 2 provides better fit than model 1 does. Meanwhile, their performance results for one-step-ahead forecasts reveal that the results are not statistically different for two models.

Using the estimates of p, q, and m for the OLS procedure as initial values, the nonlinear least squares estimation algorithm of the SAS/STAT package is applied to estimate the parameters. Table 11–2 includes estimation results of the nonlinear least squares estimation procedures applied to the U.S. data. Parenthesized numbers indicate standard errors for the parameter estimates. One of the major findings is that the mean squared errors (MSE) of model 2 are consistently smaller than those of model 1 for all the product classes studied, indicating that model 2 provides better fit of the model to the data. Other findings from the table warrant the following points:

- Estimated values for the parameters p, q, and m by the nonlinear estimation procedures appear to be fairly stable throughout the product classes as indicated by the ratio of the estimates to the standard error. Furthermore, the differences of the estimated values of p and q between these two procedures appear to be negligibly small.

- Regarding the potential market size, m, model 1 provides larger values than model 2 does for six out of eight cases. On the other hand, the standard errors of model 1 are always larger than those of model 2. This suggests that model 2 provides more stable estimates than model 1 does.

Table 11–3 summarizes prediction performance of the Bass model for the U.S. market. The OLS predictions of the peak time and peak magnitude are obtained by using equations (8) and (9), respectively. The results show that the model performs fairly well. The predicted years for the previously mentioned four products (refrigerators, black and white TV sets, radios, and vacuum cleaners) are the only exceptions with some discrepancies between the actual and predicted periods. This is considered to be mainly due to the lack of observations during the war. On the other hand, the nonlinear estimation procedures predict peak years and peak sales accurately for such products as vacuum cleaners, calculators, and electric washers.

For further analysis, we only use the estimating equation of model 2 to analyze the data of Japanese and Korean markets. Table 11–4 shows the estimation results for the Japanese durable goods. The Bass model fits remarkably well with the data as depicted by extremely high R^2 values and significant F statistics. Estimates by nonlinear algorithm for the parameters m, p, and q lie within a plausible range, with small standard errors. Consequently, the model predicts time of peak and its magnitude accurately as indicated in table 11–5.

The Bass model also demonstrates its good fit to durables in the Korean market, and it predicts peak period and magnitude with small margin, as evidenced in tables 11–6, and 11–7, respectively. The OLS coefficient esti-

Table 11-2
NLS Estimation Results of the Bass Model for the U.S. Market

Product	Model 1				Model 2			
	m	p	q	MSE	m	p	q	MSE
Electric refrigerators	101603 (7973)	0.000035 (0.000023)	0.1779 (0.0183)	300172	82331 (7254)	0.0001 (0.000048)	0.1618 (0.0168)	299255
Black and white TVs	78636 (8041)	0.0117 (0.0038)	0.3844 (0.0606)	1664571	76698 (5779)	0.0116 (0.0038)	0.3880 (0.0626)	1554452
Electric washing machines	100499 (28980)	0.0001 (0.0001)	0.1487 (0.0376)	404414	81626 (28159)	0.0002 (0.0002)	0.1309 (0.0308)	375897
Room air conditioners	19080 (1510)	0.00207 (0.0008)	0.3821 (0.0391)	34147	18322 (1122)	0.0020 (0.0007)	0.3871 (0.0406)	30961
Passenger cars	54525 (3500)	0.00014 (0.000071)	0.2874 (0.0238)	224899	55404 (1896)	0.0001 (0.000067)	0.2889 (0.0227)	199172
Vacuum cleaners	75792 (6376)	0.000055 (0.000033)	0.1658 (0.0168)	114532	63336 (5662)	0.0001 (0.000061)	0.1513 (0.0157)	107772
Calculators	140855 (13151)	0.0084 (0.0023)	0.4218 (0.0539)	2991476	136116 (10386)	0.0081 (0.0023)	0.4302 (0.0559)	2647279
Radios	103832 (14314)	0.0007 (0.0006)	0.3775 (0.0686)	6510338	115027 (5796)	0.0007 (0.0006)	0.3800 (0.0614)	5594718

Note: Numbers in parentheses represent standard errors.

Table 11–3
Comparison of OLS and NLS Forecasting Performances for the U.S. Market

Product	Time of Peak				Magnitude of Peak			
		Predicted				Predicted		
		NLS				NLS		
	OLS	Model 1	Model 2	Actual	OLS	Model 1	Model 2	Actual
Electric refrigerators	21.70	27.94	26.86	30 (1950)	4413	4521	3334	6200
Black and white TVs	8.12	8.82	8.79	10 (1955)	8050	8024	7891	7757
Electric washing machines	12.17	24.22	23.88	22 (1948)	4052	3739	2678	4616
Room air conditioners	9.06	13.58	13.55	8 (1956)	1879	1843	1791	1828
Passenger cars	23.06	26.65	26.61	29 (1929)	3900	3921	4005	4791
Vacuum cleaners	14.85	17.34	16.66	16 (1947)	3154	3144	2398	3801
Calculators	8.05	9.11	9.06	9 (1978)	15809	15449	15198	15322
Radios	25.32	16.69	16.58	20 (1941)	8859	9834	10969	13642

Table 11–4
Parameter Estimation for the Japanese Market

Product	F Statistic*	Adj. R²	OLS			NLS			MSE
			m	p	q	m	p	q	
Electric refrigerators	421.75	0.99	22626	0.0031	0.6116	18279 (384)	0.0019 (0.0004)	0.7618 (0.0321)	10904
Black and white TVs	75.54	0.93	40505	0.0098	0.4958	33671 (935)	0.0020 (0.0005)	0.5862 (0.0362)	84142
Electric washing machines	180.36	0.94	86824	0.0057	0.1810	81887 (4501)	0.0046 (0.0006)	0.1933 (0.0145)	102762
Room air conditioners	144.12	0.92	53337	0.0019	0.2662	50371 (3977)	0.0006 (0.0003)	0.2789 (0.0288)	130534
Passenger cars	204.00	0.997	47501	0.0001	0.3620	43736 (984)	0.0001 (0.000014)	0.3916 (0.0101)	6290
Vacuum cleaners	202.56	0.96	73028	0.0048	0.2155	68821 (5105)	0.0037 (0.0006)	0.2309 (0.0191)	80377
Calculators	123.81	0.93	573339	0.0034	0.3768	553494 (64793)	0.0004 (0.0002)	0.3850 (0.0455)	18075

Note: Numbers in parentheses represent standard errors.
* All F statistics are significant at the .01 level.
Source: *Monthly Statistics of Japan*, Bureau of Statistics, Japan.

Table 11–5
Forecasting Performance of the Bass Model for the Japanese Market

Product	Time of Peak			Magnitude of Peak		
	Predicted			Predicted		
	OLS	NLS	Actual	OLS	NLS	Actual
Electric refrigerators	8.57	7.84	8 (1963)	3495	3499	3421
Black and white TVs	7.76	9.65	10 (1962)	5221	4968	4885
Electric washing machines	18.50	18.86	18 (1970)	4182	4149	4349
Room air conditioners	18.44	21.95	23 (1979)	3600	3528	4534
Passenger cars	24.00	21.32	22 (1973)	4299	4284	4471
Vacuum cleaners	17.23	17.23	18 (1973)	4113	4100	4724
Calculators	12.36	17.67	18 (1980)	55008	53395	60356

Table 11–6
Parameter Estimation for the Korean Market

Product	OLS					NLS			
	F Statistic	Adj. R²	m	p	q	m	p	q	MSE
Electric refrigerators	29.31***	0.78	8426	0.0009	0.5714	6824 (552)	0.000038 (0.000056)	0.6951 (0.1237)	28516
Black and white TVs	467.63***	0.98	52114	0.0017	0.4458	44384 (879)	0.0003 (0.000067)	0.5189 (0.0215)	51350
Electric washing machines	5.25*	0.59	1971	0.0270	0.6085	1573 (230)	0.0150 (0.0120)	0.8072 (0.2597)	3440
Room air conditioners	7.67**	0.60	299	0.0160	0.4262	257 (46)	0.0098 (0.0063)	0.5004 (0.1498)	47
Passenger cars	13.23**	0.78	610	0.0160	0.6540	470 (33)	0.0069 (0.0045)	0.8868 (0.1634)	178
Radios	46.60***	0.84	80688	0.0041	0.2809	72981 (6038)	0.0030 (0.0012)	0.3085 (0.0437)	649357

Note: Numbers in parentheses represent standard errors.

*Significant at the .10 level.
**Significant at the .05 level.
***Significant at the .01 level.

Sources: *The Major Statistics of Korean Economy*, Kyongje Kihoegwon, Seoul, South Korea. *Yearbook of Industrial Statistics*, Statistical Office of the United Nations, New York.

Table 11-7
Forecasting Performance of the Bass Model for the Korean Market

Product	Time of Peak			Magnitude of Peak		
	Predicted			Predicted		
	OLS	NLS	Actual	OLS	NLS	Actual
Electric refrigerators	11.30	14.13	14 (1979)	1207	1186	1445
Black and white TVs	12.50	14.62	15 (1980)	5852	5763	5863
Electric washing machines	4.88	4.86	5 (1979)	327	329	343
Room air conditioners	7.66	7.71	8 (1979)	33	33	39
Passenger cars	5.66	5.44	6 (1979)	104	106	112
Radios	14.81	14.84	13 (1976)	5834	5740	6717

mates for Y_{t-1} and Y^2_{t-1} are significant at .10 or higher with proper coefficient signs for all the products studied.

Conclusion

The main objective in this chapter is analyzing the data on consumer durables for three different countries (the United States, Japan, and Korea) using the OLS and NLS estimation procedures. The Bass model appears to be capable of capturing the diffusion process for the products fairly well not only in the U.S. market but also in Japanese and Korean markets. Two important topics of managerial interest are the time at which sales peak and the magnitude of sales at that point. As expected, the predicted time of peak of the diffusion by the nonlinear estimation outperforms OLS prediction for the majority of products. On the other hand, as far as the prediction of magnitude of the peak is concerned, the OLS estimation performs comparably well to the NLS estimation. Regarding nonlinear estimation, our experience indicates that nonlinear least squares estimation is sometimes quite sensitive to specification of initial values for the parameters. The OLS estimation prior to the nonlinear estimation serves to provide useful values of the parameters for this purpose.

References

Bass, Frank M. (1969). "A New Product Growth Model for Consumer Durables," *Management Sciences* 15 (January): 215–27.

Dodds, Wellesley (1973). "An Application of the Bass Model in Long-term New Product Forecasting," *Journal of Marketing Research* 10 (August): 308–11.

Dodson, Joe A., and Eitan Muller (1978). "Models of New Product Diffusion through Advertising and Word-of-Mouth," *Management Science* 24 (November): 1568–78.

Heeler, Roger M., and Thomas P. Hustad (1980). "Problems in Predicting New Product Growth for Consumer Durables," *Management Science* 26 (October): 1007–20.

Jain, Dipak, and Ram C. Rao (1987). "Effect of Price on the Demand for Durables." Working paper. School of Management and Administration, University of Texas at Dallas.

Kotler, Philip, Liam Fahey, and Somkid Jatusripitak (1985). *The New Competition.* Englewood Cliffs, N.J.: Prentice-Hall.

Mahajan, Vijay, Charlotte H. Mason, and V. Srinivasan (1986). "An Evaluation of Estimation Procedures for New Product Diffusion Models," in *Innovation Diffusion Models of New Product Acceptance,* Vijay Mahajan and Yoram Wind, eds. Cambridge, Mass.: Ballinger, pp. 203–32.

Mahajan, Vijay, and Eitan Muller (1979). "Innovation Diffusion and New Product Growth Models in Marketing," *Journal of Marketing* 43 (fall): 55–68.

——— (1986). "Determination of Adopter Categories Using Innovation Diffusion Models." Working paper 86-101. Edwin L. Cox School of Business, Southern Methodist University, Dallas, Texas.

Nevers, John V. (1972). "Extensions of a New Product Growth Model," *Sloan Management Review* 13 (winter): 78–89.

Robinson, Bruce, and Chet Lakhani (1975). "Dynamic Price Models for New Product Planning," *Management Science* 21 (June): 1113–22.

Rogers, Everett M. (1983). *Diffusion of Innovations,* 3rd ed. New York: Free Press.

Schmittlein, David C., and Vijay Mahajan (1982). "Maximum Likelihood Estimation for an Innovation Diffusion Model of New Product Acceptance," *Marketing Science* 1 (winter): 57–78.

Srinivasan, V., and Charlotte Mason (1986). "Nonlinear Least Squares Estimation of New Product Diffusion Models," *Marketing Science* 5 (spring): 169–78.

Tigert, Douglas, and Behrooz Farivar (1981). "The Bass New Product Growth Model: A Sensitivity Analysis for a High Technology Product," *Journal of Marketing* 45 (fall): 81–90.

Part VI
Consumer-Behavior Models for New-Product Evaluation

T his part presents two chapters dealing with behavioral components of consumers' new-product evaluations. The first chapter was originally presented at the workshop and later was published in *Journal of Marketing Research*. Although methodologies are unrelated, the two chapters have an underlying common objective of measuring consumer response in terms of preference and/or buying intentions. Each chapter is an example of a unique method applied to the evaluation of consumer response that may be utilized within a new-product–testing process.

Chapter 12 by Imran Currim, Robert Meyer, and Nhan Le presents research using an algorithm termed the Concept Learning System (CLS) for modeling both compensatory and noncompensatory decision structures. The CLS represents decisions as hierarchical or sequentially conditioned in the spirit of consumer-choice behavior as modeled by decision nets. From the time of an earlier publication by Peter Wright (1973) in *Journal of Marketing,* much debate has been expressed as to the true process of consumer decisions, given the apparent robustness of linear models in capturing alternatively hypothesized noncompensatory decisions. The chapter by Currim, Meyer, and Le presents a different research viewpoint: the null hypothesis about the form of the consumer-choice rule is a hierarchical or heuristic model that in fact may be robust for *compensatory* decisions.

As pointed out by the authors, model misspecification of consumer-choice rules may impact negatively upon marketing programs and tactics. New-product positioning is an example whereby methodologies at least implicitly assume the evaluation process to be linear and compensatory. If models of the evaluation process are structurally misspecified, then resulting perceptual maps may be suspect. The authors' study of household coffee purchases via the CLS illustrates this point nicely. For their coffee data, the CLS model suggests much more complexity and conditional evaluation of product attributes and brands on the part of consumers compared to a logistic regression model of the same behavior. In the context of new-product research, traditional methodologies that assume the consumer is using a linear compensatory rule in the purchase of coffee brands would not reveal a richer decision process that structurally may be more accurate.

The next chapter, written by one of the editors of this book, presents an application of an existing model for the concept-evaluation stage of product development. The methodology it outlines does not argue for or against a specific structural model of the evaluative process, but rather takes issue with the methodological conduct of concept/product testing commonly encountered in practice, under the assumption that the evaluative process is linear and compensatory.

The research makes use of sample-group covariance structures as presented in LISREL (Joreskog and Sorbom [1984]). Evaluative variables leading to purchase intentions are assumed to be latent or unobservable, yet a set of observed variables (measured from the concept/product test) allow estimation of the set of latent variable variances and covariances specified by the model. The example developed in the chapter utilizes consumer-panel data from tests of competing brand formulations of a food product. Of interest are differences in structural parameters between any two brands representing a common product concept that is designed to be positioned along a known preference vector.

The response scales reported in the chapter are representative measurements taken by vendors of this type of field research. Of these types of scales, intent-to-purchase responses are frequently used to forecast initial purchases of a prospective new brand (Urban and Hauser [1980]). To assess the potential success of a concept via various brand prototypes (or existing brands), concept evaluation is conducted prior to placing quantities of the disguised brand or prototype with panel members. Subsequent measurements of brand evaluations and purchase intentions are taken after a fixed period of in-home consumption. Thus, one important research question embedded in the forecasting problem is how well do various brand formulations or prototypes "match" with the concept under study?

It should be noted, however, that such field methodologies are limited by the number of "brands" consumers can realistically use and evaluate for in-home–use tests, not to mention the costs of constructing panels and conducting the tests. Hence, pairwise comparisons of brands using independent but disaggregated portions of the total sample are common practice. This issue is discussed in chapter 13 and an alternative procedure is suggested.

Although not discussed in detail in the version of Menasco's writing presented here, specific issues of model development relevant to concept testing are identified. The interested reader is referred to more extensive discussions of these issues in other published work as indicated in the chapter. For instance, the identification problem for multiple group models is an important consideration for the specification of both factor-analytic and structural models.

References

Joreskog, Karl G., and Sorbom, Dag (1984). *LISREL, Analysis of Linear Structural Relationships by the Method of Maximum Likelihood.* Chicago: National Educational Resources.

Urban, Glen L., and Hauser, John R. (1980). *Design and Marketing of New Products.* Englewood Cliffs, N.J.: Prentice Hall.

Wright, Peter (1973). "Use of Consumer Judgment Models in Promotion Planning," *Journal of Marketing* 37 (October): 27–33.

12
Disaggregate Tree-Structured Modeling of Consumer-Choice Data

Imran S. Currim
Robert J. Meyer
Nhan T. Le

W e describe a new approach to individual-choice analysis in which decision trees represent the process consumers use to integrate product-attribute information when making choices. The method departs from other procedures for tree-structured modeling of choice data by allowing decision trees to be estimated at the individual level with normally available data and without a need to prespecify the form of the decision policy.

The approach centers on an algorithm for inferring expert decision rules proposed in artificial intelligence by Quinlan (1983). Similar to AID (Morgan and Sonquist [1963]) and CART (Breiman et al. [1984]), the algorithm builds treelike models of individual decision making by successively partitioning choice data by the product attributes that best discriminate chosen from unchosen options. Once a decision model is estimated for each individual in a sample, three secondary analyses are performed.

1. The heterogeneity of decision rules is examined in terms of the relative importance of attributes in choice, the accuracy of predictions in a holdout sample, and the extent to which each tree is suggestive of a compensatory or noncompensatory decision rule.

2. Segments of consumers sharing similar tree structures are derived.

3. Predictions are generated of the likely effects of changes in marketing-mix variables on aggregate market shares.

We first provide background by reviewing current methods for deriving hierarchical models of discrete choice data. We then describe the central modeling algorithm and the approach we use to make aggregate inferences about consumer-decision strategies. An application of the proposed model-

Reprinted with minor alterations from *Journal of Marketing Research*, Vol. XXV (Aug. 1988), 253–65, published by the American Marketing Association.

ing system to the coffee purchases of a consumer panel is reported as well as an empirical comparison with disaggregate and aggregate logit analysis. We conclude with implications for current research in consumer-choice analysis in marketing.

Background

Hierarchical-Choice Models in Marketing

Consumers often process product-attribute information in a contingent way. When purchasing a soft drink, for example, a consumer may consider price only after first determining that a drink is acceptable on other dimensions such as brand, flavor, or sugar content. Because such decision processes are thought to arise frequently in consumer markets (e.g., Bettman [1974], Gensch [1987], Hauser [1986], Lehmann and Moore [1986], choice analysts in marketing have long sought means for formally modeling them. Modeling efforts have been of two types, those representing contingent processing rules as a decision tree or attribute hierarchy (e.g., Lehmann and Moore) and those representing them as interactions in a linear or log-linear model (e.g., Batsell and Polking [1985]).

In most current methods for estimating hierarchical-choice models, the analyst first hypothesizes a decision tree that represents the sequence with which consumers might consider product attributes. The ability of this hypothesized tree to explain choice behavior then is compared with that of other structures. The model having the highest fit is accepted as the "true" decision sequence. Well-known examples include Tversky and Sattah's (1979) PRETREE and McFadden's (1986) nested logit models, both of which characterize choice as a process in which options are sequentially eliminated if they fail to satisfy a set of ordered attribute criteria. (For further discussion, see Currim [1982], Dubin [1986], Lehmann and Moore [1986]). Closely related are the hierarchical models of decision making proposed for the study of market structure by Grover and Dillon (1985), Kalwani and Morrison (1977), Urban et al. (1984), and others. Though the latter representations are not choice models per se (they do not yield individual probabilities of brand choice), their hierarchical structure is thought to reflect the process by which consumers evaluate brand features when making choices (Urban et al.).

A limitation of these procedures is that they are difficult to apply to the study of how *individual* consumers make brand choices. In most applications, the analyst estimates one decision tree for a sample or segment and then assumes this process holds for each consumer (e.g., Dubin [1986], Urban et al. [1984]). The assumption of homogeneity is often likely to be untenable, but the analyst usually has little recourse; individual-level estimation is hindered by both the need for a large number of repeated choices to define brand choice or switching probabilities (Rao and Sabavala [1981]) and, more generally, the need to fit models repeatedly by trial and error (a process that becomes cumbersome as the number of possible trees increases).

Though several researchers have recently sought means for overcoming these drawbacks, the solutions are still rather limited. For example, Gensch and Svestka's (1984; also Gensch [1987]) HIARCH estimates the parameters of a hierarchical elimination rule at the individual level, but requires measures of the relative importance of product attributes to each consumer—something usually unavailable. Likewise, DeSarbo et al. (1987), Rao and Sabavala (1981), and others have explored the possibility of estimating decision trees by using hierarchical clustering algorithms that do not require prior hypotheses about tree form. These procedures, however, appear most applicable to aggregate studies of decision making and do not yield trees that predict probabilities of brand choice as a function of product-attribute values.

In response to the difficulties involved in applying traditional hierarchical-modeling procedures, several researchers have suggested that conditional-choice processes might be represented more flexibly within linear models recognizing cross-effects or interactions among attributes (e.g., Batsell and Polking [1985], Cooper [1987], Meyer and Eagle [1982]). The rationale behind this approach is that one can represent a wide variety of conditional as well as unconditional (linear additive) judgment processes within one modeling framework and without a need for prior hypotheses about the form of a decision hierarchy (Batsell and Polking). Unfortunately, this generality comes at a cost: the data requirements for fully interactive models are often substantial and are difficult to meet in natural (nonexperimental) field settings. In practice, the analyst is faced with many of the same limitations that inhibit applications of hierarchical-modeling procedures: one must either restrict application to the aggregate level (e.g., Cooper) or have prior hypotheses about the restricted set of attribute interactions likely to be significant at the individual level (e.g., Batsell and Polking; Green et al. [1981]; Lynch [1985]).

Inductive-Learning Algorithms in Artificial Intelligence

Within the field of artificial intelligence, there has recently been interest in the development of algorithms that enable machines to "learn" the rules underlying concepts (Cohen and Feigenbaum [1982]). An often-used example is disease diagnosis: given examples of a number of diseases and their associated symptoms, the objective of the algorithm is to infer a parsimonious set of "if-then" rules that would allow diseases to be diagnosed from a set of symptoms (e.g., Michalski [1983]). The primary motivation of the work has been to reduce the traditional reliance of expert systems on human experts. In principle, expert knowledge bases could be developed merely by studying examples of decisions made by experts and could be automatically refined as new examples became available.

Though learning algorithms have not been used widely as an approach to developing *descriptive* models of decision making (Smith et al.'s 1984 work appears to be the only exception), this application seems to be a natural one. The appeal of the approach is that learning algorithms can be used as *exploratory* model-building tools in instances where the number of previous decisions may be small. Hence, they raise the possibility of allowing decision-tree models of consumer choice to be estimated efficiently at a true disaggregate level.

We report an application of one inductive-learning algorithm to the analysis of consumer–decision-making strategies. The algorithm, called CLS (for concept learning system), is applied to the inference of individual-level tree models of decision making from discrete panel data. The algorithm is part of a more general consumer-modeling system that both summarizes the types of decision-making strategies in a sample and assesses the likely consequences of those strategies on aggregate market shares.

The CLS Modeling System

The Algorithm

CLS (Quinlan [1983]) is a nonparametric classification procedure for inferring "if-then" rules that relate a set of predictor variables (such as product attributes) to a discrete outcome criterion (such as choice). The CLS algorithm parallels a larger literature of parametric and nonparametric approaches to tree-structured modeling, such as Breiman et al.'s (1984) CART, Morgan and Sonquist's (1963) AID, and Perreault and Barksdale's (1980) CHAID. Though similar in the basic model-building process, the CLS algorithm differs from these procedures in the nature of the criterion used for branching and the approach used to determine optimal tree size. The more important difference for our purposes, however, is the domain of application. Whereas tree-structured modeling procedures traditionally have been used as tools for analyzing interactions among variables in an aggregate database, our focus is on their use as a tool for building a system of disaggregate models.

Assume that an analyst observes a consumer making repeated purchases from a set of brands and after each purchase records whether each brand was chosen or unchosen. Associated with each brand is a set of nominally valued attributes, each taking N levels, $N \geq 2$. For example, an attribute might be a measure of whether a product comes with a lifetime warranty or is above or below a threshold price (cases in which N equals 2) or the product's color (N greater than 2).

As in CART, the CLS algorithm uses this battery of attributes to infer a decision tree that discriminates chosen from unchosen options. The implementation can be summarized in terms of a four-step algorithm.

1. For each product attribute x, define a splitting criterion $C(x)$ that is a measure of the ability of that attribute to discriminate chosen from unchosen options. Based on information theory (e.g., Shannon [1948]), $C(x)$ is a measure of the classification power of x or its entropy. Formally, let $j = 1,...,N_x$ be the number of levels associated with attribute $x(N \geq 2)$ and let $f_{j|x}$ be the number of choice options having level j of x. $C(x)$ is defined as

$$C(x) = -\sum_{j=1}^{N_x} f_{j|x}[p(\text{chosen}|j,x)\log_2 p(\text{chosen}|j,x) \tag{1}$$
$$+ p(\text{unchosen}|j,x)\log_2 p(\text{unchosen}|j,x)]$$

where $p(\text{chosen}|j,x)$ is the probability (estimated from the sample proportion) of an option being chosen that has level j of attribute x and $p(\text{unchosen}|j,x)$ is the probability that it is not chosen given j and x.

2. Define that attribute with the smallest criterion as the starting attribute or primary "root" of the decision tree. Then partition the data into N_x splits, where N_x is the number of levels associated with attribute x. For example, if color were the starting attribute, we would partition the data into several sets containing just those options that are red, just those that are blue, and so on. If there is a tie in determining the attribute with the lowest criterion value, the starting attribute is selected at random.

3. Within each split, recalibrate the discrimination criterion for each remaining attribute and define the attribute that best discriminates chosen from unchosen options as the root of a secondary branch of the decision tree.

4. Continue to apply this heuristic to successive splits of the data until either all instances have been classified or a stopping criterion is reached (e.g., until there is no longer a significant increase in the proportion of explained choices).

The decision to use an entropy measure as the splitting criterion is somewhat arbitrary; because branching decisions are made only by considering the *order* of an attribute with respect to $C(x)$, derived tree structures should be robust across ordinally equivalent measures of discrimination. Breiman et al. (1984) report a comparison of several alternative discrimination measures including the entropy statistic used here and note few salient differences in derived tree structures. Consequently, the entropy criterion is retained largely because of its relative ease of computation and its links to the literature in information theory.

Similar to CART (Breiman et al. [1984]) and CHAID (Perreault and Barksdale [1980]), the CLS algorithm also extends to multiple-classification problems in which the analyst seeks to model the ability of a set of predictors to discriminate among several nominal outcomes. For example, the approach could be extended to the problem of modeling how product attributes combine to yield decisions on whether to accept, reject, or be undecided toward an option or discriminate among multiple chosen brands on the basis of buyer characteristics.

A Worked Example. To provide an intuitive feel for how the algorithm can be used to recover a heuristic choice rule, we offer a simplified worked example for the case of a conjunctive decision policy. Imagine that a respondent has been asked to look through a list of nine one-bedroom apartments (table 12–1), where each is described by rent and distance to work. Suppose the respondent decides whether or not an apartment is acceptable by employing the following heuristic: declare acceptable any apartment that is not more than $500 per month and is within 2 miles of work.

To apply the algorithm to these data, we first convert continuous measures of rent and distance to the following dichotomous indicators: ≤ $450, ≤ $500, and ≤ $600, ≤ 1½ miles, ≤ 2 miles, and ≤ 3 miles.[1] In step 1, two indicators, rent ≤ $500 and distance ≤ 2 miles, have identical minimum criterion $(C(x))$ values of 3.81; hence we choose one at random, say rent ≤ $500, to create the first node of the decision tree. (see figure 12–1.)[2] The original set of nine apartments is now partitioned into two sets, one con-

Table 12–1
Options Used in the Apartment-Choice Example

Apartment Number	Rent per Month ($)	Miles from Work	Judgment (1 = Yes, 0 = No)
1	450	1.5	1
2	500	1.5	1
3	600	1.5	0
4	450	2	1
5	500	2	1
6	600	2	0
7	450	3	0
8	500	3	0
9	600	3	0

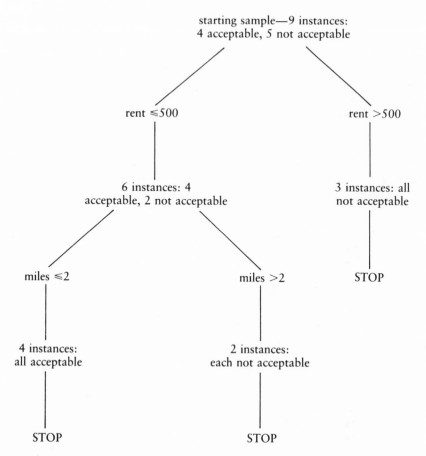

Figure 12–1. Decision Tree Generated by CLS Algorithm for Apartment-Choice Example

taining six profiles and the other three profiles. Because this second set describes only unacceptable apartments, no further partitioning of this set is required. For the first set, however, we compute a new set of criterion values. The new attribute with the lowest criterion value is distance $\leq$ 2 miles ($C(x)$ = 0).

The set of six apartments is now partitioned into two sets, the first comprising four profiles, all of which are judged acceptable, and the second comprising two profiles, neither of which is acceptable. Here we stop, having explained the original set of judgments. The decision tree inferred by the algorithm (figure 12–1) can be described by the predicate calculus expression,

accept if (rent $\leq$ 500) and (distance $\leq$ 2 miles); else reject, which is precisely the rule considered.

Problems of Noise and Rule Uniqueness. An inherent difficulty in applications of CLS or any tree-structured analysis method is that data cannot be expected to be error-free as in the preceding example. Choice data will be marred by the effects of unobserved variables, measurement error, and instability in preference structures. Consequently, when one infers a classification tree for a given context, only a portion of the structure will reflect systematic variation in the effect of each predictor of an outcome. In addition, because the selection of an attribute node at one stage determines the structure of a tree at later stages, the chance introduction of a single noisy attribute can cause changes in structure of an entire tree.

The first implication of this problem is that the ability of a tree to explain the data that generated it will be an inadequate measure of the tree's validity as a predictive tool. Because the objective is to classify all instances, the estimation fit may be high regardless of the true validity of the model. Hence, in application one must initially partition the data set into estimation and validation samples and measure model fit by the correspondence of the tree to these holdout observations.

A more difficult problem is identifying error within the tree structure itself. In other words, which portions of the proposed tree represent reliable effects and which random noise? The most commonly adopted approach is to use a stopping rule whereby branching is halted when the increase in information about classification provided by the addition of an attribute is below some threshold level (e.g., Perreault and Barksdale [1980], Quinlan [1983]). Unfortunately, as noted by Breiman et al. (1984), the use of such rules does not guarantee an optimal predictive tree; plots of changes in explanatory ability across modeling iterations often show "local plateaus" in which significant improvements in fit follow periods of little change in overall model performance.[3] Because of this problem, Breiman et al. suggest that decision trees probably are best estimated by first building a tree without stopping constraints and then successively *deleting* branches until a significant decrease in the model's explanatory ability is encountered.

In our implementation of the CLS algorithm, we follow this procedure by first estimating a tree that maximizes the fit to an estimation sample and then successively deleting those attributes that impose the smallest decrease in the overall model chi-square.[4] In the case of large samples, this process continues until the decrease in descriptive validity (fit in the estimation sample) exceeds that expected by chance variation in the data. In the case of small samples (as are common when one is building disaggregate decision models), "optimal tree size" is more difficult to determine statistically. Here, any stopping decisions ultimately will be arbitrary, as reliably detecting statistically significant differences will be impossible. In such cases, the stopping decision could be made subjectively, but in applications we have adopted the more conservative approach of using the complete tree inferred from the estimation sample, accepting the possibility that at least some of the structure will be unreliable.

Consumer-Choice Analysis Using CLS

The CLS algorithm has been integrated in a general modeling system[5] designed to offer six levels of analysis of individual choice data:

1. Predicate calculus and graphic representations of each derived decision tree with a summary of each partitioning history.
2. Descriptive and predictive validities of a given derived tree.
3. Summaries of the relative frequency with which each product feature appears across all choice paths (a measure of feature importance suggested by Bettman [1984]) and a measure of the degree of symmetry exhibited by each tree, reflecting the extent to which the absence of a given product feature can be compensated in choice by the presence of another.
4. Histograms of the distribution of descriptive validity, predictive validity, and tree symmetry across the sample.
5. Segmentation of individuals with matching tree structures.
6. Predictions of the likely effect of changes in product-attribute values on aggregate choice behavior.

The first output presumably would be most useful when CLS is applied to small-sample problems, when the analyst's prime interest is in building models of a single decisionmaker. In general, however, the latter, more aggregate, analyses are presumed to be the prime interest.

The aggregate implications of a derived set of decision trees are explored through the use of a choice simulator. The simulator generates a set of predictions of the likely choice frequencies for each option in a market under alternative product-attribute configurations. The procedure is straightforward. A factorial array of product attribute levels first is generated for each brand. Each combination of levels then is passed through the decision tree derived for each respondent. This step in turn yields a prediction for each respondent of whether he or she would choose or not choose a brand given that set of attributes. These individual-level predictions are summed across respondents to yield a prediction of the likely aggregate choice share for each brand/attribute combination.

We stress that predicted relative-choice frequencies are not market-share forecasts per se, as these relative frequencies are not sum-constrained across brands. Unlike simulators used in applications of conjoint analysis (e.g., Green et al. [1981]), the CLS procedure does not derive choices by declaring the chosen option to be the one with the maximum predicted utility in a set. Rather, an option is predicted to be chosen simply if a given "if-then" decision structure is satisfied, which allows for the possibility of predictions of multiple or no choices in a given context. If an analyst wants forecasts to sum to unity in a given context, he or she should normalize predictions across brands.

CLS Applied to Analysis of Consumer-Panel Data

In this section, we report results of an application of the CLS modeling system to UPC scanner-panel data. Our objective is to illustrate the types of analyses yielded by the CLS algorithm and consumer-modeling system. In addition, we compare these results with those obtained by logit analysis, one of the dominant methods used to analyze similar data (e.g., Cooper [1987], Guadagni and Little [1983]).

The Data

The data are a two-year record of regular–ground-coffee purchases made by two hundred households in a Marion, Indiana, UPC scanner panel. This sample of two hundred was part of a larger dataset describing the coffee purchases of two thousand households provided by Information Resources, Inc. The smaller sample was selected because it had the greatest frequency of purchasing the five leading brands of regular ground coffee. A broader sampling of households could have been considered, but we restricted our focus to minimize the presence of individual households with few purchases.

The five brands of coffee considered in the analysis were Chock-Full-o'Nuts, Folgers, Hills Brothers, Maxwell House, and Mellow Roast. Chock-Full-o'Nuts, Folgers, and Maxwell House were the three major-share brands. All brands had considerable variance in price levels across stores and weeks. The category was reasonably active in feature and display promotions, with the exception of Mellow Roast, which was not supported during the period of observation.

For each household, the data provided a record of each brand purchased in a given week, the store chain in which it was purchased, and the other brands that were available. The data were prepared for analysis by initially sorting these purchase records by household, week, and chain. Within these strata, the characteristics of each available brand (e.g., price and whether it was featured or displayed) were represented as a row vector and the dependent variable was a binary (0,1) indicator of whether the brand had been chosen by the household in a given week and chain.

Associated with each choice record were six sets of explanatory variables.

1. The name of the considered brand, coded in terms of five dichotomous dummy variables.

2. A binary indicator of whether the given brand was featured in a newspaper ad during the given week.

3. A binary indicator of whether it was included in a special store display.

4. The brand's price per ounce, net of any coupons redeemed.

5. A translation of this continuous variable into seventeen dichotomous cumulative net-price indicators for use in estimating CLS tree models. The indicators took the value 1 if the net price was below a threshold value and 0 otherwise. Prices ranged from ≤ nine cents per ounce to > twenty-four cents per ounce in one-cent-per-ounce increments.

6. Three dichotomous indicators denoting the chain in which a given brand was purchased.

The two measures of price reflected differences in how this variable was to be modeled in comparing the CLS and logit procedures; in the CLS procedure, price was to be modeled as a series of dichotomous variables, whereas in logit it was to be treated as a single cardinal measure (following traditional practice). The brand-name and store-chain variables were introduced to capture unique effects of branding and store environment that were not reflected in featuring, display, and price activity.

The mean number of weeks in which at least one coffee purchase was made across all households was thirty-two, which corresponded to an average of 160 brand purchase/nonpurchase records per household. These data were split for each household; one half was used for model estimation and the other half was set aside as a holdout for predictive validity tests.

Results

Household Decision Policies. We applied the CLS algorithm to each household's data to derive two hundred household-level models of choice. Because of the small number of observations available in each partition (hence the difficulty of performing significance tests), no attempt was made to refine each tree after estimation; the derived model for each household is simply the one that maximizes fit to the estimation.

On average, the CLS tree models do well in recovering the brand choices observed in both the estimation and validation samples. Only 3 percent of the derived trees yield prediction rates of less than .9, with an average of

.971. More importantly, however, there is only a small drop-off in prediction rates when the derived trees are applied to the validation sample. Eighty-nine percent of the trees yield prediction rates greater than the chance level of .668 with an average fit across respondents of .834.[6]

To provide means for summarizing the diversity of tree structures in the sample, we examined the degree of symmetry of each derived decision tree. The symmetry index was a 0-to-1 measure of the extent to which the absence of a given desired product feature (e.g., being off display) could be compensated for in choice by the presence of another positive feature (e.g., being low in price).[7] Proportions close to 1 implied a more balanced or compensatory decision structure, whereas values closer to 0 implied a more skewed or noncompensatory structure. Most derived trees suggest a mix of compensatory and noncompensatory elements; there are few instances of either highly skewed (noncompensatory) or perfectly symmetric (compensatory) structures, with 75 percent of households yielding trees with symmetry ranging from .4 to .7. The average symmetry index across respondents is .559.

A caveat to be stressed in interpreting the measures of tree symmetry is that the structure of a given tree may be influenced by "noise" or inconsistency in choices, which will tend to encourage "false" symmetric structures. To explore this issue, we examined the extent to which there was a systematic relationship between tree symmetry and a model's predictive validity. The hypothesis was that if the symmetry were primarily a by-product of noise in the choice (or measurement) process, validation fits should be lower for trees having a more symmetric structure. The results indicate no significant relationship between symmetry and fit ($r = .06$), suggesting that the effect of noise on tree structures is not biased toward symmetric structures.

Decision-making Segments. To provide a more graphic summary of the types of decision strategies used by households in the sample, we summarize in figure 12–2 the results of grouping households that share identical tree structures through the first two levels of branching.[8] The grouping suggests three major decision styles: one in which price is the initial discriminator (35 percent), one in which brand is the initial discriminator (33 percent), and one in which feature is the initial discriminator (27 percent). The remaining 5 percent of the trees have either "on display" or a "store chain" as the initial attribute. An intuitively attractive aspect of these graphs is that they resemble the brand and form partitions of markets that frequently arise in aggregate studies of market structure (e.g., Grover and Dillon [1985], Kalwani and Morrison [1977]).

A perhaps more interesting aspect of these graphs is the pattern of secondary attributes considered after the initial roots. They indicate how different attributes are conditioned by whether a brand satisfies a given primary attribute and how such interactions vary across the sample. For example,

Form 1: price primary (35% of all panelists)

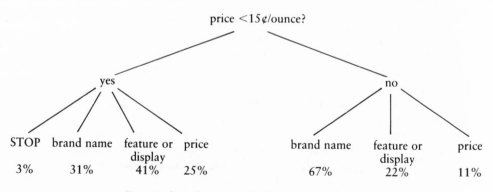

Form 2: brand primary (33% of all panelists)

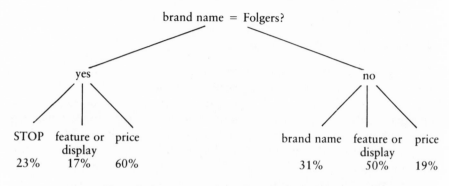

Form 3: feature primary (27% of all panelists)

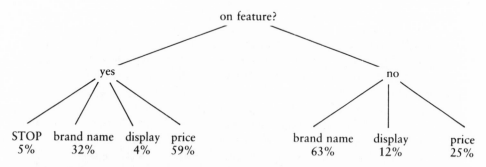

Figure 12–2. Modal Tree Structures in IRI Panel

Note: Percentages below each parent note reflect distribution of secondary nodes across panelists.

consider the 33 percent of households that followed a brand-primary structure. The modal decision rule is a simple one. If a given brand was a household's favorite, only one other attribute was relevant as a precursor to choice:
its price. If the price was acceptable, the brand was purchased; if not, either
it was rejected or other factors (such as features or displays) were considered.
When "off brands" were purchased, they tended only to be those featured
or displayed.

There are also important variations about such modal patterns. For example, 23 percent of the brand-primary segment considered *only* brand name
in their decisions, displaying a complete insensitivity to other marketing instruments. Likewise, though some households were "brand loyalists," there
were surprisingly few "price loyalists." We found only one instance of a
household willing to buy any brand that met a primary-price threshold.
Rather, price appeared to serve as a filter before the consideration of either
brand name or promotion.

Aggregate-Sales-Response Analysis

In many applied contexts, the nature of individual decision-making policies
is of less importance than the aggregate consequences of those policies. To
demonstrate CLS's approach in such cases, we explored the likely aggregate
effects of a change in product attributes on choice proportions. Following
the simulation procedure described before, we derived estimates of the likely
proportion of households that would buy each brand given different combinations of price per ounce, feature, and display, holding competitors' pricing and promotional activities constant at the previous (estimation) year's
mean values. Figure 12–3 shows these predictions for the two largest-share
coffee brands, Folgers and Maxwell House.

An inspection of the graphs suggests a rather intriguing result: at the
household level, decision processes are represented as contingent and often
complex, but when the decision trees are aggregated they yield a surprisingly
simple market-level view of how changes in brand attributes affect brand
shares. Across brands, the graphs suggest a simple negative S-shaped effect
of price and positive effects of features and displays. In addition, these effects
appear largely additive; an aggregate regression analysis fit to the simulation
surface across brands fails to support interactions between price and either
feature or display and shows only a small (negative) interaction ($p < .10$)
between feature and display. The latter result implies that the gains in share
likely to be obtained when a brand is both featured *and* displayed will be
less, on average, than the sum of the gains accruing to a feature or display
alone.

These results illustrate the potential danger of drawing inferences about
individual-level processes from the study of aggregate response patterns (e.g.,

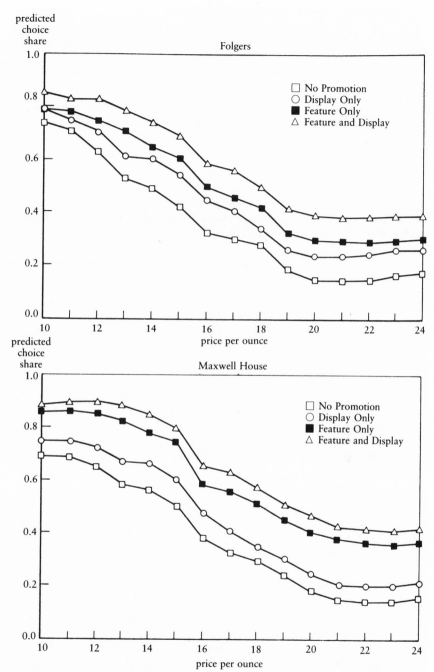

Figure 12-3. Proportion of Panelists Choosing Folgers and Maxwell House Coffees under Alternative Combinations of Prices per Ounce, Features, and Displays as Predicted by CLS Choice Simulator

Figure shows how individual decision trees are smoothed by aggregation.

Urban et al. [1984], Tversky and Sattah [1979]). In our example, the aggregate analysis masks an important finding that surfaces in the disaggregate analyses: the sample of households is very heterogeneous in its decision-making styles (at least three distinct segments are evident) and attributes often have contingent effects on choice. Though the choice simulation is useful for aggregate-level predictions of brand shares, it is less useful for gaining insights into the behavioral process that underlies these shares.

A Comparison with Disaggregate Logit Analysis

A natural question that arises in the evaluation of any new methodology is the extent to which its insights converge with those provided by more established methods. To address this issue, we compared the analysis of coffee purchases provided by CLS with that of another method, disaggregate logit analysis (McFadden [1986]). Logit analysis was used as a comparison both because of its increasing importance as a method for analyzing consumer-panel data at the individual level (e.g., Guadagni and Little [1983]) and because it is a contrasting approach to modeling dependencies among attributes (e.g., Batsell and Polking [1985], Cooper [1987]). We compared the methods on their ability to predict households' coffee purchases in a holdout sample at the disaggregate level and on their insights about the relative importance of factors in brand choice.

Two different specifications of the linear utility equation within a logit model were considered: one in which the effects of price, displays, features, and brand name were assumed to be mutually independent and one that allowed for dependencies or interactions among predictors. Formally, binary brand-choice data were represented in terms of the dichotomous choice model

$$Y_i = \frac{1}{1 + e^{\beta'X_i}},\tag{2}$$

where Y_i is a 0–1 measure of whether or not brand i was chosen and $\beta'X_i$ is a linear combination of the brand's price (expressed as a cardinal measure), dummy-effect codes for feature, display, and brand name, and a similar effect code for store chain.[9] In the interactive form, this set of predictors was expanded to include all the cross-products among brand names, prices, and promotions. The parameter vector β' was estimated by maximum likelihood using the SAS supplemental procedure LOGIST. Expression 2 was estimated at two different levels of aggregation: at the individual household level (yielding two hundred sets of parameter estimates), termed the *disaggregate analysis,* and at the aggregate level (which is most common in practice), termed the *aggregate analysis.*

The simple (nine-parameter) additive forms of logit yield levels of predictive validity comparable to those provided by the CLS models (which are estimated with an average of twelve data partitions per household) at both the aggregate and disaggregate levels. Specifically, the average rate of correspondence is .851 for the disaggregate logit, .799 for the aggregate logit, and .834 for the CLS system, all significantly greater than chance. (See note 6.) This level of comparability is similar to that found in other comparisons of tree with linear discriminant models (Breiman et al. [1984]) and reported attempts to fit linear logit models to data known to have a noncompensatory component (e.g., Einhorn et al. [1978], Johnson and Meyer [1984]).

In the case of the twenty-two-parameter aggregate logit, adding interactions yields a nominal increase in predictive validity to .806. In contrast, there is clear evidence that such effects could *not* be efficiently supported at the household level. When interactions are included at the household level, predictive accuracy decreases to .604, which is actually *below* chance levels of prediction. Exploring this failure in further detail, we find that only 23 percent of the household-level variance-covariance matrices are of full rank, implying that interaction analyses could be possible only at the aggregate level.

As a final point of comparison, we examined the diagnostic information each approach yielded about the average relative importance of different predictors of brand choice. In table 12–2, we report measures of the relative importance of brand price, featuring, displays, and the different brand-specific effects implied by each method of analysis. In the case of the CLS system, we report two measures of predictor importance: the relative number of

Table 12–2
Estimates of Attribute and Brand Importance Derived by CLS and Logit

	Price and Promotional Effects		
	Relative Frequency with Which an Attribute Appeared in a CLS Decision Tree[1]	*t-statistic Revealed by a Logit Model Fit to the CLS Simulation Surface*[1]	*Logit t-statistic*[1]
Predictor			
Feature	.268 (1)	19.44 (1)	42.0(1)
Price	—	−16.03 (2)	−15.56 (2)
Display	.153 (2)	8.53 (3)	11.49 (3)
Brand-specific effects			
Maxwell House	.117 (3)	0[a] (1)	0[a] (2)
Folgers	.133 (2)	−3.68 (2)	2.28 (1)
Chock-Full-o'Nuts	.153 (1)	−7.76 (3)	−5.78 (3)
Hills Brothers	.039 (4)	−13.15 (4)	−16.86 (4)
Mellow Roast	.036 (5)	−14.14 (5)	−17.66 (5)

[1]Importance rank is in parentheses.

[a]Maxwell House is the referent brand in these analyses.

choice "routes" containing a given predictor (a measure of importance suggested by Bettman [1974]) and *t*-statistics derived from a logistic regression fit to the response surfaces reported in figure 12–3. (The latter analysis was used to derive a single measure of the global importance of price that would be comparable to that yielded by the logit.[10]) The logit-effect measures we report are the *t*-statistics derived for the single aggregate logit equation estimated across all disaggregate data.[11] The results indicate a high degree of convergence. Both modeling approaches identify featuring as the dominant brand attribute influencing brand choice, followed by price and displays. Among the brand-specific effects, there is some variance among the procedures, but all identify Chock-Full-o'Nuts, Folgers, and Maxwell House as being the dominant brands and Hills Brothers and Mellow Roast as being less preferred.

In sum, the comparison of the CLS and logit approaches suggests that the two are comparable in terms of aggregate predictive validity and the diagnostic information they yield about the primary determinants of choice behavior. The primary difference is in the ability to represent interactive or contingent attribute effects at the household level. Such effects are implicit in CLS models, but data sparsity precluded their representation at the household level in linear or logistic models.

Discussion

We describe and illustrate an approach to the estimation of hierarchical models of consumer choice that departs from previous methods for such analysis in two ways.

1. The estimation of models is explicitly at the individual level.
2. The analyst need not make assumptions about the form of the hierarchy or dependency among attribute effects.

The approach appears comparable to logistic modeling techniques in predictive validity and its ability to detect the aggregate determinants of choice in a category, but has the advantage of permitting the study of interactive or conditional attribute effects at a disaggregate level.

Though the support we offer for the approach is positive, cautions for its use should be emphasized. It is tempting to interpret derived production systems as actual sequential decision processes, but care should be taken in doing so without some convergent process evidence on how decisions are made in a given context. Specifically, *any* model of data is inherently paramorphic and CLS is no exception. Hence, while one might be led to describe a tree as suggesting that consumers "first consider attribute A, then B," the more proper translation is that choice is explained best when the conjunction "if A and B" is satisfied.

The method is subject to many of the same statistical caveats that apply to all tree-structured modeling procedures, such as AID and CART. (See, e.g., Breiman et al. [1984] for a discussion.) For example, the final structure of a given tree may be sensitive to which product attribute forms the root or parent node of the tree (something that has chance elements associated with it). Likewise, as with any estimated model, instabilities in tree structures will become more pronounced with diminishing sample sizes or whenever the discriminability indices are driven more by chance elements. It is because of these concerns that we tend to focus on aggregates of individual trees on the presumption that individual trees may be unreliable but forecasts based on a pooling of trees will be more reliable.

Implications for Modeling in Marketing

We contrast the CLS procedure with one conventional modeling procedure, logit analysis. In its ideal application, however, we view CLS as being a complementary rather than competing approach to the analysis of choice data. The greatest advantage of logit (or any linear modeling method), which CLS cannot match, is its parsimony in capturing simple compensatory decision rules and the presence of a rich theoretical basis that supports detailed hypothesis testing. In contrast, linear models are not as well suited for capturing *nonadditive* or noncompensatory decision rules at low levels of aggregation. Hence, if analysts have reason to suspect that individual-level decisions are made through noncompensatory or conditional processes or if a central concern is studying the pattern of heterogeneity in nonadditive rules, CLS may be an attractive alternative analysis approach.

In addition, the CLS modeling system might be used as a *preliminary* data-analysis tool. For example, the graphic representation of how attributes interact provided by the choice simulator (figure 12–3) offers a potential tool for guiding the a priori selection of interactive functional forms without the need for extensive exploratory nested model tests. Figure 12–3 would have suggested that a simple additive-demand model would be likely to provide a good account of aggregate response patterns—and this is indeed the case. Similarly, the clustering algorithm could be used to identify market segments that are likely to have similar response patterns. Once such exploration has been completed, techniques could be used to parameterize the response surface and/or test hypotheses.

Another potential application of the approach, which we do not explore thoroughly here, is to use CLS as a tool for studying the structure of competition among brands in a market. As we noted at the outset, hierarchical models of product choice, such as those generated by CLS, have long been important as aggregate representations of the structure of competition within a market (e.g., Kalwani and Morrison [1977]). Unfortunately, most traditional approaches to such analysis have been based on the assumption that the market of interest is homogeneous in its perceptions of market structure, causing some authors to argue that the insights yielded about competition can be inappropriate (e.g., Kahn et al. [1986], Grover and Dillon [1985]).

Future research should explore the extent to which the individual-level hierarchical models offered by CLS might be used to overcome this limitation. If the production rules generated by CLS can be shown to reflect actual elimination strategies, the algorithm could be used to infer perceived competitive structures at the individual level, with the matching procedure being used to identify market segments with similar substitution patterns. Central to such an exploration would be an expansion of the array of alternative methodologies with which CLS is compared; for example, a comparison with the competitive structures yielded by switching patterns (e.g., Kalwani and Morrison [1977]) and interpurchase times would be of interest.

Finally, the usefulness of alternative learning algorithms might be explored. An advantage of CLS is that it is easily implemented and has theoretical links to established literatures in tree-structured modeling. A disadvantage, however, is that there is no guarantee that the derived rules will appear "logical" to the analyst or be the most parsimonious representation of a given decision policy. Hence, future research could explore more sophisticated rule-learning algorithms being developed within artificial intelligence, such as Michalski's (1983) STAR and INDUCE procedures.

Notes

1. Rent and distance are coded dichotomously for simplicity. If one had an a priori reason to suspect that each level of a factor had a unique contingent decision rule associated with it, we might prefer to treat each factor as being fully nominal, hence yielding multiple branches from each node.

2. To illustrate this calculation, for rent $\leq$ \$500 we compute, from expression 1 (using log base e),

$$
\begin{aligned}
C(x) = & - (\text{number chosen}| \leq \$500)\log(P(\text{chosen}| \leq \$500)) \\
& - (\text{number not chosen}| \leq \$500)\log(P(\text{not chosen}| \leq \$500)) \\
& - (\text{number chosen}| > \$500)\log(P(\text{chosen}| > \$500)) \\
& - (\text{number not chosen}| > \$500)\log(P(\text{not chosen}| > \$500)) \\
= & - 4\log(4/(4 + 2)) - 2\log(2/(4 + 2)) \\
& - 0\log(0/(0 + 2)) - 2\log(2/(0 + 2)) \\
= & \ 3.81.
\end{aligned}
$$

3. For illustration, consider the problem of using the CLS algorithm to analyze the following choice data

Choice	Attribute A	Attribute B
1	1	0
0	1	1
0	0	0
1	0	1

where choice outcomes have been generated by the rule

choice = 1 if $A = 1$ and $B = 0$ or $A = 0$ and $B = 1$.

This case is a difficult one because neither attribute has independent discriminatory power; therefore there would be no statistical rationale for initially splitting the data. Only after an initial partition is *forced* on the data is the existence of a perfect discriminatory rule evident.

4. Formally, at any given stage we prune the attribute x that yields the smallest change in discriminatory ability, as defined by the chi square statistic suggested by Quinlan (1983):

$$X^2(x) = \sum_{j=1}^{m} \{[N(j|\text{chosen}) - N'(j|\text{chosen})]^2/N'(j|\text{chosen})$$
$$+ [N(j|\text{unchosen}) - N'(j|\text{unchosen})]^2/N'(j|\text{unchosen})\}$$

where $N(j|\text{chosen})$ is the number of chosen options at a given stage possessing level j of attribute x and $N'(j|\text{chosen})$ is the *expected* number of chosen options under independence. Specifically, $N'(j|\text{chosen}) = N \cdot P(j) \cdot P(\text{chosen})$, where N is the total number of options to be classified at a given stage and $P(j)$ and $P(\text{chosen})$ are the unconditional probabilities that a randomly chosen option will have attribute level j and be chosen, respectively.

5. Copies of the CLS-modeling software for implementation on IBM PC-ATs are available from the second author upon request.

6. The .668 rate is the relative proportion of unchosen options in the holdout sample and reflects the proportion of correct predictions that would be made if the most likely naive outcome (not chosen) were predicted for each brand on each occasion. Though panelists indeed allocated their choices across five brands, the naive rate is less than .8 because choice-set sizes were frequently smaller than five in individual weeks (in some weeks, for example, information was available on only three competing brands) and panelists occasionally chose multiple brands on the same shopping occasion (this happened on about 4 percent of the occasions).

7. Symmetry is defined by the index

$$SIM = \left(\sum_{k=1}^{m} \left[(N_k P_k P_k') \Big/ \sum_{k=1}^{m} N_k \right] \right) \Big/ .25$$

where $k = 1, ..., m$ subscripts the m dichotomous product features appearing in a tree. N_k is the number of times that feature appears in a choice path within that tree, P_k is the relative proportion of these appearances that are *affirmative* (e.g., "if A . . ."), and P_k' is the relative proportion of these appearances that are *disaffirmative* ("if *not* A . . ."). The denominator of .25 is the maximum value the numerator can take on, that when $P_k = P_k' = .5$ for all k, and hence serves to standardize the index to vary between 0 and 1. A perfectly balanced tree (yielding an index of 1) by this definition is one having an equal blend of conditions and their complements. We should also note that the index weights each product by its sample size across all choice paths; hence, for example, trees having balance in their primary attributes (or root nodes) will be judged as more symmetric than ones having balance only in minor attributes.

8. Our decision to limit grouping to identical first- and second-order structures reflects the fact that the number of possible groups expands exponentially with the number of levels one considers. Hence nontrivial clusters of respondents having the same tree tend to vanish beyond the first two levels.

9. We also explored an aggregate multinomial representation of these data, with results similar to those reported here. We focus on the binary representations because they most closely mirror the models derived by the CLS procedure. Because of data sparsity, the multinomial logit with interactions was not consistently estimable (convergent parameter estimates could not be obtained) at the individual level for a large number of panelists.

10. Because price was defined in terms of seventeen dichotomous variables, the CLS procedure would not yield a single "global" measure of its importance. One could note the relative frequency with which *any* price level appeared in a model, but such an index would be biased (upward) by the larger number of levels associated with that factor than with others (price would have sixteen more "chances" of entering a model than, for example, feature or display). Because the multiple levels do not have independent probabilities of entering by chance (the inclusion of one in a tree diminishes the likelihood of another being included), there is no obvious method for controlling for the bias; the correction "divide all relative frequencies by the number of levels" would be correct only under the assumption of sampling independence.

11. The average rank-ordering of attribute effects across the disaggregate models mirrors that of the single aggregate equation. We report the aggregate model to provide greater comparability with the logit fit to the CLS simulation surface, which also can be seen as an aggregate model.

References

Batsell, Richard R., and John C. Polking (1985). "A New Class of Market Share Models," *Marketing Science* 4 (summer): 177–98.

Bettman, James R. (1974). "Toward a Statistics for Consumer Decision Net Models," *Journal of Consumer Research* 1 (June): 71–80.

Breiman, Leo, Jerome H. Freidman, Richard A. Olshen, and Charles W. Stone (1984). *Classification and Regression Trees.* Belmont, Calif.: Wadsworth International.

Cohen, Paul R., and Edward A. Feigenbaum (1982). *The Handbook of Artificial Intelligence,* vol. 3. Los Altos, Calif.: William Kaufmann.

Cooper, Lee G. (1988). "Competitive Maps: The Structure Underlying Asymmetric Cross Elasticities," *Management Science,* 34 (June): 707–723.

Currim, Imran S. (1982). "Predictive Testing of Consumer Choice Models Not Subject to Independence of Irrelevant Alternatives," *Journal of Marketing Research* 19 (May): 208–22.

DeSarbo, Wayne, G. DeSoete, J. Douglas Carroll, and Venkatram Ramaswamy (1987).

"A New Stochastic Ultrametric Unfolding Methodology for Assessing Competitive Market Structure and Deriving Market Segments." Working paper. Wharton School of Business, University of Pennsylvania, Philadelphia.

Dubin, Jeffrey A. (1986). "A Nested Logit Model of Space and Water Heat System Choice," *Marketing Science* 5 (spring): 112–24.

Einhorn, Hillel, Don N. Kleinmuntz, and Benjiman Kleinmuntz (1979). "Linear Regression and Process-Tracing Models of Judgment," *Psychological Review* 86 (May): 464–85.

Gensch, Dennis (1987). "A Two-Stage Disaggregate Attribute Choice Model," *Marketing Science* 6 (summer): 223–39.

Gensch, Dennis, and J. Svestka (1984). "A Maximum-Likelihood Hierarchical Disaggregate Model for Predicting Choices of Individuals," *Journal of Mathematical Psychology* 28 (June): 160–78.

Green, Paul E., J. Douglas Carroll, and Steven M. Goldberg (1981). "A General Approach to Product Design Optimization via Conjoint Analysis," *Journal of Marketing* 45 (summer): 17–37.

Grover, Rajiv, and William R. Dillon (1985). "A Probabilistic Model for Testing Hypothesized Hierarchical Market Structures," *Marketing Science* 4 (fall): 312–35.

Guadagni, Peter M., and John D.C. Little (1983). "A Logit Model of Brand Choice Calibrated on Scanner Data," *Marketing Science* 2 (summer): 203–38.

Hauser, John R. (1986). "Agendas and Consumer Choice," *Journal of Marketing Research* 23 (August): 119–212.

Johnson, Eric J., and Robert J. Meyer (1984). "Compensatory Choice Models of Noncompensatory Processes: The Effect of Varying Context," *Journal of Consumer Research* 11 (June): 528–41.

Kahn, Barbara E., Donald G. Morrison, and Gordon P. Wright (1986). "Aggregating Individual Purchases to the Household Level," *Marketing Science* 5 (summer): 260–8.

Kalwani, Manohar U., and Donald G. Morrison (1977). "A Parsimonious Description of the Hendry System," *Management Science* 23 (May): 467–77.

Lehmann, Donald R., and William L. Moore (1986). "Two Approaches to Estimating Hierarchical Models of Choice." Working paper. Graduate School of Business, Columbia University, New York.

Lynch, John G. (1985). "Uniqueness Issues in Decompositional Modeling of Multiattribute Overall Evaluations: An Information Integration Perspective," *Journal of Marketing Research* 12 (February): 1–19.

McFadden, Daniel (1986). "The Choice Theory Approach to Marketing Research," *Marketing Science* 5 (fall): 275–97.

Meyer, Robert J., and Thomas C. Eagle (1982). "Context-Induced Parameter Instability in a Disaggregate-Stochastic Model of Store Choice," *Journal of Marketing Research* 19 (February): 62–71.

Michalski, Ryszard S. (1983). "A Theory and Methodology of Inductive Learning," in *Machine Learning: An Artificial Intelligence Approach*, R.S. Michalski, J.G. Carbonell, and T.M. Mitchell, eds. Palo Alto, Calif.: Tioga, pp. 83–134.

Morgan, J.N., and J.A. Sonquist (1963). "Problems in the Analysis of Survey Data, and a Proposal," *Journal of the American Statistical Association* 58 (September): 415–34.

Perreault, William D., and Hiram C. Barksdale (1980). "A Model-Free Approach to Analysis of Complex Contingency Data in Marketing Research," *Journal of Marketing Research* 18 (November): 503–15.

Quinlan, J. Ross (1983). "Learning Efficient Classification Procedures and Their Application to Chess End Games," in *Machine Learning: An Artificial Intelligence Approach,* R.S. Michalski, J.G. Carbonell, and T.M. Mitchell, eds. Palo Alto, Calif.: Tioga, pp. 463–82.

Rao, Vithala R., and Darius Jal Sabavala (1981). "Inference of Hierarchical Choice Processes from Panel Data," *Journal of Consumer Research* 8 (June): 85–96.

Shannon, C.E. (1948). "A Mathematical Theory of Communication," *Bell Systems Technological Journal* 27 (July): 379–423.

Smith, Terence R., William A.V. Clark, and John W. Cotton (1984). "Deriving and Testing Production-System Models of Sequential Decision Making," *Georgraphical Analysis* 16 (October): 191–222.

Tversky, Amos, and Shumel Sattah (1979). "Preference Trees," *Psychological Review* 86 (November): 542–73.

Urban, Glen L., Philip L. Johnson, and John R. Hauser (1984). "Testing Competitive Market Structures," *Marketing Science* 3 (Spring): 83–112.

13

Using Multiple-Group–Covariance Structures for Evaluating Concept/ Product Tests

Michael B. Menasco

A number of methodologies are available for employing concept and product tests as predictors of market success (Shocker and Srinivasan [1979]). An alternative to these methodologies is proposed in this chapter for the evaluation of concept/product tests. Concept/product testing is a common industry method for testing new products (Moore [1982], Trebi and Flesch [1983], Batsell and Wind [1980]). The modeling presented here illustrates the use of multiple-group–covariance structures to match concepts with brand prototypes. The methodology is most applicable to panel research for which independent samples of category users evaluate both a product concept and various brand prototypes or brand reformulations.

This research procedure is illustrative of the design phase of new-product development (Urban and Hauser [1980]). That is, we are primarily concerned with finding a concept closest to a preference vector in perceptual space. It is assumed that a preference vector has been previously established and a concept is developed to be positioned along the preference vector via consumer evaluations of brand prototypes or reformulations. One or more brand prototypes may best represent the concept and thus be a candidate(s) for further development and market testing.

In the example developed subsequently, a latent variable model is developed from panel data in which respondents evaluated both a single concept and two product reformulations. The field methodology is a competitive test designed to position the concept with the most appropriately matching brand (Moore [1982]). The product category is a packaged food reformulated with NutraSweet. Five brand reforms varying by predetermined amounts of NutraSweet were evaluated by panel members.

Background

A brief summary is presented in this section on the analysis of multiple-group–covariance structures. This discussion and later presentation of results is offered with the assumption that researchers using latent structural analysis have a working knowledge of the LISREL program. Other software programs and structural models are available (Bentler [1985]); however, LISREL (Joreskog and Sorbom [1984]) is a program for which a majority of researchers in the field should be most familiar. A complete discussion of model specification and estimation beyond the presentation of this section can be found in Joreskog and Sorbom (1984) and Joreskog (1971).

As with single-group estimation, hypothesized latent models are specified and estimated so as to reproduce the original N group matrices of observed variances/covariances. Each group matrix, S^g, is estimated by its corresponding matrix, Σ^g, derived from the latent model that is specified. In simultaneously estimating all models, the following fitting function is minimized.

$$F = \sum_{g=2}^{G} (N_g/N)F_g, \tag{1}$$

where, for estimation by maximum likelihood,

$$F_g = \log |\Sigma^g| + tr(S^g \Sigma^{g-1}) - \log |S^g| - (p + q).$$

N_g is the sample size for each group, $g = 1,2,3, \ldots, G$; and N is the sample size of all groups together. p and q are the number of observed dependent and independent variables, respectively. A chi-square goodness-of-fit measure under the assumption of multivariate normality is given by N-$g(2)$ (minF) with degrees of freedom equal to the number of observed variances and covariances in all samples less the number of parameters to be estimated in all population models. This chi-square measures the fit of all models over all groups.

Assuming that the hypothesis of equality of covariances over groups is rejected and that a common factor model holds over groups of the form, $y = \Lambda_y \eta + \epsilon$, then additional measurement and structural tests may be performed.[1] Their general forms are as follows:

Measurement model:

$$\Lambda_y^{(1)} = \Lambda_y^{(2)} = \cdots = \Lambda_y^{(G)} \tag{2}$$

$$\Theta_\epsilon^{(1)} = \Theta_\epsilon^{(2)} = \cdots = \Theta_\epsilon^{(G)} \tag{3}$$

Structural model:

$$\Psi^{(1)} = \Psi^{(2)} = \cdots = \Psi^{(G)}$$

and/or

$$\mathbf{B}^{(1)} = \mathbf{B}^{(2)} = \cdots = \mathbf{B}^{(G)} \qquad (4)$$

If groups exhibit differences in variances/covariances, it is expected that differences are due to differences in population models of either a measurement or structural form. Any number of group hypotheses may be formulated. Tests of equality may be made in the aggregate as given by (2), (3), and (4); or individual parameter estimates within common pattern matrices may be constrained to be equal as less strong tests of invariance.

Panel Data

Panel members were assigned to one of twenty ordered pairs of the five brand reforms. Each respondent (in-home) evaluated the concept and then "tried" the two brand reforms over a fixed time interval for each brand. Panel members responded to a set of concept-evaluation scales (prior to product use) and a set of product-evaluation scales after each use period. Observed variables (evaluative scales) were measured using five-or seven-point scales anchored by the adjectives listed for each of the following attributes. Internal scale points were indicated by degree of the adjective; e.g., for a scaling of "excellence": excellent, good, . . ., very poor.

Concept evaluation:

Y1. Concept hedonic scale [family] (like–dislike)

Y2. Concept hedonic scale [children] (like–dislike)

Y3. Concept value at a given price per 12-ounce box (very good–very poor)

Y4. Concept difference relative to other brands (very different–not different)

Y5. Concept advantage relative to other brands (great–not great)

Y6. Willingness to buy at a given price per 12-ounce box (definitely would–definitely would not)

Product evaluation:

Y7. Overall reaction after taste (extremely like–extremely dislike)

Y8. Overall taste (excellent–very poor)

Y9. Overall texture in the mouth (excellent–very poor)

Y8. Willingness to buy if available

Tests of Models and Hypotheses

For the present example, the goal is to determine which brand reform fits best with the product concept. The parameters of interest are the structural-path components as specified in figure 13–1. Thus, we initially test hypotheses represented by equation 4. Tests of the measurement model are presented in a later section. Differences in path coefficients (between groups) from the concept factor to latent factors of the product model may indicate which of the two brand-reform evaluations are influenced to a greater or lesser degree by concept evaluation. Such diagnostics could be used as a decision-aid to developing a brand most suited to preference positioning. Further, one brand reform may influence purchase intentions to a greater degree than the other given perceptible differences in taste.

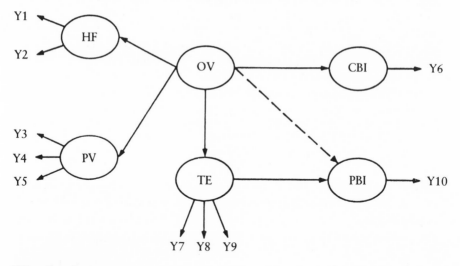

CBI: concept-buying intention
HF: hedonic factor
OV: overall evaluative factor
PBI: product-buying intention
PV: perceived value (concept)
TE: taste-evaluation factor (brand)

Figure 13–1. Structural Model of Two-Group Concept/Product Evaluation

Statistical Tests. Pairwise tests of models may be conducted such that one model is nested within a previous model, and differences in chi-square values test hypotheses of equivalence between group-parameter matrices of interest. Fit of each of a single multiple-group model is given by its respective probability of achieving a chi-square equal to or less than the value produced by the specified model (minimum of the fitting function). A level of probability of $p > .05$ is generally considered to be indicative of adequate statistical fit. A second measure of practical fit, defined as ρ, is also used (Bentler and Bonnett [1980]). Rho is a normed index calculated by taking the difference in chi-square between an estimated (hypothesized) model and a null (unsaturated) model relative to the null model. Both hypothesized and null models are adjusted for degrees of freedom. Values of $\rho = .95$ indicate good fit of the hypothesized model to the sample variance/covariance matrix, S. The rationale for the use of ρ is no different than an application to single-group estimation. In multiple-group analysis, the null model is estimated for all groups (with a single chi-square measure-of-fit), and any substantive (though different) model for each group is nested within its respective null model. Hence, the χ^2s for multiple-group estimation are also numerically comparable between null and hypothesized models as in single-group analysis.

Concept Model. A second-order–factor model of hedonic and perceived-value constructs was specified. The model is illustrated in figure 13–1 as part of the entire structural model that was estimated. This initial concept model was estimated from all 298 responses in order to establish an appropriate evaluative model leading to concept purchase-intention. The concept model was then included in the two group analyses (figure 13–1). The sample data fit the concept model fairly adequately with $\chi^2 = 14.01$ (df = 7) and $\rho = .965$ and was thus considered a good representation of concept evaluation leading to purchase intention.

Product-Evaluation Model. Given that brand reforms differed only on level of sweetness, an evaluative taste factor was hypothesized to affect stated purchase intentions for that brand. Since no brand was paired with itself during the use test, responses were pooled over the two trial periods to form the variance/covariance matrices of evaluative responses to each brand tried. The groups who tried brand reforms with the highest and lowest levels of NutraSweet differed in covariance structures, but the difference only approached significance ($p = .07$). Other possible pairwise comparisons to include pooling of brand responses produced no other significant differences. For purposes of illustration, we shall consider the differences in variances and covariances between brand reform 1 ($n = 116$) and brand reform 5 ($n = 118$) sufficiently significant to warrant further investigation. Henceforth, brand reforms 1 and 5 are referred to as brands 1 and 2, respectively.

Test of Equivalence of Parameter Matrices in Beta. Estimates of latent factor variances may be biased by specification of invariance for Λ_y given an initial test of the measurement model. If this is the case, subsequent estimation of free parameters in **B** (between groups) will also be biased.[2] Thus, one way to proceed is to conduct tests of invariance for the group matrices of beta, while allowing parameters of other matrices to be made without constraints. On the other hand, one may start with tests of the measurement model in an effort to find equivalent parameter estimates between groups and then proceed to the structural tests. The former appears to be the simpler and most parsimonious approach and it is presented as the testing procedure in the following paragraphs.

Estimation of Free Elements of Beta between Groups. Specification of the model presented in figure 13–1 is equivalent to the test of a common-factor model between groups. This is so because the structural paths from the higher-order factor (in the figure 13–1 model) account for the correlations between latent variables as if the model were instead specified in psi. The model must be identified in Λ_y, since the diagonal elements of ψ are properly interpreted as residuals of the structural (regression) equations. The model fits marginally by the chi-square measure ($\chi^2 = 80.01$, $p = .043$) but practically well by the rho index ($\rho = .97$). One correlated measurement error was allowed between the concept variables measuring buying intention and concept value, since both evaluative questions occurred sequentially and *both* were stated in reference to a given price per box. No other model modifications were justified on grounds of practicality or theory. An expected correlation between the residuals of the measures of concept- and brand-buying intentions did not materialize, likely due to the three path estimates (β_{46}, β_{43}, and β_{56}) accounting for the covariance between both factors on buying intention. All things considered, the joint hypothesis of common structures and structural paths appears reasonable.

Table 13–1 presents standardized parameter estimates of beta from this model estimation. All estimates are significant in both groups; however, some estimates differ in magnitude indicating more or less structural effects between groups. A model of invariance between group matrices of beta yielded $\chi^2 = 102.18$, $p = .003$. A nested test is significant with χ^2 (diff) = 22.17, $p < .01$. As explained previously, this test is constructed so that the less restricted model with a chi-square of 80.01 is nested within the latter model specifying constraints between the two groups for the beta matrix. The researcher could also specify tests for individually common elements of the **B** matrices. In the interests of space, only results of the aggregate test are discussed, although upon inspection of table 13–1, the estimates of β_{16} and β_{26} exhibit the greatest differences between groups. The result is unexpected since all respondents evaluated the same concept prior to product use. How-

Table 13–1
Standardized Estimates of Beta for Brand Model

	Brand 1	*Brand 2*
OV $\longrightarrow$ HF β_{16}	.663	1.140
OV $\longrightarrow$ PV β_{26}	.985	.556
OV $\longrightarrow$ TE β_{36}	.338	.505
OV $\longrightarrow$ PBI β_{46}	.151	.176
OV $\longrightarrow$ CBI β_{56}	.557	.849
TE $\longrightarrow$ PBI β_{43}	.649	.867

ever, variations in sampling representativeness may be reflected in these estimated parameters. Group 2 respondents reported relatively more children under the age of 12 at home than did group 1 respondents. Note that the estimated beta weights are inverse in magnitude between the two groups, indicating the hedonic factor to have a greater association with overall evaluation (OV) in group 2, while perceived value (PV) is instead more highly correlated with OV in group 1. Overall evaluation by respondents in group 2 also has a much greater effect upon concept-buying intention (CBI).

Other parameter differences also indicate that the concept has a better "match" with brand reform 2. Overall evaluation is more highly correlated with taste evaluation (TE) (OV ----> TE), while TE also has a greater effect upon product-buying intention in group 2 (TE ----> PBI). Thus, the concept best represents a brand that possesses a greater amount of NutraSweet, and that brand should result in higher reported buying intentions, other factors being equal. To further refine the brand concept, one could employ a test of structured means (Joreskog and Sorbom [1984]) to test for differences in means of latent variables. The procedure is beyond the scope of this chapter, however, a model of structured means can be specified simultaneously with tests of the **B** matrices.

Measurement Model. We now consider an assessment of the measurement model in this example. As indicated in note 2, choice of a scale metric can alter outcomes of subsequent statistical tests dependent upon which method of scale metric is used. The approach to tests of the measurement model in this example considers tests of hypotheses by fixing the scale in the factor loadings rather than in latent variable variances, since the former method yields less restricted models when equality constraints are employed.

1. Given $\Sigma^{(1)} \neq \Sigma^{(2)}$, the hypothesis $v(y)^{(1)} = v(y)^{(2)}$ is tested. The test is easily constructed in LISREL by specifying psi in the null model to be invariant between groups. A chi-square difference test may then be employed for the free and invariant versions. For the present example, the hypothesis of equal variances of observed variables between groups is rejected [χ^2 (diff) $= 23.29$, df $= 10$, $p < .01$].

2. The test of measurement error, $\theta_\epsilon^{(1)} = \theta_\epsilon^{(2)}$, is conducted by specifying parameter estimates in θ_ϵ to be invariant between the two groups. (The other matrices, Λ_y and ψ are unconstrained.) This hypothesis, too, is rejected [χ^2 (diff) $= 22.53$, df $= 9$, $p < .01$]. The nested test in this case is made in conjunction with the common-factor model of the five lower-order factors ($\chi^2 = 73.56$, df $= 52$).

3. If $[\lambda^2 v(\eta)]^{(1)} \neq [\lambda^2 v(\eta)]^{(2)}$, no restrictions can be placed upon the factor loadings or the variances of the factors because of the very reason that the first two hypotheses were rejected. A reasonable way to proceed is to test for invariance of factor loadings by allowing the other parameter matrices to be freely estimated in both groups. The hypothesis of equal factor loadings is rejected: χ^2 (diff) $= 11.61$, df $= 5$, $p < .05$.

Nested comparisons were again made with the common-factor model. It can be fairly concluded that the two populations differ in both factor loadings and measurement error over a common evaluative model of concept and brand reforms. Thus, the researcher may wish to investigate further reasons for these differences. Ex post hypotheses can be formulated concerning brand evaluation. For example, estimates of factor loadings on the taste-evaluation factor may be held invariant between groups, under the hypothesis that evaluations of observed variables of brand 2 are more pertinent than those of brand 1. Perhaps measurement error may be assessed in terms of trial effects for a specific brand reform. Responses to scale items may have been affected by the order in which brands were tried.[3] A method factor representing order of trial might be included in the model in an attempt to achieve homogeneity of observed errors between groups.

Extensions of the Method

This chapter has outlined a latent-variable methodology for evaluating the match between concepts and competing brand prototypes. Consistent with recommendations by Batsell and Wind (1980), latent-variable modeling allows the researcher to specifically assess measurement error in concept/product tests. The approach presented in this chapter is also applicable to multiple concepts in which matched samples evaluate different concepts in either a monadic or competitive test (Moore [1982]). In this regard, the following is offered as a means of improving the research methodology of concept/product tests commonly encountered in practice.

1. Evaluative, preference, and intention data should be collected consistent with an underlying or hypothesized behavioral model. This eliminates the need to collect data on variables that have only a peripheral influence upon the choice process and reduces the necessary initial data reduction and analysis.

2. With a variance/covariance methodology, testing two or more brands in subsequent use tests is not necessary and in fact may confound results of modeling. As discussed in the section on the testing of measurement error, for the present example, trial effects may have contributed to differences in measurement error between groups. This is an effect that is unwanted when testing for differences in factor loadings and structural parameters between groups.

3. Latent constructs may or may not exhibit the same degree of covariation but may well represent different mean levels of those constructs between groups. In the preceding example, the structural model estimated between populations was significantly different. However, the two groups might also differ in estimated means on one or more constructs, say for the taste-evaluation and product-buying-intention factors. An analysis of structured means (Joreskog and Sorbom [1984]) could be employed to model differences between groups in the means of these variables. Results can be used as an additional diagnostic to such methods as conjoint analysis in determining the appropriate level of the taste dimension leading to purchase intention.

In conclusion, structural equation modeling can be viably used in various applications of new-product research. Other uses include comparisons of new-product evaluations to benchmark evaluations of existing brands, and other anchor-point criteria. Modeling by structural equations is a natural application for these types of test criteria.

Notes

1. The models presented in this chapter use the four LISREL matrices, Λ_y, θ_ϵ, ψ, and B, for purposes of continuity between presentation of measurement and structural models. Parameter estimates may be obtained in LISREL by specifying models using only the four y matrices.

2. As in single-group analysis, two commonly accepted methods may be used to identify factor-analytic models for multiple groups. The scale of measurement

(model identification) may be set by fixing elements of the matrix of estimated factor loadings (Λ_y) or by fixing the diagonal elements of the estimated variance/covariance matrix of latent variables. The convention is to set fixed elements to the value 1.0. Either method yields the same model fit and standardized estimates of parameters unless equality constraints are imposed (Long [1983]). When equality constraints are imposed, model fit and estimates of parameters may vary widely dependent upon which method of scale metric is used. This is partly due to the additional restrictions imposed on models of invariance in which the scale is set in ψ. In general, however, for structural (path) models, the scale metric is set in Λ_y since the diagonal elements of ψ are properly considered residual errors in equations. Still, a model decremented by specification of invariance in factor loadings between groups will affect subsequent free estimates of beta in both groups.

3. Although aggregate variance/covariance tests for trial differences were nonsignificant, the small numbers for individual brand responses per trial period precluded a large sample test of trial effects per brand. It may be that trial order did affect the variance of responses for one or more of the five brand reforms.

References

Batsell, Richard R., and Yoram Wind (1980). "Product Testing: Current Methods and Needed Developments," *Journal of the Market Research Society* 22: 115–39.

Bentler, Peter M. (1985). *Theory and Implementation of EQS: A Structural Equations Program*. Los Angeles: BMD Statistical Software.

Bentler, Peter M., and D.G. Bonnett (1980). "Significance Tests and Goodness of Fit in the Analysis of Covariance Structures," *Psychological Bulletin* 88: 588–606.

Joreskog, Karl G. (1971). "Simultaneous Factor Analysis in Several Populations," *Psychometrika* 36: 409–26.

Joreskog, Karl G., and Dag Sorbom (1984). *LISREL VI, Analysis of Linear Structural Relationships by the Method of Maximum Likelihood*. Chicago: National Education Resources.

Long, J. Scott (1983). *Confirmatory Factor Analysis*. Beverly Hills, Calif.: Sage.

Moore, William L. (1982). "Concept Testing," *Journal of Business Research* 10: 279–93.

Shocker, Allan D., and V. Srinivasan (1979). Multiattribute Approaches for Product Concept Evaluation and Generation: A Critical Review," *Journal of Marketing Research* 16: 159–80.

Sorbom, Dag (1974). "A General Method for Studying Differences in Factor Means and Factor Structures between Groups," *British Journal of Mathematical and Statistical Psychology* 28: 138–51.

Trebbi, George C., and Edward J. Flesch "Single vs. Multiple Concept Tests," *Journal of Advertising and Research* 23: 21–26.

Urban, Glen L., and John R. Hauser (1980). *Design and Marketing of New Products*. Englewood Cliffs, N.J.: Prentice Hall.

Concluding Remarks

The keys to successful new-product development include management of the process that rigorously completes all of the steps of development while integrating customer wants throughout the process. The keys include bringing in design as an early factor in the conceptualization of consumer wants. Success requires that appropriate research tools are used to investigate concept acceptance by the consumers and it requires that pretest models be used to estimate market share during the evaluation stage. Once introduction has started, the rate of diffusion must be estimated to allow timely market-plan adjustments. The last key involves better understanding of what drives consumer acceptance of innovations.

The chapters in this book provide valuable insights into each of the keys of success in product development. Implicit however in each of the chapters is an underlying commitment to the fundamental marketing concept of a true customer orientation. As Philip Kotler introduced it many years ago, the marketing concept is a philosophy that seeks to understand customer needs and fill those needs using an integrated marketing approach. It is a marketing approach that requires all areas of the organization to be continually customer-need–driven. New-product development cannot go far wrong if the marketing concept is maintained as the principle guiding force of the organization.

About the Contributors

Frank M. Bass is the University of Texas System Eugene McDermott Professor of Management at the School of Management, the University of Texas at Dallas. He served as a president of The Institute of Management Sciences, an editor of the *Journal of Marketing Research*, and has published widely in scholarly journals on marketing topics. He was a 1986 winner of the Paul D. Converse Award for Outstanding Contributions to Marketing Theory and Science.

Imran S. Currim is associate professor of marketing, Graduate School of Business Administration, New York University. Professor Currim's articles appear in the *Journal of Marketing Research* on topics of choice models and consumer preferences. He is a past recipient of the American Marketing Association award for best article published in the *Journal of Marketing Research*.

Laurence P. Feldman is a professor of marketing at the University of Illinois at Chicago. He has over six years of experience consulting in product planning and has done extensive research in the areas of product planning and marketing and public policy.

Warren French is head of the marketing department at the University of Georgia. He is the coauthor of two books in marketing and has research interests in marketing strategy and the market behavior of senior citizens. Dr. French's works appear in the leading business and marketing journals.

Dr. Roberto Friedmann is an assistant professor of marketing at the College of Business at the University of Georgia. His research activities are in the area of consumer behavior, with a special interest in the psychological meaning of products. Dr. Friedmann consults on product development and product positioning with numerous *Fortune 500* firms.

Professor **Paul E. Green** from the Wharton School at the University of Pennsylvania is, without a doubt, a world-recognized authority in the areas of marketing research, multidimensional scaling, and conjoint analysis. Dr. Green has published many books and numerous articles at the leading edge of research methodology. He may be truly called the father of modern marketing research.

William G. Hall received his MBA in 1985 from Vanderbilt University and is a 1980 honors graduate of Vanderbilt's chemical engineering program. He serves as a member of the product development staff at Procter and Gamble in Cincinnati.

Frederick A. Johne is a distinguished member of the faculty at The City University Business School, Frobisher Crescent, London, England, where he teaches and conducts research. Prior to his academic career he was in product management and marketing research at Imperial Chemical Industries in Europe.

Philip Kotler is the Harold T. Martin Professor of Marketing at the J.L. Kellogg Graduate School of Management at Northwestern University. Dr. Kotler is a world-renowned marketing scholar and author. He has published numerous books in the marketing field and has over eighty articles in the leading journals of business and marketing. In 1985 he received the Distinguished Marketing Educator Award from the American Marketing Association.

Abba M. Krieger is a well known Professor of Statistics at the Wharton School at the University of Pennsylvania. Dr. Krieger has done extensive writing and development in the area of conjoint analysis.

Nhan Le is a graduate student in computer science at the University of California, Los Angeles.

Robert J. Meyer is associate professor of management, Anderson Graduate School of Management, University of California, Los Angeles. Professor Meyer has published articles on consumer choice theory in the *Journal of Marketing Research, Journal of Consumer Research,* and *Marketing Science*. He received his Ph.D. from the University of Iowa.

John A. Norton is assistant professor of business administration at the Colgate Darden Graduate School of Business Administration, University of Virginia. He received his Ph.D. in Management Science from the University of

Texas at Dallas. His paper with Frank M. Bass in this book won the TIMS College on Marketing Best Article Award for 1987.

Albert L. Page is an associate professor of Marketing in the College of Business Administration at the University of Illinois at the Chicago campus. Dr Page is a noted academic in industrial marketing and product planning research.

Leonard J. Parsons is a widely noted author in marketing management. He has also published in numerous marketing journals, and served on the editorial boards of many of the leading business and marketing journals in the United States. Dr. Parsons is a professor of management at Georgia Institute of Technology.

G. Alexander Rath is a principle at Tah & Associates in Chicago.

Allan D. Shocker is professor of marketing at the Curtis L. Carlson School of Management, University of Minnesota. Professor Shocker conducts research in product planning, development, and strategy, and he is a frequent contributor in these areas to major marketing journals. Professor Shocker received his Ph.D. from Carnegie Mellon University.

David K. Smith, Jr., is assistant professor of marketing, Department of Marketing and Transportation Administration, Michigan State University. Professor Smith has published in the *Journal of Marketing* on the subject of product portfolio models. His research interests also include product management, marketing strategy, and international marketing. Professor Smith received his Ph.D. from the University of Minnesota.

V. Srinivasan is the Arbuckle Professor of Marketing and Management Science at Stanford University. Dr. Srinivasan is a leading scholar in the area of marketing research and has published widely in the area of marketing research methodology and conjoint analysis techniques. His advances in the state of the art in computer-assisted consumer research are internationally known.

R. Dale Wilson is professor of marketing, Department of Marketing and Transportation Administration, Michigan State University. Professor Wilson was previously director of marketing science, BBDO, Inc. He has contributed articles on new product strategy, marketing strategy, and advertising published in major journals including in the *Journal of Marketing Research*, *Marketing Science*, and the *Journal of Advertising*. Professor Wilson received his Ph.D. from the University of Iowa.

Gordon A. Wyner is the vice president of M/A/R/C Inc., a leading national consumer research firm. He has worked extensively in the area of new-product concept testing research.

About the Editors

Professor **Walter A. Henry** is a marketing educator with interest in consumer behavior, research methodology, product development, promotion management, and strategic planning. His research has been published in the *Journal of Marketing Research, Journal of Consumer Research,* and *Journal of Advertising* and he has contributed invited chapters to several books. Prior to his academic career, Dr. Henry had ten years of management experience with Honeywell, Inc., and other major corporations. He is an active member of the American Marketing Association and Academy of International Business, and has chaired numerous panels. Dr. Henry brings to this project a wealth of experience gained through active management, over fifteen years in business academics, and many years of marketing consulting.

Michael B. Menasco has served on the marketing faculties at The University of Iowa, Washington State University, and the University of California, Los Angeles. He has published articles in the *Journal of Consumer Research, Journal of Marketing Research, Organizational Behavior and Human Performance,* and other journals in applied psychology. Professor Menasco's current research interests concern the ability of classes of utility models to predict both family purchase behavior and negotiated decisions between organizations in the private and public sectors.

Hirokazu Takada is assistant professor of marketing in the Graduate School of Management at University of California, Riverside. He received his Ph.D. in marketing from Krannert Graduate School of Management, Purdue University. His current research interests are in the analysis of competitive marketing behavior, time series analysis and econometric modeling of marketing problems, analysis of diffusion process of new products, and international marketing research. He is currently a member of American Marketing Association, The Institute of Management Science, and The American Statistical Association.